Down Home Feasts

Down Home Feasts

The Native Cuisines of America's Gulf States

Sallie Y. Williams
and Nancy G. Cortner

Taylor Publishing Company

DALLAS, TEXAS

Down Home Feasts was developed jointly by Taylor Publishing
Company and Media Projects Incorporated

Published by Taylor Publishing Company
under the direction of:

Randy Marston, President
Arnie Hanson, Publisher
Robert Frese, Senior Editor
Kathy Ferguson, Art Director

Produced by The Cookhouse Press of
Media Projects Incorporated

Executive Editor: Carter Smith
Project Editor: Ellen Coffey
Editorial Assistants: Charlotte McGuinn Freeman,
                                Michael Wong
Principal Photography: Dan Barba
Designer: Bernard Schleifer

Library of Congress Cataloging-in-Publication Data

Williams, Sallie Y.
  Down home feasts.

  1. Cookery, American—Southern style. 2. Cookery—
Gulf States. I. Cortner, Nancy G. II. Title.
TX715.W7292   1986   641.5976   86-3751
ISBN 0-87833-526-9

Printed in the United States of America

FIRST EDITION
0 1 2 3 4 5 6 7 8 9

frontispiece: Oakleigh, headquarters of the
Historic Mobile Preservation Society
opposite: Holiday Country Ham

CONTENTS

➤

INTRODUCTION

To most of us the term "down home Southern cooking" conjures up visions of tables laden with simple, hearty, home-cooked fare—fried chicken and fish, hush puppies or corn bread, black-eyed peas or okra, perhaps, and inevitably, peach or strawberry shortcake.

While the foregoing is certainly an accurate vision, the South has always had a more sophisticated cuisine as well. Consider the evidence of a letter written in 1848 by Mrs. George H. Fry of Mobile, Alabama, to Rebecca Jones Robinson:

"I want to tell you about our party. There were 328 invitations out but the night was very bad, not more than half came, which was fortunate as the rooms were just comfortably filled. . . . Our house was as light as day, having thirty solar lamps and sixty candles throughout the house.

"I suppose you would like to know what we had for supper. Well, roast turkeys, boiled turkeys, hams, alamode beef, gumbo, broiled oysters, pickled oysters, chickens, salaman punch, vanilla ice-cream, orange ice, pineapple ice, charlotte russe, calves-foot jelly, blamange, a very little sponge and almond cake as cake is not the rage, now-a-days. Then there was punch, wine, and champaign—pyramids of it unexploded, thank fortune."

Such a down home feast might well have been prepared by a staff of cooks in a plantation kitchen similar to the one at the left. The staff is no more, and the Gulf South, like every region in America, has undergone revolutionary changes in its culinary ways. As a 1985 *Time* cover story proclaimed, Americans have discovered our amazingly rich and diverse foodstuffs and the joy of imaginative cooking.

Plantation kitchen

And for the first time, European chefs are coming to our country not to teach but to learn. They are returning to their restaurants to receive raves from patrons for such very American dishes as Corn Fritters and Pecan Pie.

The first stop on any of these "learning" trips would have to be the Gulf South. Traditionally Southerners demanded from local restaurants food at least as good as what they prepared at home. In New Orleans, Dallas and other cities, restaurants vied with each other to find and keep the very best chefs. What couldn't be raised or produced locally was brought in from far away if necessary, but one of the sources of Southern pride has always been to produce something wonderful to eat out of whatever was at hand.

The Gulf South has a marvelous culinary heritage. Much was learned from Native Americans about indigenous American culinary resources; and the Spanish, French, Germans, Africans, and Orientals are just a few of the groups of American émigrés who brought to these shores an affection for cooking and the skills to do it well. Now we are returning the favor as we begin to share with other nations the uniquely American cuisine we have built on the cornerstone of their culinary traditions.

We could begin in Key West, where seafood reigns supreme, as it does all along the Gulf and Atlantic coasts. The nearly tropical atmosphere of Florida most often calls for lighter fare than that which is traditional in other regions, but such delicacies as Conch Salad, delicious lobster dishes, red snapper so fresh it has lost none of its color, all make dining a pleasure. Miami, with its Cuban influence, is where you will find a hearty Arroz con Pollo at its best. But don't overlook the perfect simplicity of stone crab claws with mustard mayonnaise, followed by a rare steak and Key Lime Pie. Add Hearts of Palm Salad and have a meal fit for a king. Tarpon Springs and other communities on the Gulf Coast have a Greek heritage second to none. Eggplant Caviar, Plaki, and Rice Custard with Lemon Sauce are as at home on a menu here as they are

Annual Greek Heritage Festival,
Pensacola, Florida

in Piraeus. The area abounds with festivals in celebration of the residents' cultural "roots," and food is always the centerpiece.

Mobile, Alabama, has always been a food lover's paradise. The French had settled Mobile before they moved on to New Orleans, and the culinary sophistication they brought with them has endured. The excesses of the Ante-Bellum days may have disappeared, but the pride in serving the freshest and the finest from the fields, the gardens and the Gulf persists.

It has been written that Natchez, Mississippi, had the highest per capita income in America in the 1850s, when "Cotton was King." Even today, the Natchez dining table seen on page twelve may be awaiting fish, chicken and ham, four or five vegetables and several "sweets"—such is the rich culinary bounty in some plantation homes.

Louisiana, with its definitely French atmosphere, would have to be a main stopping place on any tour. From the time that errant husbands brought home a *médiatrice* (a French loaf slathered with butter or Creole garlic mayonnaise and filled with fried oysters) to placate their angry wives, to the present-day passion for Blackened Redfish at K-Pauls, Louisiana has long been considered by Americans and foreigners alike to be one of the culinary centers of the world. The contrast of the refined Creole dishes, those American interpretations of French and Spanish originals, to the heartily delicious Cajun fare with its roots deep in France's Brittany coast has fascinated diners for a hundred and fifty years. Today these dishes are all the rage, suddenly discovered by San Franciscans and New Yorkers—as if we haven't known how good they were all along!

Texas is the barbecue capital of the world. "Barbecue," it has been written, "is any four-footed animal, be it mouse or mastodon, whose dressed carcass has been roasted whole. . . ." Almost anything is barbecued these days, and it doesn't need to be whole—fish steaks do nicely, and two-legged animals such as chicken and turkey certainly aren't anything to neglect. But Texas isn't all barbecue and fiery hot Tex-Mex dishes. The skill and creativity of practitioners of Nouvelle Cuisine with a Texas flair have produced truly original culinary delights, from Pickled Catfish to Persimmon Mousse. The flavors of Texas main dishes are today—as always—enhanced with peppers both blazingly hot and mild, but the preparation techniques are as sophisticated as the results are delicious.

For those who prefer to do their traveling in an armchair and their dining in their own home, *Down Home Feasts* provides the perfect passport to the home of all these tastes and many more. Don't hesitate; start your trip now. Bon appétit!

SALLIE Y. WILLIAMS

Menus

FLORIDA

Alligators sunning themselves in the sluggish waters of the Everglades; the Space Shuttle roaring into the sky; Disney characters on parade; acres of orange groves spreading over the gently undulating countryside of the interior; Spanish moss hanging from silvery-gray live oak trees near the legendary site of Ponce de Leon's fountain of youth: All these things are Florida—but it is also much, much more.

Frequently we forget just how large and diverse a region Florida is. The universal image seems to consist of beaches, palm trees, orange groves and senior citizens enjoying the sunshine after having lived for many years in one of the less gentle climates of our country.

That narrow view could not be farther from the truth. Florida is a veritable microcosm of the United States. It is a warm-weather melting pot, its citizens counting a hundred nations in their background.

Nowhere is this diversity more apparent than in the myriad cuisines that are represented in this southernmost of our states. From the genteel Old South atmosphere of Pensacola to the Greek-American community at Tarpon Springs and on to the Cuban-American enclave near Miami, Florida abounds in culinary delights to please a wide variety of tastes.

Seafood is the star attraction here. Freshness counts, especially along the long stretches of coastline. Succulent grouper is often presented in a luscious tomato sauce; thick steaks of swordfish grilled on an open fire are a culinary experience not to be missed. The gifts of the sea appear in every form and flavor: kabobs, salads, casseroles, grills—anything goes, and everything is delightful.

Enormous tracts of Florida's land are given over to raising cattle—so enormous in fact that you will think you are in Texas. You can drive by the same ranch for twenty-five miles! Not surprisingly, the beef is delicious. Vegetables are wonderfully fresh; salads abound, and are uncommonly good—especially in Key West, where the only constraint on a salad is the limits of the chef's imagination.

Desserts are a Florida specialty. Fruit is everywhere—usually in your own back yard—and a few minutes' work outdoors will yield enough to form the basis of a pie, a cake or a sorbet.

Florida cuisine encompasses many pleasures, from the spicy favorites of the southernmost regions to the old-fashioned classics served in central Florida and in the "panhandle" to the west toward Alabama. Don't wait—start now on your culinary tour of the Sunshine State.

Feijoada Completa

Brazil is the original home of Feijoada, an aromatic combination of black beans, beef, garlic and spicy pork sausage. Served with mounds of snowy rice, this dish with a Portuguese heritage reaches new heights when accompanied by fresh, lightly cooked spinach and chunks of creamy ripe banana. The tang of a freshly made Lemon Sherbet finishes things off on a proper note.

Caviar means celebration, and this easy-to-make appetizer sets the stage for an evening of fun. Follow with cold Florida salads from the sea for a do-ahead party that will do you proud.

Brazilian Festive Fare

Feijoada Completa

Salsa Forte

Corn Muffins

Lemon Sherbet

Summer Cold Buffet

Caviar Pie

Smoked Fish Salad

Curried Chicken and Shrimp Salad

Frozen Charlotte Russe

Smoked Fish Salad

The influence of the sea on Florida cuisine is evident in these menus, where the emphasis is on fish and shellfish main courses. Conch is versatile and can be enjoyed as chowder, steaks, or even fritters. Hopping John, a hearty combination of beans or peas and rice, is a classic; nutritionally sound, it is also delicious. Hearts of Palm are featured in a crunchy salad; the yellow Florida Key lime is the basis for a glorious pie closely akin to Lemon Meringue.

Florida abounds in wild game. Roast Leg of Venison and Turnip Pudding are the centerpieces of a menu to celebrate the victorious hunter's return.

Dinner in the Keys

Conch Chowder
Broiled Swordfish with Sauce Dijon
Ginger Stir-Fry
Coconut Pecan Cake

Waterfront Repast

Stuffed Flounder
Hopping John
Fennel, Endive and Mushroom Salad
Guava Turnovers

Mary Snyder's Seafood Dinner

Cold Avocado Soup
Seafood Kabobs
Seasoned Rice
Hearts of Palm Salad
Key Lime Pie

Game Dinner Deluxe

Roast Leg of Venison
Turnip Pudding
Green Peas Sautéed with Jicama
Pear and Quince Tart

Saturday Night Company Dinner

Baked Sea Trout
Spinach Casserole
Artichoke Salad
Lemon Ice Cream

Florida Patio Lunch

Potato Leek Soup
Shellfish and Melon Salad
Mint Sherbet with Spanish Almond
Cookies

ALABAMA

The cuisine of Alabama, like those of its four sister states on the Gulf of Mexico, derives from two basic influences: first, from the natural resources of the land itself (native fruits, vegetables and grains; fish, fowl and game; other crops and domesticated animals to which the land is well suited) and, second, from the cultural heritage of its settlers.

While most people associate the French influence in America with New Orleans, few realize that Mobile was the capital of the Louisiana Territory before New Orleans in the eighteenth century and that, in the nineteenth century, many Bonapartists emigrated to Alabama after Napoleon's defeat (in Marengo County—named for a Napoleonic victory—an attempt was made to establish a wine and olive colony). Southern Alabama was also briefly under Spanish and English control, but it is the French presence that most influenced its culinary tastes.

Rich natural resources have always been the predominant factor, however, in determining what Alabamans sat down to "at table."

In southern Alabama it is, of course, the bounty of the Gulf that makes possible the great gumbos and broad variety of fish and seafood dishes popular throughout the area.

"Up country," in west central Alabama, the loam-heavy soil is so dark and rich that several counties have been termed "the black belt." The vegetables grown here and the game and fish taken from the timberlands in this area are beyond compare.

Southern staples such as black-eyed peas, okra, yams, corn—and all manner of corn breads—are menu favorites. And the hunting seasons offer the wonderful possibilities of venison, wild turkey, dove, quail and wild duck dishes.

In other parts of Alabama cattle raising is a major industry, and the state is also home to one of America's largest commercial poultry farms.

From country food at its freshest and best to high-style "Frenchified" cuisine, Alabama offers wonderful culinary options. Enjoy them.

Mallard Duck Dinner

Alabama's multiple heritage is evident in this eclectic selection of culinary celebrations.

The Caribbean comes alive in the tangy goodness of a West Indian seafood salad. Roast wild duck—preferably brought to the kitchen by your favorite hunter—is succulent and delicious. The creamy Lemon/Orange Trifle—a reminder of England's influence—is a special ending for a special meal.

Mobile's proximity to the Gulf of Mexico ensures an abundance of wonderfully fresh seafood. Red snapper, poached and served garnished with dill, makes the perfect main course for a warm-weather dinner celebration.

Desserts are rich and satisfying, including Old English favorites like Syllabub and Ginger Pudding.

Mallard Duck Dinner

West Indies Salad
Roast Wild Duck
Wild Rice Pilaf
Green Beans with Almonds
Lemon/Orange Trifle Dessert

Dinner in Mobile

Crab Meat Norfolk
Frozen Tomato Salad
Corn Pudding
Refreshed Fruit

Old-Time Alabama Supper

Pork Chop Casserole
Spicy Black-Eyed Peas
Green Beans with Tomatoes
Spoonbread
Bread and Butter Pickles
Ginger Pudding

Company Dinner

Cold Watercress Soup
Roast Pork Fillets with Prunes
Squash Soufflé
Sally Lunn Bread
Syllabub

Elegant Fish Dinner

Cheese Biscuits
Cold Poached Red Snapper with Dill
Rice Salad
Sliced Tomatoes
Lady Baltimore Cake

Alabama Sunday Lunch

Oyster Stew
Mrs. Smith's Baked Duck
Corn Bread Stuffing
Green Beans
Peppermint Stick Ice Cream

Even the most dyed-in-the-wool football fanatic has to eat sometime. Serve them this imaginative lunch, and score a touchdown of your own. Crispy Fried Shrimp with Spicy Pecans is as easy to eat as popcorn; you will need to make plenty to satisfy a Saturday appetite. Cole Slaw and Hush Puppies (even if you don't have a hound dog to throw the cornmeal nuggets to) are classic accompaniments. Strawberry Shortcake—strawberries are available all year long now—is outstanding, made with biscuits or spongecake.

Alabama Fried Chicken is legendary, and it yearns for cotton-eyed peas and grits as accompaniments. Stir some stewed tomatoes into the grits, and pass crispy Corn Sticks for a perfect meal. And if you have never tasted Black Bottom Pie, you have a chocolate-lover's delight in store when you sample this marvelous dessert.

Saturday Football Lunch

Fried Shrimp with Spicy Pecans
Cole Slaw
Hush Puppies
Strawberry Shortcake

Down Home Chicken Feast

Fried Chicken
Smothered Cotton-Eyed Peas
Stewed Tomatoes and Garlic Grits
Corn Sticks
Black Bottom Pie

Fried Shrimp and Spicy Pecans

MISSISSIPPI

Mississippi is nearly the heart of the Deep South. Plantation life flourished here, especially along the great Mississippi River. Natchez was a major stop on the riverboats' journey both north and south. Cotton was the crop, and Mississippians prospered. South, near the Gulf Coast, the influence was French; more to the north the settlers had moved in from other parts of the country, such as Virginia, South Carolina and Georgia.

Cotton is no longer king, but the "Big Muddy" is still a major North-South highway, and time has not affected the inborn hospitality, good humor and love of good food that is alive and well in all of Mississippi. From the seafood of the Gulf Coast to the beef—and rabbit, and squirrel—of the interior, the state is famous for dishes that truly melt in the mouth.

Catfish, which used to come straight from the great Mississippi, are now commercially farmed, and the crop of this succulent white-fleshed fish provides a dependable, year-round supply for connoisseurs everywhere. There is even a restaurant in Natchez, down by the river, that serves nothing but catfish—every way you can think of.

Greenville is in the middle of pecan country. The pecan, a truly native American nut, was known to the Native Americans even before any Europeans arrived on these shores. Considered by locals to be the best-tasting nuts in the world, pecans are added to just about anything. Stuffings, vegetables, breads, and desserts of all kinds are enhanced by their taste.

While some French influence on Mississippi fare survives to this day, dishes are usually simple, relying on the fine quality of the ingredients. Sauces are used to complement the natural flavors of foods. And desserts are an obsession, from the simplicity of the perfect Banana Pudding to the dense complexity of Mississippi Mud Cake.

Classic Country Picnic

Fried Chicken
Fried Whole Bream
Turnip Greens
Black-Eyed Peas
Biscuits
Blackberry Jam Cake

Picnicking is a Mississippi tradition. The "light collation" taken along of an afternoon is usually substantial enough for an army, and this classic menu includes crisply Fried Chicken and Bream accompanied by bowls of savory turnip greens that have been simmered with ham, as well as moist and tender Black-Eyed Peas with Bacon. Blackberry Jam Cake, long a favorite, is a must for the finale.

Venison, pheasant and rabbit appear on Mississippi tables as often as they are available, and in every conceivable form.

Easter calls for ham, of course, and Mississippi is famous for Stuffed Ham, this time with Clove and Mustard Seed Dressing, to be eaten with the fiery goodness of Hot Pepper Jelly.

Hunters' Delight

Venison Stew
Brussels Sprouts with Bacon Dressing
Corn Muffins
Banana Pudding

First Hunt of the Season

Braised Pheasant
Pecan Rice Dressing
Cold Dill Beans
Dixie Fried Corn
Rice Custard with Lemon Sauce

Easter Sunday Dinner

Stuffed Ham with Clove and Mustard
  Seed Dressing
Hot Pepper Jelly
Yams with Rum Glaze
Hot Cabbage Creole
Sunshine Cake

Early Fall Supper for Friends

Sorrel Soup
Rabbit with Red Wine Sauce
Broccoli with Horseradish
Corn Muffins
Lemon Chess Pie

Sunday Night Supper

Eggplant Caviar and Toast Rounds
Lamb Shanks with Zucchini and Rice
Yellow Cake with Caramel Icing

Anyone who has ever eaten catfish knows just how good it is. But it seems to taste best down by the Mississippi, even though nearly all catfish are cultivated in huge "farms" these days. This catfish dish is a great introduction to the pleasures in store for you if catfish is new to your culinary repertoire. Stewed corn, thick with the goodness of fresh corn right off the cob, makes the perfect accompaniment. And there isn't a chocolate-lover anywhere who can resist the dense goodness of Mississippi Mud Cake.

For more sophisticated fare, freshly caught sautéed brook trout fills the bill. Succulent mushrooms and rich potatoes round out the menu, and another rich offering for the chocoholics who abound in Mississippi—and everywhere—finishes off the feast.

Supper on the Water

Catfish with Artichoke Sauce
Corn, Lima Beans and Tomatoes
Parker House Rolls
Mississippi Mud Cake

Fisherman's Fancy

Florentine Mushrooms
Trout Veronique
Potatoes with Cheese Sauce
Three Bean Salad
Chocolate Pie

Catfish with Artichoke Sauce

LOUISIANA

The mention of Louisiana evokes images of beautiful old homes surrounded by huge oak trees festooned with swags of Spanish moss; or of the vast rolling Mississippi, alive with craft of every description, from rafts to the giant paddle-wheel palaces for which the river was known far and wide; or, perhaps, of New Orleans—with its famous French Quarter and its elegant early-nineteenth-century residences, with their wrought-iron balconies visible to admiring passersby, their sumptuous gardens and quiet interiors hidden beyond thick solid walls to keep them cool in the sultry climate.

Mention Louisiana and immediately food comes to mind. Rightly or wrongly, Louisiana still has a reputation around the world as the one place in the United States where fine food is consistently available. Nowhere else in this country does local cooking have such an illustrious heritage. Eating seems to have been raised above the level of one of life's necessities here, almost to the level of a mystical experience.

Spanish, French, African, Acadian and all the other influences naturally felt in a bustling international port have had their impact on local food. There are all levels of cuisine, from the traditional abundance of the Cajun table to the unique elegance of fine dining in the Creole style.

Seafood abounds. Shrimp and other varieties of shellfish are frequently the featured ingredient in main dishes—both on restaurant menus and for meals at home. The feisty little freshwater crayfish (or crawfish, or crawdad) is as popular here as it is in Europe and Scandinavia, where it is devoured by the ton. The sweet, succulent little creatures can be found here in bisques, étouffées (or stews), gumbos—they are even the main ingredient in Paul Prudhomme's now famous "Cajun popcorn." And indeed these crisply fried morsels eat like popcorn.

Cajun food, hot and spicy enough to scorch the mouth, or as delicate as a custard pie, is enjoying enormous popularity. It is considered one of the few truly American cuisines, as indigenous as the Native American-inspired dishes of the Northeast. Developed by the "Acadians," settlers who fled Eastern Canada in the eighteenth century, Cajun food is hearty, robust fare. When the Cajuns disappeared into the bayou country, often isolated from the outside world except by barely navigable waterways, they learned to make use of every available foodstuff. As a result, even fiery hot alligator sausage still has its place today, firmly established in Cajun cuisine.

Whether it is classic, refined Creole cooking, adapted from the cuisines of France and Spain and with African overtones, or the homely but dynamically delicious Cajun food that appeals to your fancy, Louisiana fare truly encompasses dishes to please everyone, of every taste.

Classic Cajun Lunch

Nothing in this world beats sitting down to a fine Cajun meal. Not all of this now-famous robust cuisine is so hot it burns the tongue and smarts the eyes, but hot red peppers are often used in its preparation—frequently in the form of that fiery liquid commonly known as Louisiana hot sauce or red pepper sauce. If it is not actually incorporated into the dish—as in the Oyster Loaf featured in this delightful menu—it is served on the side. Desserts are generally simple and simply satisfying. Who can resist creamy smooth Buttermilk Pie, Cassis Mousse or rich, delicious Bread Pudding with Bourbon Sauce?

Louisiana also offers a vast selection of more refined dishes, such as superb Turtle Soup, Stuffed Crabs, Pecan Rice, and oysters and eggs in so many preparations it takes weeks to sample them all. The red pepper sauce bottle, however, is never out of reach.

Classic Cajun Lunch

Creole Gumbo

Oyster Loaf

Red Beans and Rice

Green Beans Vinaigrette

Bread Pudding with Bourbon Sauce

Cajun Company Supper

Shrimp Rémoulade

Redfish Courtbouillon

Steamed Asparagus with Hollandaise

French Bread

Buttermilk Pie

Summer Supper

Creole Turtle Soup
Chicken with Artichokes
Green Rice
Watercress Salad
Chocolate Almond Soufflé

Louisiana Sunday Lunch

Beet and Claret Soup
Stuffed Crabs
Creole Tomatoes
*Brandied Rice Ring with Custard
    Cream*

Al Fresco Brunch

Grilled Pigeon
Caesar Salad
Cassis Mousse

Creole Family Festival

Oysters Bienville
Beef en Daube Gelée
Pecan Rice
Asparagus Custard
Rhubarb Ring with Strawberries

When cool breezes blow off the lake, the river or the bayou, Louisiana folk love to eat outdoors. From plantation days to today, a meal in the sunshine, or served beneath a shady tree, is a chance to meet with friends, relax and enjoy the simple pleasures of life. Any excuse will do to set up a table and serve a meal in the fresh air. Barbecued Ribs, hot and spicy, and the thinnest imaginable Pommes Frites (french fries) are the mainstays of this outdoor supper. Add zucchini with tomatoes and onions and ethereally light Cajun Rolls, and top it all off with a Southern favorite, Pecan Pie.

Pompano, a distinctively strange-looking fish that will swim right up and look you in your swim mask when you explore the waters off the Gulf Coast, is a delicious food fish, never better tasting than when it has been steamed in a tightly sealed paper package (en papillote). Add other Louisiana favorites and have a meal to remember.

Louisiana Outdoor Dining

Barbecued Ribs

Pommes Frites

Creole Zucchini

Cajun Rolls

Pecan Pie

Louisiana Dinner in the Garden

Pompano en Papillote

Stuffed Mirlitons

Green Salad

Glazed Orange Slices in Ginger Sauce

Brunch may well have been a Creole invention; certainly no one does it better than this. A beautifully laid table is just as important as the food on it, for eating often begins with the eyes. Variety meats have always been popular in the South: Here you have sweetbreads married with mushrooms. Add to the repast Eggs Sardou, a combination of poached eggs, freshly cooked artichoke hearts, silky creamed spinach and hollandaise sauce, and you have a brunch fit for a king.

Oysters and artichokes just naturally seem to go together; here they are combined in a fabulous creamy soup. Roast quail, tender and juicy, are accompanied by Dirty Rice, which is cooked with the quail giblets, or with chicken livers. Okra is a Louisiana mainstay; many say that fried okra is the best of all. Those same people will tell you Crème Caramel is the only possible dessert choice for this delightful meal.

Creole Brunch

Sweetbreads and Mushrooms with
  Cream in Pastry Shells
Eggs Sardou
Orange and Red Onion Salad
Beignets
Bananas Foster
Pralines

Bayou Country Fare

Oyster and Artichoke Soup
Quail in Red Wine with Dirty Rice
Fried Okra
Crème Caramel

TEXAS

The soul of Texas is as big as Texas itself. Even complete strangers find themselves treated to Southern hospitality that seems to have no bounds. Visitors are plied with food and drink at every possible occasion—and what food and drink it is! If one can survive the washtub-size Margaritas, there is a treat in store every time a meal is served.

Texas is a vast state, ranging from the Deep South milieu of East Texas to the arid stretches of land near the Rio Grande. The year-round heat of south Texas is in sharp contrast to the climate of the Panhandle to the north, with its frigid, snowy winters. The people of Texas are just as diverse. The influences on Texas have been many, from the French to the east to the Spanish and Mexicans of the south and west, and of course the Native Americans, who were there long before any others arrived. The Germans and the Chinese, who settled in Texas in large numbers during America's immigration boom, have added their cultural assets to the Texas melting pot; German Texas communities flourish and prosper to this day. Recently, the arrival of Southeast Asians has added still another cultural influence on Texas cuisine.

From the days of the chuck wagon, when cattle drovers signed on according to the reputation of "cookie," food has been enormously important here. It was no easy job to satisfy tired, hungry men, who had spent eight to twelve hours in a saddle, usually eating dust and dying of boredom—sometimes interspersed with short intervals of stark terror when things went wrong. The food had to be hearty, but it also had to be tasty. The cook was so concerned about the quality of the meals he prepared that he often slept with the sourdough jug in winter, just to keep his yeast from freezing.

Things have changed some in the Texas of today, but the love of good food remains. Along the Gulf Coast, seafood is perhaps the most important element in the cuisine, but as you move into the interior regions of the state, beef, poultry and pork are most often the main dishes. Beans of all kinds are served many ways, including dozens of kinds of cultivated peas—each with its own distinctive taste and texture. But it is the hot pepper that rises to great heights in Texas—each variety prized for what it alone can add to a dish.

Communal events are common, and range in size from a gathering of close friends to a meal for hundreds of guests. Sometimes these feasts are for the benefit of charitable organizations, but frequently they are simply an excuse for folks to get together and share good food and conversation. Barbecues are spectacular events, featuring whole sides of beef, vast numbers of chickens and huge piles of ribs—all basted with flaming hot sauce and washed down by a dozen different beverages.

Real Down Home Texas Dinner

Chili peppers are perhaps the most important ingredient in Texan dishes. There are at least six major varieties, each prized for its degree of hotness or the amount of flavor it can add to a special dish. Chilies con Queso, filled with hot peppers and onions and topped with a thick layer of mild, delicious Monterey Jack cheese, is a contrast of flavors, fiery hot and smooth. Chicken Mole Poblano, a complex dish with a sauce accented by bittersweet chocolate, is said to be an invention of necessity created by the sisters at a mission when the Bishop paid an unexpected visit. They threw together a little of everything they had, with results so satisfying that the dish has become a mainstay of Texas cuisine. Other menus incorporate many traditional Texas dishes, including warm Wilted Lettuce Salad, Enchiladas, Venison Chili, and Spicy Cabbage. There is a new accent along the Gulf Coast now, and Vietnamese Mackerel in Tomato Sauce fits right into the Texas culinary repertoire, as one taste will attest.

Real Down Home Texas Dinner

Guacamole

Chilies con Queso

Chicken Mole Poblano

Refried Beans

Tortillas

Flan

Family Fun Dinner

Spicy Fiesta Chicken

Wilted Lettuce Salad

Fig Soufflé

Supper at Home

Molded Gazpacho
Vietnamese Mackerel in Tomato Sauce
Southwest Broccoli
Natillas

Brunch for a Bunch

Green Enchiladas
Texas Quiche
Onion Casserole
Midsummer Salad

Fall Favorites

Seafood Diablo
Rice
Mexican Bean Pot
Persimmon Mousse

Hunters' Fare

Venison Chili
Spicy Cabbage
Old Time Rice Pudding

The Mexican and Native American influence on Texas food is vast indeed. Texans with no Spanish heritage enjoy the combinations of hot peppers and bland beans, rice or avocado just as much as their Hispanic brethren. At its best, Tex-Mex fare is good Texas food, inspired by the culinary traditions of our Mexican neighbors. Guacamole, a marvelous avocado concoction, can be either smooth and cooling or just as fiery hot as any other dish. Served with enchiladas—corn tortillas filled with any kind of chili and spiced with a blazing hot salsa—it can heighten the fire, or help put it out.

Fajitas have taken the country by storm, and here they are at their best—big flour tortillas filled with chunks of barbecued beef or chicken are accompanied by the near-ubiquitous guacamole and often by refried beans. Top with shredded Monterey Jack cheese and as much salsa verde as you can manage. Put out the fires with Texas Baked Apples.

Tex-Mex Celebration

Guacamole

Enchiladas

Chilies Rellenos

Chili Squash Bake

Pickled Okra

Sopaipilla Dulce

Tex-Mex Supper

Fajitas

Guacamole

Salsa Verde

Shredded Monterey Jack Cheese

Baked Apples

Barbecue is a way of life in Texas. Its origin may be in the Spanish *barbacoa*, the word for an American Indian green-wood framework for grilling meat and fish over an open fire. Wherever it came from, barbecue is here to stay. Texas barbecues can be as big as everything else in the state, requiring truckloads of food and dozens of people to put it together, but they can also be smaller, a gathering of twenty or so friends who do it all themselves. Whatever form it takes, the ingredients are often the same—grilled meats, including beef in the form of whole sides, quarters, or simply huge pieces of brisket; ribs, both beef and pork; sausages, frequently spicy enough to talk back; and sometimes chicken.

Today, barbecue rises to new heights, and charcoal grilling (often over mesquite chips) includes fish. This menu offers Charcoal-Baked Redfish with Roast Green Chilies, rice on the side and Skillet Corn Bread. Margarita Sorbet ends this meal on a perfect note.

Classic Texas Barbecue

Beef Brisket

Ribs

Sausages

Cole Slaw

Barbecued Beans

Watermelon

Barbecue at Its Best

Charcoal-Baked Redfish

Roast Green Chilies

Rice

Skillet Corn Bread

Margarita Sorbet

Texas Barbecue Plate

East Texas, which borders on the state of Louisiana, is more southerly than most of the western region of the state. Between Shreveport and Dallas, the food has a decidedly Southern accent as well—with just a little touch of the chili pepper to prove it really is Texas. Caviar Mousse starts things off on a party note, followed by Baked Stuffed Shrimp and Eggplant Creole. The delicate lightness of Pumpkin Pecan Soufflé is just the right touch for dessert.

There are many wonderful down home Texas dishes. These menus all incorporate some of the best: Steaks grilled with Green Chilies, Spanish Bean Soup, Corn and Chilies, and Fried Marinated Perch are just a few. Light Fish Mousse with Mustard Cucumber Dressing and Shrimp and Feta Cheese are indications that the effects of the trend toward lighter eating are also being felt here, but the accent is definitely a Texas one.

East Texas Celebration

Caviar Mousse
Baked Stuffed Shrimp
Eggplant Creole
Pumpkin Pecan Soufflé

Entertaining Friends

Steaks and Green Chilies
Zucchini and Mushrooms
Rice
Baked Pears

Texas Company Special

White Gazpacho
Shrimp and Feta Cheese
Spicy Rice
Ice Box Cake

Birthday Dinner Outdoors

Creamy Guacamole Dip
Fried Marinated Perch
Corn and Chilies
Chocolate Cake

Poolside Lunch

*Fish Mousse with Mustard Cucumber
    Dressing*
Spinach Salad
Almond Macaroons

Summer Fun Dinner

Spanish Bean Soup
Spicy Stockpot Ribs
Mexican Tomatoes
Coconut Ice Cream

Recipes

APPETIZERS

Guacamole

2   large ripe avocados
1   teaspoon lemon juice
2   teaspoons minced onion
1   large tomato, peeled, seeded and chopped
1   tablespoon chopped green chilies
    Salt to taste
    Pinch chili powder
    Fresh coriander for garnish

Peel the avocados and mash the flesh with a fork. Stir in the lemon juice, onion, tomato and chilies. Season with salt and chili powder. Garnish with fresh coriander.

NOTE: If guacamole is not to be eaten immediately, bury the avocado pits in the mixture, cover with plastic wrap and refrigerate.

Creamy Guacamole Dip

3   ripe avocados, peeled and pitted
1   small tomato, peeled, seeded and cubed
1   cup sour cream
1   tablespoon lemon juice
    Red pepper sauce to taste
1/2 teaspoon salt

In a large bowl mash the avocados; stir in the tomato, sour cream, lemon juice, red pepper sauce and salt. Mix well and serve with tortilla chips. Makes 2½ cups.

NOTE: This guacamole is also an excellent accompaniment for cold roast chicken.

Crab-Stuffed Mushrooms

1   pound mushrooms
    Salad oil
1/3 cup dry breadcrumbs
1/4 teaspoon thyme
    Salt to taste
    Freshly ground pepper to taste
2   tablespoons chopped parsley
1/2 cup lump crab meat, well picked over
2   tablespoons butter
1   tablespoon minced onion
    Red pepper sauce to taste
1/4 cup mayonnaise

Preheat oven to 400° F.

Twist the stems out of the mushrooms and dice the stems finely. Wash, dry and oil the mushroom caps. In a mixing bowl combine the breadcrumbs, thyme, salt, pepper, parsley and crab meat. In a small skillet melt the butter and sauté the onion and diced mushrooms until the onion is transparent; stir into the breadcrumb mixture. Stir in the mayonnaise and season with red pepper sauce. Fill the mushroom caps with the crab meat mixture and bake until lightly brown, about 8 minutes. Six to eight servings.

NOTE: This mixture can also be used to stuff cherry tomatoes.

Crab-stuffed Mushrooms
and Cherry Tomatoes

Caviar Mousse

1   envelope (1 tablespoon) unflavored
        gelatin
2   tablespoons cold water
½   cup boiling water
1   tablespoon strained lemon juice
1   tablespoon Worcestershire sauce
2   tablespoons mayonnaise
2   cups sour cream
½   teaspoon dry mustard
1   tablespoon grated onion
¼   teaspoon Beau Monde seasoning
1   4½-ounce jar red caviar, drained
1   tablespoon salad oil
      Lemon slices for garnish
      Paprika for garnish
      Melba rounds

Soften the gelatin in the cold water, then dissolve in the boiling water. Add the lemon juice and Worcestershire sauce and allow to cool. Combine the mayonnaise with the sour cream and add the mustard, onion and Beau Monde seasoning; add to the liquid mixture and blend well. Stir in the caviar.

Grease a 4-cup ring mold with a little salad oil, and pour in the mousse. Refrigerate for about 1 hour, until set. To unmold, place the lower half of the mold in hot water for a minute or so and gently cut around the edges of the mold with a sharp knife. Place a lightly moistened platter upside down on top of the mold; turn plate and mold over together. Serve the mousse on a glass or crystal platter, garnished with the lemon slices and paprika, and surrounded with melba rounds. Makes one 4-cup ring mold; 30 to 35 appetizer servings.

NOTES: It is best to make the mousse the morning of the day you plan to use it; do not make it ahead of time. Discard leftovers; the mousse may become bitter if stored. Beau Monde seasoning, a Southern favorite, is available in most food stores everywhere.

Eggplant Caviar

1   large eggplant, unpeeled
½   onion, very finely minced
2   tablespoons fresh lemon juice
1   tablespoon olive oil
2   cloves garlic, minced
½   teaspoon salt
¼   teaspoon red pepper sauce or to taste

Preheat oven to 350° F.

Place the eggplant in a shallow baking dish. Bake for 1 hour or until soft, turning once. Trim off the ends and slice the eggplant in half lengthwise. Place the eggplant halves cut side down in a colander and let them drain for 10 minutes. Scoop out the pulp and reserve. Cut the shells in pieces.

In a blender or food processor combine the eggplant shell, onion, lemon juice, oil, garlic, salt and red pepper sauce; process until the eggplant peel is finely chopped. Add the eggplant pulp and process until just chopped. Pack the mixture into a serving bowl and refrigerate for several hours. Serve at room temperature with toast points. Makes about 1½ cups.

Caviar Pie

1   8-ounce package cream cheese
1/4 cup heavy cream
1   small onion, minced
1   teaspoon lemon juice
1   3 1/2-ounce jar domestic sturgeon caviar
3   hard-cooked eggs

In a mixing bowl soften the cream cheese with the cream; beat in the onion. Spread the mixture in a 9-inch pie pan, shaping it like a crust. Refrigerate for 1 hour or until firm.

In a small bowl mix the lemon juice gently with the caviar; spread the mixture over the chilled cream cheese in the pie pan.

Shell the eggs and separate the whites and yolks; put them separately through a ricer. Pile the egg yolks in the center of the pie and place the whites around the edges in a circle. Makes one 9-inch pie.

Shrimp Rémoulade

1/2 tablespoon or more Creole mustard
3   tablespoons finely minced onion
2   cups mayonnaise
1/4 cup or more horseradish
1   clove garlic, minced
1   tablespoon chopped chives
1/4 teaspoon salt
1   tablespoon lemon juice
1/4 teaspoon pepper
1/4 cup chopped parsley
1   pound small shrimp, boiled, peeled and
       deveined
1/2 pound backfin lump crab meat, well
       picked over

In a mixing bowl combine all the ingredients except the shrimp and crab meat. Refrigerate for at least 1 hour. To serve, pour the sauce over the shrimp and crab meat. Six servings.

NOTE: Creole mustard is hot and spicy. If it is unavailable in your area, Dijon mustard is a good substitute.

Texas Quiche

1   unbaked pastry shell
1/2 cup grated sharp Cheddar cheese
3/4 cup grated Monterey Jack cheese
1   dried chili pepper, crushed
3   large eggs
1   cup cream
1/2 cup milk
1   teaspoon salt
     Red pepper sauce to taste
1   4-ounce can diced green chilies
1/3 cup sliced scallions

Line a pie plate with the pastry shell and chill for at least 30 minutes. Preheat oven to 350° F.

In a small bowl mix cheeses together and spread on the bottom of the pastry shell. Sprinkle chili pepper over the cheese.

In a large bowl beat the eggs slightly and whisk in the cream, milk, salt, red pepper sauce, chilies and scallions. Pour the mixture over the cheese in the pastry shell and bake for 40 to 45 minutes or until a knife inserted in the center of the quiche comes out clean. Serve hot or at room temperature. Six servings.

Eggs Sardou

4	tablespoons butter
2	pounds spinach, well washed, steamed and well drained
1	tablespoon flour
½	cup cream
½	teaspoon salt
¼	teaspoon pepper
¼	teaspoon nutmeg
¼	teaspoon sugar
2	tablespoons Pernod
8	artichoke bottoms, warmed in salt water
8	eggs, poached
1	cup hollandaise sauce

In a saucepan melt the butter, add the spinach and cook for 3 minutes. Sprinkle with the flour, stir and add the cream. Cook for 5 minutes over low heat. Add the seasonings and the Pernod.

Spoon some of the spinach onto each serving plate and arrange 2 artichoke bottoms over the spinach on each plate. Top each artichoke with a poached egg and spoon hollandaise sauce over the eggs. Serve very hot. Four servings.

Cheese Biscuits

1	cup (2 sticks) butter
½	pound grated Cheddar cheese
2	cups all-purpose flour
1	teaspoon baking powder
	Pinch salt
	Dash cayenne pepper
1	cup pecan halves

Preheat oven to 450° F.

In a mixing bowl work the butter and cheese together well; transfer to a board and add the flour. Knead the dough gently until the ingredients are well blended, but do not overwork. Pinch off small pieces of the dough and roll each in a ball. Place the balls on a cookie sheet and press each one flat with a fork. Place a pecan half on top of each biscuit. Bake for about 12 minutes. Makes about 2½ dozen.

Florentine Mushrooms

2	pounds fresh spinach, well washed
½	pound (2 sticks) butter
2	pounds fresh mushrooms, caps removed, stems chopped
3	medium onions, minced
2	cloves garlic, minced
½	cup fine breadcrumbs
1½	teaspoons salt
	Freshly ground black pepper to taste
1	teaspoon dry mustard
6	tablespoons freshly grated Parmesan cheese

Preheat oven to 375° F.

In a saucepan cook the spinach in unsalted water; drain, squeeze out any excess moisture and chop. Puree the spinach in a blender or food processor.

In a skillet melt the butter. Dip the mushroom caps in the butter, coating all sides. Place cap side down on a baking sheet. Reheat the butter and sauté the onions and chopped mushroom stems until soft. Add the spinach, garlic, breadcrumbs and seasonings; stir to combine.

Fill the mushrooms caps with the spinach mixture, mounding high. Sprinkle with the grated cheese. Bake for 10 to 12 minutes. Twenty servings.

Chilies con Queso

2   10-ounce cans whole green chilies, seeded, deveined and sliced
5   jalapeño peppers, seeded, deveined and chopped (optional)
1   medium tomato, peeled and chopped
1   large onion, sliced
2   cloves garlic, chopped
    Red pepper sauce to taste
2   pounds mild Cheddar cheese, grated
8   ounces Monterey Jack cheese, grated
8   ounces Longhorn Cheddar cheese, grated

Preheat oven to 375° F.

In a medium saucepan stir together the green chilies, jalapeño peppers, tomato and onion and simmer over low heat for 30 minutes. Stir in the garlic and red pepper sauce. Pile the pepper mixture in an ovenproof dish, top with the cheeses and bake for 30 minutes. Serve hot, accompanied by tortilla chips. Makes 4 cups.

NOTE: If you include the optional jalapeño peppers when making this dish, be sure to wear rubber gloves when preparing them.

Oysters Bienville

4   tablespoons butter
2   bunches scallions, including green tops, chopped
1/4   pound mushrooms, chopped
2   tablespoons flour
3/4   cup chicken broth
1   cup cooked shrimp, chopped
2   egg yolks
1/3   cup white wine
    Salt to taste
    Black pepper to taste
1/4   teaspoon cayenne or red pepper sauce
3   dozen oysters on the half shell
    Rock salt or kosher salt
1   cup breadcrumbs
1/4   cup grated Parmesan cheese
    Paprika

Preheat oven to 450° F.

In a skillet melt the butter and lightly sauté the scallions and mushrooms. Blend in the flour and gradually add the broth; stir in the shrimp. In a small bowl beat the egg yolks with the wine; add to the shrimp mixture, stirring constantly until thickened. Remove the sauce from the heat and season with salt and pepper.

Arrange the oysters on a bed of rock salt on an ovenproof platter. Top each oyster with a spoonful of the sauce. Sprinkle the tops with breadcrumbs, grated cheese and paprika. Bake for 10 to 12 minutes until the sauce is bubbly and the edges of the oysters have begun to curl. Six servings.

Po' Boy Oyster Loaf

1   18-inch loaf French bread
     Butter or garlic mayonnaise
2   *dozen oysters*
     Cornmeal
     Lard for frying
     Shredded lettuce (optional)

Split the top crust off the loaf of bread about
½ inch down. Scoop out some of the soft
bread inside the bottom, making a boat of it.
Brush both the top and bottom pieces with
butter or garlic mayonnaise. Toast the bread
lightly under a broiler.

   Roll the oysters in the cornmeal and fry
them in hot lard; drain. Pile the oysters in the
hollowed-out section of the bread. Top with
the shredded lettuce if desired. Close the
sandwich, cut it in half and serve. Four to six
servings.

NOTE: As a main dish for lunch or supper,
this sandwich will serve two or three.

Ham Biscuits

12   *baking powder biscuits*
1½   *cups ground ham*
 2   *teaspoons Dijon-style or Creole mustard*
½   *cup heavy cream*
      Red pepper sauce to taste

Preheat oven to 400° F.
   Split the biscuits. In a medium bowl mix
together the remaining ingredients. Spread
the mixture over the bottom halves of the
biscuits. Cover with the tops of the biscuits
and bake for 5 minutes. Serve hot. Twelve
servings.

NOTE: See the Resource Guide for
information on ordering Creole mustard if it
is unavailable in your area.

Green Enchiladas

1   *3-pound frying chicken*
4   *cloves garlic*
3   *medium green tomatoes*
1   *4-ounce can green chilies*
1   *clove garlic*
     Salt to taste
1   *cup chicken broth*
3   *tablespoons oil*
     Small piece of onion
1   *package corn tortillas*
1   *cup sour cream*
8   *ounces Monterey Jack cheese, shredded*

In a large saucepan or Dutch oven boil the
chicken with the garlic cloves in water to cover
until the chicken is very tender (at least 30
minutes). Remove the meat from the bones
and set it aside.
   Preheat oven to 350° F.
   In a medium saucepan boil the tomatoes for
15 minutes, peel, then place in a blender
along with the green chilies, garlic, salt and
chicken broth. Blend until smooth.
   In a heavy skillet heat the oil and fry the
onion until brown. Remove the onion, add the
pureed mixture to the skillet and heat for a
few minutes. In another skillet fry the tortillas

in a little oil to soften them, then dip them through the mixture in the other skillet.

Place some chicken inside each tortilla and roll up. Place filled tortillas side by side in an oblong casserole dish, spread sour cream over the top and cover with the shredded cheese. Cover the casserole and heat in the oven for about 20 to 30 minutes. Heat the remainder of the sauce and serve separately, to be poured over the enchiladas. Six to eight appetizer servings.

NOTE: If you wish to serve this dish as a main course, this recipe will provide four servings.

Spicy Pecan Ham Mold

   3   cups ground Virginia-style ham
         (1 pound)
   1   8-ounce package cream cheese,
         softened
  1/3   cup chopped chutney
 1 1/4 teaspoons red pepper sauce
   1   cup chopped pecans
        Parsley sprigs for garnish (optional)

In a small bowl combine the ham, cream cheese, chutney and red pepper sauce; mix until smooth. Stir in 2/3 cup of the pecans. Line a 4-cup mold or bowl with clear plastic wrap and pack the ham mixture firmly into the mold. Refrigerate for 1 to 2 hours. Turn the mold out onto a serving platter; gently remove the plastic wrap. Press the remaining pecans on the sides and top of the mold. Garnish with parsley, if desired. Serve with thin slices of rye bread. Makes about 4 cups.

Venison Sashimi

 1 1/2 tablespoons water
   1   tablespoon wasabi (Japanese
         horseradish)
   1   pound fillet of venison, partially frozen
   3   tablespoons soy sauce

In a small bowl mix together the water and wasabi to form a paste. Slice the partially frozen venison into paper-thin strips. Arrange the venison strips around the mound of wasabi on a serving plate. Serve accompanied by the soy sauce in a small bowl. Six or more servings.

NOTES: Partially freezing the meat makes it much easier to cut in paper-thin strips. Venison is a very rich meat; when it is served in this manner, you may find that a little goes a long way.

Hot Artichoke Dip

   1   4-ounce can artichoke hearts, drained
         and coarsely chopped
   1   cup freshly grated Parmesan cheese
   1   cup homemade mayonnaise
   2   cloves garlic, minced
        Dash fresh lemon juice

Preheat oven to 350° F.

In a medium bowl combine all ingredients and mix well. Pack the mixture in an ovenproof casserole and heat for about 10 minutes until it is thoroughly warm and the cheese is melted. Eight to ten servings.

Highlands Bar and Grill's Mini Crab Cakes

9   tablespoons unsalted butter
3   eggs
1   tablespoon water
1   pound fresh lump crab meat, well picked
      over
3¼ cups fresh breadcrumbs,
      lightly packed
1   small shallot, minced
¼   cup chopped parsley
2   tablespoons fresh lemon juice
1   tablespoon chopped parsley
      Red pepper sauce to taste
¾   teaspoon salt
¼   teaspoon freshly ground black pepper
1   tablespoon peanut oil
¼   cup dry white wine
1   teaspoon lemon juice
1   tablespoon chopped parsley
      Lemon wedges for garnish
      Parsley sprigs for garnish

In a small skillet melt 4 tablespoons of the butter; set aside to cool.

In a large bowl lightly beat 1 egg with the water. Add the crab meat, half of the breadcrumbs, the cooled melted butter, the shallot, 2 tablespoons lemon juice, ¼ cup parsley, 2 tablespoons of the lemon juice, the red pepper sauce, ½ teaspoon of the salt and the black pepper; stir well to combine. Shape the mixture into 12 small cakes about ½ inch thick.

Place the remaining 1½ cups breadcrumbs in a shallow bowl. In another shallow bowl lightly beat the remaining 2 eggs with 2 tablespoons of water. Dip each crab cake first in the eggs, then in the breadcrumbs, pressing lightly so the crumbs adhere. Shake off any excess. Set the cakes on a rack.

In a large skillet melt 1 tablespoon of the remaining butter in the oil over moderately high heat until foaming. Add the crab cakes, reduce the heat to medium and fry until a golden crust forms on the bottom, about 3 minutes. Turn and cook the other side until lightly browned, about 3 minutes. Remove and set aside.

Pour off any fat from the skillet. Add the white wine and the 1 teaspoon lemon juice and bring to a boil over moderately high heat. Boil until reduced by half, about 2 minutes. Remove from the heat and whisk in the remaining 4 tablespoons butter, 1 tablespoon at a time. Stir in 1 tablespoon parsley and season with the remaining ¼ teaspoon salt and a pinch of black pepper. Garnish each serving with a lemon wedge and a sprig of parsley. Serve the sauce on the side. Six servings.

Scalloped Oysters

2   cups crushed saltine crackers
1   quart oysters, drained,
      liquor reserved
⅔   cup minced parsley
⅓   cup minced scallions
½   cup (1 stick) butter
      Seasoned salt or Creole seasoning to
      taste
      Pepper to taste
      Light cream

Preheat oven to 350° F.

Place a layer of cracker crumbs in a greased 1½-quart casserole; cover with a layer of oysters. Sprinkle the oysters with the seasonings and dot with some of the butter. Repeat the layers, ending with the crumbs and butter. Measure the oyster liquor and combine it with an equal amount of cream. Pour the liquid over the oysters and bake for 20 minutes or until bubbling. Serve very hot. Six to eight servings.

Oysters Rockefeller

2	bunches scallions, including green tops, finely chopped
¼	cup chopped fresh parsley
1½	cup (1 stick) butter or margarine
2	pounds fresh spinach, washed, steamed, drained and finely chopped
	Salt to taste
¾	tablespoon anchovy paste
2	tablespoons Worcestershire sauce
	Red pepper sauce to taste
2	tablespoons horseradish
2	teaspoons basil
1	teaspoon marjoram
2	tablespoons Pernod
1	tablespoon bitters
3	dozen oysters on the half shell
	Rock salt or kosher salt

Preheat oven to 450° F.

In a large skillet sauté the scallions and parsley in the butter for 20 minutes; cool. Remove and puree until smooth. Return the puree to the skillet; add the spinach, salt, anchovy paste, Worcestershire sauce, red pepper sauce, horseradish, basil and marjoram and bring to a full boil. Remove from the heat; add the Pernod and bitters.

Arrange the oysters on a bed of rock salt on an ovenproof platter. Top each oyster with a spoonful of the sauce and bake until the tops are slightly browned and the edges of the oysters have begun to curl. Six servings.

Oyster Spinach Quiche

1	white onion, chopped
2	tablespoons butter
1	pound fresh spinach, washed, steamed and drained
2	tablespoons flour
1	teaspoon salt
¼	teaspoon pepper
¼	teaspoon nutmeg
	Cayenne pepper to taste (optional)
2	eggs, beaten
1¼	cups half and half cream
2	tablespoons grated Parmesan cheese
1	dozen oysters, drained
1	unbaked 9-inch pie shell

Preheat oven to 400° F.

In a saucepan sauté the onion in the butter; stir in the spinach and cook for 2 minutes. Add the flour and seasonings and stir to combine. In a medium bowl combine the eggs with the cream and Parmesan cheese; beat well and stir into the spinach mixture. Place the oysters in the pie shell and cover them with the spinach mixture. Bake for 50 to 55 minutes. Serve very hot. Six servings.

Oyster Pan Roast

2   tablespoons butter
1   teaspoon chili sauce
    Dash Worchestershire sauce
    Dash red pepper sauce
    Salt to taste
    Freshly ground black pepper to taste
1/4 cup heavy cream
1   dozen oysters and their liquor
2   slices of buttered toast

In a skillet melt the butter; add the chili sauce, Worcestershire sauce, red pepper sauce, salt and pepper. Stir in the cream. Add the oysters and their liquor and cook them just until they are plump and the edges are curled. Place the oysters on slices of toast on preheated soup plates and pour the pan juices over them. Two servings.

Oysters Bayou

2   tablespoons butter
1   tablespoon flour
3   scallions, minced
2   tablespoons minced parsley
1/4 cup white wine
1/2 cup oyster liquor
1   cup pureed artichoke hearts
12   oysters, drained
     Salt to taste
     White pepper to taste
1/8 teaspoon cayenne pepper
     Red pepper sauce to taste
1/2 teaspoon Worcestershire sauce
1/3 cup breadcrumbs

1/4 cup grated Parmesan cheese
     Minced parsley for garnish
1   teaspoon butter

Preheat oven to 375° F.

In a saucepan melt the butter and stir in the flour. Add the scallions and parsley and cook over low heat, stirring occasionally, for 3 minutes or until the vegetables are soft. Stir in the wine and the oyster liquor and continue to cook over low heat for 5 minutes. Add the artichoke puree, oysters and seasonings; cover and simmer for 10 minutes. Pour into 2 buttered ramekins or gratin dishes, top with the breadcrumbs and cheese, sprinkle with the minced parsley and dot with the remaining butter. Bake for 10 minutes or until hot and bubbly. Two servings.

Anchovy Puffs

1/2 cup (1 stick) butter, softened
1   3-ounce package cream cheese
1   cup flour
1   can anchovies, rinsed, dried and mashed
    Finely chopped pecans

Preheat oven to 400° F.

In a mixing bowl cream together the butter and cream cheese. Beat in the flour; chill. Roll out the pastry very thin and cut into rounds with a 2-inch cutter. Place a small amount of mashed anchovies and a few chopped pecans on each pastry round. Moisten the edges with water, fold in half and press the edges together with a fork to seal the puffs tightly.

Bake for about 10 minutes or until brown. Serve hot. Makes about 4 dozen.

NOTE: These may be made several days ahead and stored in the refrigerator.

Artichoke Squares

2 6-ounce jars marinated artichoke
    hearts
1 onion, chopped
1 clove garlic, minced
2 cups coarsely grated zucchini,
    drained
4 eggs, slightly beaten
½ cup or more seasoned cracker
    crumbs
    Salt to taste
    Freshly ground pepper to taste
1 teaspoon oregano
    Red pepper sauce to taste
8 ounces (2 cups) grated sharp Cheddar
    cheese
3 tablespoons minced parsley

Preheat the oven to 325° F. Grease a 7- x 11-inch ovenproof casserole.

Drain the marinade from 1 jar of artichokes and reserve. Drain the marinade from the other jar of artichokes and discard. Chop the artichokes and set aside.

In a skillet sauté the onion, garlic and zucchini in the reserved marinade until transparent; do not brown. In a mixing bowl combine the beaten eggs with the crumbs, salt, pepper, oregano and red pepper sauce; mix well. Combine the egg mixture with the

cheese, parsley, artichokes and zucchini mixture. Pour into the casserole and bake for 30 minutes or until set when lightly touched. Let cool slightly, cut into squares, and reheat for about 10 minutes. Serve hot. Eight to ten servings.

Asparagus Canapes

1 1-pound loaf thinly sliced white bread,
    crusts removed
8 ounces Roquefort cheese,
    crumbled
1 8-ounce package cream cheese,
    softened
1 tablespoon mayonnaise
1 egg, beaten
½ teaspoon Worcestershire sauce
1 tablespoon grated onion
2 pounds fresh asparagus,
    steamed until
    just tender
    Melted butter

Preheat oven to 350° F.

Roll out the bread slices with a rolling pin. In a mixing bowl beat together the cheeses, mayonnaise, egg, Worcestershire sauce and onion. Spread the mixture on the bread and top each slice with 1 asparagus spear. Roll up each bread slice and cut into 3 pieces. Dip each piece in melted butter. Place on an ungreased cookie sheet and bake for 15 minutes. Makes 5½ dozen.

NOTE: These can be frozen before baking.

SOUPS

Oyster Stew

2   cups milk
2   cups light cream
1   pint small oysters
4   tablespoons butter
    Salt to taste
    Celery salt to taste
    White pepper to taste
    Paprika to taste

In a large saucepan combine the milk and cream and scald the mixture. Drain off and reserve nearly all the liquor from the oysters, leaving about 2 tablespoons. In a large skillet melt the butter; add the oysters with the 2 tablespoons liquor and cook just until the edges of the oysters begin to curl. Remove the oysters and set aside; add the milk and cream, the reserved oyster liquor and the seasonings to the skillet. When the mixture begins to bubble, add the reserved oysters. Heat through and serve hot. Six servings.

Potato and Leek Soup

1   tablespoon butter
4   leeks, cut in ½-inch slices
1   onion, diced
4   medium potatoes, peeled and
        diced
4   cups chicken broth
1   cup sour cream
    Pepper to taste

In a large saucepan melt the butter; add the leeks and onion and cook, covered, until the vegetables are tender, stirring occasionally. Add the potatoes and broth and simmer, covered, for 40 minutes. Add the sour cream; heat to serving temperature but *do not boil*. Season with pepper and serve at once. Eight servings.

Sorrel Soup

¼   pound sorrel
¼   pound watercress
¼   cup (½ stick) butter
1   medium potato, peeled and
        chopped
1   teaspoon fresh thyme
3   cups chicken stock, heated
1¼ cups buttermilk

Chop the sorrel and the watercress and stew them gently in the butter in a heavy kettle for about 5 minutes. Add the potato and the thyme, and stir in the stock. Cover and simmer for 35 minutes or until the potato is soft. Cool slightly, then pour the mixture into a blender. Puree the mixture and pour it into a serving bowl. Stir in the buttermilk and chill. Check the seasonings and adjust if necessary. Four to five servings.

NOTE: To serve the soup hot, substitute a mixture of half milk and half cream for the buttermilk and reheat gently before serving.

Creole Turtle Soup

½   cup (1 stick) butter
4   tablespoons flour
2   large onions, finely chopped
1   green pepper, finely chopped
2   ribs celery, minced
2   tablespoons chopped fresh parsley
6   cloves garlic, minced
3   pounds turtle meat, including any eggs
    and turtle bones
2   quarts beef broth
2   quarts hot water
1   pound tomatoes, peeled, seeded and
    chopped
2   bay leaves
1   lemon, sliced
¼   teaspoon ground allspice
¼   teaspoon ground cloves
½   teaspoon basil
½   teaspoon thyme
¼   teaspoon marjoram
½   teaspoon cayenne
1   tablespoon Worcestershire sauce
⅓   cup sherry
    Salt to taste
    Freshly ground black pepper to taste
    Chopped hard-cooked eggs for garnish
    Chopped parsley for garnish
    Lemon slices for garnish

In a large heavy kettle make a roux with the butter and flour, cooking slowly and stirring constantly until it is a rich brown color, about 20 to 30 minutes. Add the onions, green pepper, celery, chopped parsley and garlic; cook, stirring occasionally, until the vegetables are soft and translucent.

Dice the turtle meat into ½-inch cubes and add it to the kettle. Add the bones, if any, to the kettle.

Add the beef broth, hot water, tomatoes and bay leaves to the kettle; bring to a boil. Reduce the heat, partially cover the kettle and simmer for 2 hours. Remove the bay leaves.

Add the lemon slices and the seasonings, except for the salt and pepper, and mix well. Partially cover the kettle again and simmer over *very* low heat for at least 2 more hours, preferably as much as 4 hours. Stir occasionally, scraping the bottom of the pot.

About 30 minutes before serving add the sherry and the turtle eggs, if any. Remove the lemon slices and turtle bones. Season the soup with salt and freshly ground black pepper. To serve, ladle the soup from the bottom of the kettle upward into preheated soup bowls. Garnish each serving with a sprinkling of chopped eggs and chopped parsley, and float a thin slice of lemon on top. Ten to twelve servings.

Spanish Bean Soup

1   cup dried navy beans, soaked overnight
    and drained
5   cups chicken broth
½   cup chopped celery
½   cup chopped onion
½   cup chopped carrots
1   tablespoon chopped fresh parsley
½   cup diced lean cooked ham
1   bay leaf
1   tablespoon tomato paste
1   teaspoon Worcestershire sauce

½ teaspoon dried basil
½ teaspoon dried oregano
   Red pepper sauce to taste
   Grated Romano cheese
   (optional)

In a large pot combine the beans, chicken broth, vegetables and parsley and bring to a boil. Cover, reduce heat and simmer for 45 minutes.

Add to the pot all other ingredients except the cheese; cover and simmer for an additional 30 minutes. Remove the bay leaf. Sprinkle each serving with Romano cheese, if desired. Six servings.

Collard Greens Soup

½ cup dried northern beans
2 quarts water
2 small ham hocks
½ pound beef short ribs
1 teaspoon salt
2 potatoes, diced
1½ pounds fresh collards, chopped
½ medium onion, chopped
½ green pepper, seeded and
   chopped
1 pound smoked sausage
   (Kielbasa), cut in
   pieces
3 tablespoons bacon drippings

Soak the beans overnight in water to cover. Drain. In a large pot place the water, ham hocks, short ribs and salt. Bring to a boil, removing the foam with a skimmer. Lower the heat and simmer for 30 minutes. Add the beans and simmer until tender. Add the potatoes and collard greens. Sauté the onion, green pepper and sausage in the bacon drippings until the onion is transparent; add to the soup. Bring to a boil and cook, uncovered, for 10 minutes. Cover the pot and simmer until the potatoes and greens are done. Check the seasonings and adjust if necessary. Serve hot. Eight to ten servings.

White Gazpacho

3 medium cucumbers, peeled, seeded and
   cut into chunks
3 cups well-seasoned chicken broth
3 cups sour cream
3 tablespoons white vinegar
2 tomatoes, peeled, seeded and chopped
½ cup sliced scallions
½ cup chopped parsley
1 avocado, peeled, seeded, chopped and
   sprinkled with lemon juice

In a food processor combine the cucumber chunks with a little of the chicken broth. In a large bowl combine the cucumber puree with the remaining chicken broth, sour cream and vinegar; stir just enough to mix. Chill in the refrigerator for several hours. Serve the soup accompanied by the tomatoes, scallions, parsley and avocado in separate bowls. Six servings.

NOTE: Yogurt may be substituted for the sour cream, or 2 cups of yogurt and 1 cup of sour cream may be used.

Crawfish Bisque

3   dozen crawfish
3   tablespoons lard or butter
3   tablespoons minced parsley
1/3 cup minced scallions
1/4 cup minced shallots
6   slices fresh bread, soaked in water
    Salt to taste
    Freshly ground pepper to taste
    Cayenne pepper to taste

BISQUE

1   tablespoon lard or bacon grease
1/2 onion, minced
1/2 green pepper, minced
2   tablespoons flour
2   tablespoons tomato paste
    Juice from the crawfish heads
6–8 cups crawfish cooking water
    Salt to taste
    Pepper to taste
    Red pepper sauce to taste

Boil the crawfish in water just to cover until they turn red. Drain and reserve the cooking water. Separate the heads from the tails. Chop up the tail meat.

Preheat oven to 400° F.

In a skillet melt the lard or butter and sauté the tail meat for 1 minute. Add the parsley, scallions and shallots and cook for 2 minutes. Squeeze out the bread slices and stir them into the mixture. Season the mixture with the salt, pepper and cayenne. Stuff the mixture into the crawfish heads. Arrange the heads on a baking sheet and bake for 5 to 6 minutes to brown.

To make the bisque, melt the lard in a heavy pot. Add the onion and green pepper and sauté until the onion is transparent. Stir in the flour and cook until brown. Stir in the tomato paste, juice from the crawfish heads and cooking water. Simmer for at least 1 hour. Season with the salt, pepper and red pepper sauce. Add the stuffed heads and heat thoroughly. Serve at once over freshly cooked rice. Six to eight servings.

NOTE: See the Resource guide for information on ordering crawfish (crayfish).

Mary Snyder's Cold Avocado Soup

4   large avocados, peeled and
      chopped
2   tablespoons lemon juice
2   cups chicken broth
1   green pepper, chopped
2   cups heavy cream
    Salt to taste
    Pepper to taste
    Red pepper sauce to taste

Combine the avocado, lemon juice, chicken broth and green pepper, reserving a few pieces of the avocado for garnish and sprinkling them with lemon juice to prevent darkening. Puree the avocado mixture in a blender or food processor until smooth. Stir in the heavy cream and season with the salt, pepper and red pepper sauce. Chill. Serve very cold, garnished with the reserved avocado. Eight servings.

Grouper Chowder

2   pounds new potatoes, diced
1   large onion, sliced
3/4   pound salt pork, cubed
6   large tomatoes, peeled,
      seeded and
      chopped
1   large grouper, filleted,
      fillets cut into
      pieces
1/2   teaspoon pepper
1/4   teaspoon red pepper sauce
      Lemon slices for garnish

In a saucepan boil the potatoes and onion for 15 minutes in water to cover. In a small skillet fry the salt pork until golden; add the pork and drippings to the potatoes. Add the tomatoes and simmer for 15 minutes. Add the fish and simmer for 45 minutes more; season with the pepper and red pepper sauce. Garnish each serving with a slice of lemon. Eight to ten servings.

Conch Chowder

6   large conch, cleaned
1/4   pound salt pork, finely diced
1   medium onion, chopped
1   rib celery, chopped
1/2   green pepper, seeded and chopped
1   tablespoon oregano
1   teaspoon lime juice
      Salt to taste
      Pepper to taste
1/2   cup light cream

Pound the conch with a meat mallet or hammer until thin; cut into small dice.

In a skillet fry the salt pork; remove and set aside. Add the onion, celery and green pepper to the fat remaining in the skillet and cook until tender.

Place the conch in a heavy kettle. Add the salt pork, cooked vegetables, 6 cups water, the oregano and the lime juice; simmer for 1 hour or until the conch is very tender. Season with salt and pepper and stir to combine; add the cream to thicken the chowder slightly. Reheat if necessary but do not boil. Serve immediately. Six to eight servings.

Beet and Claret Soup

10   medium beets, peeled and sliced
2   pounds tomatoes, peeled, seeded and
      chopped
6 1/2   cups chicken stock or broth
2 1/3   cups dry red wine (Bordeaux or
      Beaujolais)
2   teaspoons sliced fresh ginger
3/4   cup strained fresh orange juice
      Paper-thin orange slices for
      garnish

In a large saucepan combine the beets and tomatoes. Add the chicken stock, wine and ginger. Cover tightly and simmer until the beets are very tender, about 1 to 2 hours. Strain the mixture carefully; do not press down on the tomatoes or the soup will be cloudy. Sitr the orange juice into the strained soup and reheat before serving. Garnish each serving with a slice of orange. Ten servings.

Cold Watercress Soup

1   bunch watercress
3   tablespoons butter
2   bunches scallions
2   cups hot chicken or beef stock
2½   cups buttermilk
     Salt to taste
     Pepper to taste

Wash and chop the watercress, including the stems. In a saucepan melt the butter; add the scallions and watercress and sauté gently, stirring occasionally, for about 8 minutes. Pour in the stock and simmer for 20 minutes; cool. Stir in the buttermilk. Season well with salt and pepper. Puree the mixture in a blender, then chill for at least 2 hours before serving. Four servings.

George Washington Carver's Peanut Soup

1   cup ground roasted peanuts
1   quart milk
½   teaspoon salt
1   small onion, finely minced
     Freshly ground black pepper
1   rib celery, finely chopped
1   teaspoon celery seed
1   tablespoon cornstarch
¼   cup cold milk

In a large saucepan simmer the peanuts, milk, salt, onion, pepper, celery and celery seed for 15 minutes, stirring to keep from burning.

In a small bowl stir the cornstarch into the cold milk, making a smooth paste. Stir the cornstarch paste into the soup and cook over low heat until the soup is thick and smooth. Strain the soup and serve very hot. Four to six servings.

Florida Fish Chowder

1   cup diced potatoes
1   cup sliced carrots
½   cup diced celery
1   clove garlic, minced (optional)
½   teaspoon salt
2   tablespoons or more butter
1   medium onion, thinly sliced
1–2 pounds snapper, grouper, snook or other
     firm-meat fish, skinned, boned and cut
     into 1-inch pieces
1   teaspoon Worcestershire sauce
1   teaspoon salt
¼   teaspoon pepper
1½   cups milk
1½   cups half and half cream
     Small bunch dill, snipped

In a saucepan cook the potatoes, carrots, celery, garlic and salt in water to cover until almost tender. Drain. In a large saucepan melt the butter; add the onion and cook over low heat until transparent. Add the fish and the Worcestershire sauce; cook for 1 minute, stirring gently. Add the vegetables and water and simmer for 10 minutes. Add the salt, pepper, milk and cream; bring to a boil over low heat. Add most of the dill and stir gently to combine. Sprinkle a little dill over each serving. Six to eight servings.

Squash Soup

2 tablespoons butter
1 medium onion, finely chopped
4 cups peeled, chopped winter
     squash
1 large potato, diced
2 medium tomatoes,
     peeled, seeded and
     chopped
4 cups chicken stock,
     canned chicken broth
     or water
   Salt
   Freshly ground black pepper
   Hot pepper sauce
   Chopped celery leaves
   Chopped parsley
2 tablespoons butter
   Light cream
   Croutons

In a soup pot melt the butter and cook the onion until it is tender but not brown. Add the vegetables and the stock or broth. Season with the salt, pepper, hot pepper sauce, celery leaves and fresh parsley to taste. Cook the vegetables until they are tender. Puree the mixture in a food mill, blender or food processor. Rinse the pot and return the soup to it. Add the butter and cream and heat through. Serve the soup with croutons. Six servings.

NOTE: For a special presentation, serve the soup in the hollowed-out squash.

Oyster and Artichoke Soup

½ cup (1 stick) butter
2 bunches scallions, chopped
1 large onion, minced
½ cup chopped celery
3 cloves garlic, minced
3 cups artichoke hearts,
     quartered (fresh
     or canned)
3 tablespoons flour
4 cups chicken stock
½ teaspoon crushed red pepper
1 teaspoon salt
1 tablespoon Worcestershire
     sauce
1 quart oysters, drained
     and chopped,
     liquor reserved
2 cups half and half cream
   Red pepper sauce to taste

In a heavy kettle melt the butter; sauté the scallions, onion, celery and garlic until soft. Add the artichokes. Sprinkle with the flour and stir to coat well, but do not brown. Add the stock and seasonings. Cover and simmer for 1 hour. Add the oysters and their liquor; simmer for 10 minutes but do not boil. Puree the mixture in a food processor or blender. Return the soup to the kettle, add the cream, and heat through. Add the red pepper sauce. Serve the soup hot or cold. Six to eight servings.

NOTE: This soup is best when made the day before.

Creole Crawfish Bisque

2   quarts water
1   onion, quartered
1   lemon, quartered
2   tablespoons salt
1   3-ounce bag crab boil
3   pounds live crawfish
1   onion, diced
4   scallions, chopped
2   cloves garlic, minced
1   rib celery, diced
2   tablespoons butter
1   teaspoon Worcestershire sauce
½   teaspoon red pepper sauce or more to
       taste
3   tablespoons minced parsley
3   slices bread, soaked in stock and
       squeezed out
1   pound cooked and peeled crawfish tails
     Paprika to taste
     Salt to taste
     Pepper to taste

BISQUE

1   cup (2 sticks) butter
1   cup flour
2   ribs celery, diced
1   onion, diced
4   scallions, diced
2   cloves garlic, pressed
3   tablespoons tomato paste
1   pound tomatoes, peeled, seeded and
       chopped

In a large pot bring the water and the next 4 ingredients to a boil and cook for about 15 minutes. Add the live crawfish and let boil for 10 minutes. Turn off the heat, cover the pot and let it stand for another 10 minutes. Drain, reserving the stock. Cool and pick over the crawfish, saving the fat and the cleaned heads and shells as well as the meat.

In a skillet sauté the diced onion, chopped scallions, minced garlic and diced celery in the butter until the vegetables are wilted. Combine the sautéed vegetables with the Worcestershire sauce, red pepper sauce, minced parsley and bread slices; add all of the crawfish meat, including the additional pound of cooked crawfish tails, and some of the crawfish fat. Reseason to taste with the paprika, salt and pepper. Stuff the mixture into the cleaned crawfish heads.

To make the bisque, in a heavy kettle melt the butter; blend in the flour a little at a time and cook slowly, stirring constantly, until the roux is a light brown, about 15 minutes. Add the diced celery, onions and scallions, the pressed garlic cloves and the remaining crawfish fat; continue to stir and cook to a dark brown. Add the tomato paste and chopped tomatoes and stir to combine. Slowly add the reserved stock to the kettle, then cook the bisque for 30 to 45 minutes. Adjust the seasonings if necessary. Gently add the stuffed crawfish heads to the bisque, then cook for 15 minutes more. Serve in large bowls over steamed rice. Eight to ten servings.

NOTE: See the Resource Guide for information on ordering crawfish (crayfish) and crab boil seasoning.

Minestrone Soup with Pesto Sauce

1   cup dried navy beans
4   cups chicken broth
    Salt to taste
1   small head cabbage, shredded
4   carrots, peeled and sliced
2   medium potatoes, peeled and diced
10 large tomatoes, peeled, seeded and
        chopped
2   medium onions, chopped
1   rib celery, chopped
2   cloves garlic, minced
1/4 cup olive oil
1   cup broken thin spaghetti
    Chopped parsley
1/4 teaspoon pepper
    Pesto Sauce (see Accompaniments
        section)

Soak the beans overnight in water to cover.
Drain. In a large pot add 6 cups of water to
the chicken broth and bring to a boil. Add the
beans and salt and simmer until the beans are
almost tender. Add the cabbage, carrots,
potatoes and tomatoes and simmer for 10
minutes.

   In a skillet sauté the onion, celery and garlic
in the olive oil until the onion is transparent;
add the mixture to the soup. Add the
spaghetti, parsley and pepper and simmer
until the spaghetti is tender. Serve with a
spoonful of Pesto Sauce added to each bowl.
Ten servings.

NOTE: The soup may be prepared ahead of
time and reheated to serve.

Conch Chowder with Tomatoes

3   cups conch meat, chopped
    Flour for dredging
1/4 pound bacon, chopped
2   medium onions, chopped
6   tomatoes, peeled, seeded
        and chopped
3   cups fish stock or clam juice
1/2 teaspoon fennel seed
1/2 teaspoon thyme
1/2 teaspoon oregano
1/2 teaspoon black pepper
3   large potatoes, peeled and cut into
        1/2-inch cubes
1   cup heavy cream
1/4 cup finely chopped parsley
1/4 cup finely chopped dill

Toss the conch in the flour. In a large skillet
fry the conch with the bacon and onion until
lightly brown. Stir in the tomatoes and simmer
for 15 minutes; add the fish stock or clam
juice and seasoning. Simmer for 2 hours or
until the conch is tender, adding more liquid
if necessary during the cooking. Add the
potatoes and enough liquid to cover and
simmer until the potatoes are tender. Stir in
the cream and heat thoroughly. Adjust the
seasoning. Serve in small bowls garnished with
the parsley and dill. Eight to ten servings.

NOTE: Many fine seafood purveyors across the
country often have conch. See the Resource
Guide for information on ordering conch if it
is unavailable in your area.

SALADS

Creamy Tomato Aspic

2   tablespoons unflavored gelatin
1/2 cup warm water
16 ounces vegetable juice cocktail
3   3-ounce packages cream cheese
1   cup chopped celery
1/2 green pepper, seeded and chopped
2   tablespoons lemon juice
1   cup homemade mayonnaise
1   tablespoon Worcestershire sauce
    Salt to taste
1–2 teaspoons red pepper sauce

In a small bowl soften the gelatin in the warm water. In the top of a double boiler heat the vegetable juice; add the cream cheese and beat until smooth. Add the gelatin and stir until dissolved. Cool the mixture, then add the remaining ingredients in the order given. Pour into an oiled 1-quart mold and chill until set. Six to eight servings.

NOTE: Garnish the aspic with sautéed butterflied shrimp for an elegant presentation.

Smoked Fish Salad

2   cups smoked fish, diced
1/2 cup garbanzo beans (chick peas)
1/2 medium head lettuce, torn into 2-inch pieces
1   large avocado, peeled and cut into 1-inch cubes
1   medium tomato, peeled, seeded and chopped
1   cup chopped celery
1/4 cup chopped scallions
1/2 cup grated carrot
1   cup shredded mild Cheddar cheese
1/2 cup homemade mayonnaise thinned with 3 tablespoons buttermilk
1   4-ounce package tortilla chips, lightly crushed

In a mixing bowl combine all of the ingredients except the mayonnaise and the chips. Toss gently, but mix well. Add the dressing and the chips, toss gently and serve immediately. Eight servings.

Shellfish and Melon Salad

1/4 cup heavy cream
1/2 ounce Scotch whisky
    Pinch curry powder
1   cup homemade mayonnaise
1   cup drained 1-inch melon cubes (honeydew, casaba or Spanish melon)
2   cups cooked small shrimp, or picked over crab meat, or lobster meat, in chunks
    Lettuce leaves
    Paprika

In a bowl combine the cream, whisky, curry powder and mayonnaise; mix until smooth. Stir in the melon and shellfish gently. Arrange a bed of lettuce leaves on a chilled platter and mound the salad over the lettuce. Garnish with a sprinkling of paprika. Four servings.

Molded Gazpacho

2   envelopes unflavored gelatin
4½   cups tomato juice
2   large tomatoes, peeled, seeded and
     chopped
1   small onion, quartered
1   medium cucumber, peeled and seeded
     Salt to taste
     White pepper to taste
     Red pepper sauce to taste
1   teaspoon Worcestershire sauce
1   tablespoon lemon juice
¼   cup olive oil
2   tablespoons wine vinegar

TOPPING

1   cup sour cream or homemade
     mayonnaise
½   cup chopped scallions, including some
     green tops
¼   cup chopped green pepper

In a large saucepan soften the gelatin in the tomato juice and simmer over low heat until completely dissolved. In a blender or food processor puree the tomatoes, onion and cucumber. Add the pureed vegetables to the gelatin mixture, then add the seasonings, including the oil and vinegar. Cool. Pour the mixture into a lightly oiled 1½-quart mold and chill for several hours or overnight.

To make the topping, combine the ingredients in a small bowl.

To serve, unmold the salad onto a serving platter and garnish with the topping. Eight to ten servings.

Frozen Tomato Salad

1   envelope unflavored gelatin
⅓   cup warm water
9   large tomatoes, peeled, seeded and
     chopped
1⅓   cups homemade mayonnaise
     Juice of 1 lemon
3   teaspoons finely chopped scallions
1   teaspoon Worcestershire sauce
     Red pepper sauce to taste
     Freshly ground black pepper to taste

In a small bowl dissolve the gelatin in the warm water. Combine all the ingredients in a food processor and process until well blended. Pour the puree into a freezer tray and freeze until firm, stirring occasionally. When frozen, scoop out individual servings with an ice cream scoop and refreeze. Serve with additional homemade mayonnaise as an accompaniment. Six to eight servings.

Three Bean Salad

½   cup dried red kidney beans
½   cup dried white kidney beans
½   cup dried chick peas
¾   cup finely chopped scallions
2   cloves garlic, minced
2   tablespoons finely chopped parsley
1   small green pepper, seeded and coarsely
     chopped
1   teaspoon salt
     Freshly ground black pepper to taste
3   tablespoons wine vinegar
½   cup fine quality olive oil

Soak the red and white kidney beans and the chick peas separately overnight in water to cover; drain. In separate saucepans cover the beans with salted water and simmer until tender; drain thoroughly.

In a large bowl combine the red and white kidney beans, chick peas, scallions, garlic, parsley and green pepper. Add the salt, pepper and wine vinegar and toss gently with a large spoon. Add the olive oil and toss again. Let stand for at least an hour before serving to develop the flavor. Six to eight servings.

Artichoke Salad

VINAIGRETTE

1/3	cup olive oil
1	tablespoon plus 2 teaspoons white wine vinegar
2	teaspoons lemon juice
1	large clove garlic, finely minced

1 1/2	cups (1/2 pound) cooked artichoke hearts, cut up
4	ounces mozzarella cheese, cut in julienne strips
4	ounces feta cheese, crumbled
1/2	cup very thinly sliced celery
1/4	cup minced fresh parsley
1/4	cup minced fresh mint or basil leaves
2	tablespoons capers
	Salt to taste
	Freshly ground pepper to taste

To make the vinaigrette, beat together the olive oil, vinegar, lemon juice and garlic. Let stand for at least an hour before preparing the salad to develop the garlic flavor.

In a salad bowl combine the artichokes, mozzarella, feta, parsley, mint or basil and capers. Season with salt and pepper. Toss the salad with the vinaigrette. Serve chilled or at room temperature. Four servings.

Midsummer Salad

1/2	watermelon, cut into balls
1	large cantaloupe, cut into balls
1	large honeydew melon, cut into balls
1	cup fresh pineapple chunks
1	cup seedless green grapes, cut in half if large
1	cup strawberries, cut into halves or large pieces
1/2	cup sugar
1/2	cup water
1	tablespoon grated lemon peel
1	tablespoon grated orange peel
1/2	cup sweet white wine
1/4	cup lemon juice
3	tablespoons lime juice

In a glass serving bowl mix together all the fruit. In a small saucepan mix together all the remaining ingredients; stir until the sugar is dissolved. Boil the sugar syrup for 5 minutes; cool. Pour the syrup over the mixed fruit and chill for a few hours or overnight. Ten to fifteen servings.

Curried Chicken and Shrimp Salad

4   cups cooked chicken, cubed
2   cups tiny boiled shrimp
1   can (1 pound 4 ounces) water chestnuts,
      drained and sliced
1   pound seedless green grapes, halved
1   cup sliced celery
1/4 cup sliced almonds, toasted
1   cup homemade mayonnaise
2   tablespoons curry powder or to taste
1   tablespoon soy sauce
    Juice of 1 lemon

In a mixing bowl combine the chicken, shrimp, water chestnuts, grapes, celery and almonds. In a small bowl combine well all the other ingredients; add the dressing mixture to the chicken mixture and toss well, being careful not to break up the shrimp. Chill for several hours. Serve over lettuce. Twelve servings.

Shrimp and Rice Salad

2   pounds large raw shrimp
2¼   cups raw rice
½   cup heavy cream
1   cup homemade mayonnaise
1   red pepper, seeded and finely chopped
1   green pepper, seeded and
       finely chopped
1   head leaf lettuce
1–2 cups Sauce Verte (see Accompaniments
       section)

Place the shrimp in a large saucepan with 4 cups boiling salted water and simmer just until they turn pink; do not overcook. Drain, reserving the cooking liquid; shell and devein the shrimp and let them cool to room temperature.

In the saucepan bring 2¼ cups of the reserved liquid to a rapid boil, add the rice and stir once. Cover, reduce the heat to the lowest possible flame and cook, without stirring, for 20 minutes. Remove the cover and toss the rice with a fork; cool.

In a bowl beat together the cream and mayonnaise, add the peppers and rice and toss to combine. Line a serving platter with the lettuce, pile the rice mixture on top and arrange the shrimp around the rice. Serve with Sauce Verte. Six to eight servings.

Fennel, Endive and Mushroom Salad

1   small bulb fennel, sliced thin
2   Belgian endive, sliced crosswise
1   cup sliced mushrooms
3   tablespoons minced fresh parsley
3   tablespoons crumbled Roquefort
      cheese
    Freshly ground pepper to taste

VINAIGRETTE

3   tablespoons olive oil
2   teaspoons lemon juice
1   teaspoon white wine vinegar

In a serving bowl combine the salad ingredients.

To make the viniagrette, blend the ingredients well in a small bowl or covered jar. Toss the salad with the dressing just before serving. Four servings.

Caesar Salad

1	clove garlic, crushed
1	egg
1/4	teaspoon dry mustard
1/4	teaspoon freshly ground black pepper
1/2	teaspoon salt
1/2	cup grated Parmesan cheese
6	tablespoons olive oil
6	anchovy fillets, rinsed and dried
4	tablespoons fresh lemon juice
1	clove garlic, finely minced
	Worcestershire sauce to taste
2	heads Romaine lettuce, torn and chilled
2	cups croutons

Rub a salad bowl generously with the crushed garlic clove. Break the egg into the salad bowl and stir briskly with a fork until the egg is slightly beaten. Add the mustard, pepper, salt, 1/4 cup of the Parmesan cheese and the olive oil; mix well. Add the anchovy fillets and mash them into the dressing. Stir in the lemon juice. Toss with the garlic and Worcestershire sauce. Add the lettuce to the salad bowl and toss. Sprinkle with 1 cup of the croutons and 1/2 the remaining Parmesan cheese and toss again. Add the remaining croutons and Parmesan cheese and toss. Serve immediately. Four to six servings.

Duck and Orange Salad

3	cups julienne strips lean cold roast duck
1	small Bermuda onion, thinly sliced
3	tablespoons fresh lemon juice
1/4	teaspoon salt
	Freshly ground black pepper to taste
6	tablespoons olive oil
1/4	teaspoon dry mustard
	Peel of 1 orange, grated
1	tablespoon butter
1	small clove garlic, crushed
1/4	cup coarsely chopped walnuts
3	medium oranges, peeled, thinly sliced crosswise and seeded
	Salt to taste

In a large bowl combine the duck and onion. In another bowl combine the lemon juice, salt, pepper, oil, mustard and orange peel and blend thoroughly. Pour over the duck, cover and let marinate in the refrigerator for 2 hours, stirring occasionally.

In a small skillet heat the butter; add the garlic and cook until golden. Add the walnuts and cook, stirring, until they are lightly browned. Remove the garlic.

Add the orange slices to the duck mixture, toss, and season with salt. Garnish with the walnuts and serve. Four servings.

Tomato Aspic

2 envelopes unflavored gelatin
3½ cups tomato juice or vegetable juice
cocktail
⅓ cup minced green pepper
1 tablespoon grated onion
⅓ cup finely chopped celery

In a small bowl sprinkle the gelatin over 1 cup of the juice. When the gelatin is soft, pour the mixture into a saucepan and heat it gently until the gelatin is dissolved. Cool, stir in the remaining juice and chill slightly. Stir in the green pepper, onion and celery; pour the mixture into a lightly oiled mold and chill until firm. Unmold on lettuce and fill. Six servings.

NOTE: Foods for which this mold is a welcome accompaniment include cold boiled shrimp, lobster salad and chicken salad.

Shrimp in Aspic

1½ tablespoons unflavored gelatin
½ cup dry white wine
3 cups hot white fish stock or canned
chicken broth
Few drops fresh lemon juice
2 egg whites, beaten until frothy
4–5 ripe tomatoes, peeled, seeded and
quartered
½ pound cooked shrimp, peeled and
deveined
Watercress

2 cups mayonnaise,
flavored with a little
tomato paste or tomato juice

In a small bowl let the gelatin soften in the wine for 3 to 5 minutes. In a saucepan heat the stock or broth over low heat until hot, add the gelatin and stir until it is completely dissolved. Add the lemon juice and egg whites and bring to a boil, whisking constantly. Remove the pan from the heat without disturbing the mixture and let it stand for 5 minutes. Bring the mixture to a boil again, whisking, remove it from the heat and let it stand for 5 minutes. Repeat the process once more. Strain the mixture through a double layer of cheesecloth into a bowl and let it cool. (The mixture must remain liquid. If it starts to thicken, heat it slightly over low heat.)

Cover the bottom of a lightly oiled 1-quart mold with a layer of aspic and chill until partially set. Arrange the tomato quarters, rounded sides down, in the aspic and cover them with aspic. Chill until partially set. Arrange some of the shrimp on the aspic and chill. Continue to fill the mold, alternating layers of aspic and shrimp, chilling the mold each time a layer of aspic is added. Chill, covered, until firm.

Before serving, unmold the salad and fill the center of the ring with watercress. Serve with the tomato-flavored mayonnaise.

VARIATION: Prepare the first layers as directed above, but substitute tomato aspic for the last layers. This will produce an attractive, two-layered molded salad.

Tomato Aspic with Shrimp

Bayley's Restaurant's West Indies Salad

1   *medium onion, finely chopped*
1   *pound fresh lump crab meat, well picked over*
    Salt to taste
    Pepper to taste
4   *ounces salad oil*
⅓   *cup cider vinegar*
½   *cup ice water*

Spread half of the chopped onion in the bottom of a glass serving bowl. Cover with the crab meat and then the remaining onion. Sprinkle with salt and pepper. Pour the oil, vinegar and ice water over the ingredients in the bowl. Cover and marinate for 2 to 12 hours. Toss lightly before serving. Six servings.

Ham and Grapefruit Salad

3   *grapefruit, peeled and sectioned*
2   *avocados, peeled and sliced*
¾   *pound cold Virginia-style ham, cut into julienne strips*
¾   *cup finely chopped celery*
3   *tablespoons fresh lemon juice*
3   *tablespoons olive oil*
    Salt to taste
    Freshly ground white pepper to taste
6   *tablespoons sour cream*
1   *cup garlic mayonnaise*
    Lettuce leaves

In a ceramic or glass bowl combine the grapefruit sections, avocado slices, ham, celery, lemon juice, oil, salt and pepper; toss gently. Marinate the mixture in the refrigerator for 30 minutes.

In a small bowl combine the sour cream and garlic mayonnaise and blend until smooth. Add ½ the mayonnaise mixture to the grapefruit mixture and toss. Serve the salad on a bed of lettuce leaves and pass the remaining dressing in a separate bowl. Six servings.

Pork and Rice Salad

1½   *tablespoons Dijon mustard*
1   *teaspoon salt*
2   *tablespoons fresh lemon juice*
2   *tablespoons fresh orange juice*
½   *cup olive oil*
     Red pepper sauce to taste
2½   *cups julienne strips of cold cooked pork*
¼   *cup finely chopped parsley*
3   *cups cold cooked rice*
2–3 *oranges, peeled and sectioned*
1   *small red onion, thinly sliced*
     Watercress for garnish

In a large bowl combine well the mustard, salt, lemon juice and orange juice. Add the oil and beat vigorously. Add the red pepper sauce. Pour the mixture over the pork and marinate for 30 minutes at room temperature. Add the parsley and rice, mix and adjust the seasonings if necessary. Refrigerate, covered, for several hours or overnight.

Combine the orange sections and onions with the pork mixture. Toss gently, arrange on a platter and chill. Remove the salad from the refrigerator about 1 hour before serving. Garnish with the watercress. Four servings.

Cold Dill Beans

1   *cup salad oil*
1   *cup white vinegar*
¼   *cup water*
1   *clove garlic, minced*
1   *tablespoon sugar*
2   *teaspoons dry mustard*
1   *teaspoon celery seed*
1   *teaspoon dill weed*
¼   *teaspoon salt*
   Freshly ground black pepper to taste
3   *pounds green beans, tips removed, steamed until just tender*
1½   *white onions, thinly sliced*

In a saucepan mix together the first 10 ingredients. Add the beans and heat to boiling; cool. Layer the beans and the onion slices in a shallow pan and pour the marinade over them. Cover and refrigerate for at least 24 hours before serving. Serve cold. Eight to ten servings.

Fruit and Wine Salad Mold

1   *cup fresh fruit (sliced bananas, orange and grapefruit sections, apples, pears, or whatever is in season)*
1   *3-ounce package lemon-flavored gelatin*
1   *cup boiling water*
½   *cup dry white wine*
½   *cup reserved fruit juice or water*
½   *cup halved seedless grapes*
½   *cup heavy cream, whipped*

Dice the fruit and reserve the juices from the orange or grapefruit. In a heatproof bowl dissolve the gelatin in the boiling water. Cool, and stir in the wine and fruit juice or water. Pour ⅓ of the gelatin mixture into a 1-quart mold, add the grapes, and chill until partially set. Top the grapes with a layer of fruit, add ⅓ more gelatin and chill again until partially set.

Chill the remaining gelatin mixture until partially set and fold in the whipped cream. Top the mold with the cream mixture and chill until firm. Unmold onto a platter to serve. Four servings.

NOTE: Fresh pineapple can be used in gelatin only if it is first simmered for 10 minutes and drained.

Cole Slaw

¹/₂	*head white cabbage, washed and chilled*
1	*small onion, finely minced*
1	*dill pickle, finely minced*
¹/₄	*pound Roquefort cheese, finely crumbled*
1	*rib celery, finely minced*
1	*teaspoon salt*
1	*tablespoon horseradish*
¹/₂	*cup homemade mayonnaise*

In a large bowl combine the cabbage, onion, pickle, cheese and celery. Add the seasonings and the mayonnaise and toss well. Serve immediately. Six servings.

VARIATION: For a colorful presentation, red cabbage can be substituted for some or all of the white cabbage.

Boiled Dressing Cole Slaw

¹/₂	*cup cider vinegar*
¹/₃	*cup water*
2	*tablespoons sugar*
2	*tablespoons flour*
2	*teaspoons dry mustard*
2	*teaspoons salt*
¹/₂	*cup heavy cream*
2	*tablespoons butter*
4	*eggs, lightly beaten*
2	*pounds firm white cabbage, shredded*
1	*cup grated scraped carrots*

In a large saucepan combine the vinegar, water, sugar, flour, mustard and salt and beat until the mixture is smooth. Place over medium heat and, whisking constantly, add the cream and butter. Cook until the butter melts and the sauce comes to a simmer. Stir 2 or 3 tablespoons of the hot liquid into the beaten eggs and then pour the egg mixture into the sauce, beating constantly. Reduce the heat and continue to beat until the sauce thickens. Turn the sauce into a deep bowl and cool to room temperature.

Add the shredded cabbage and grated carrots to the sauce, toss together gently but thoroughly and taste for seasoning. Cover and refrigerate for 2 or 3 hours before serving. Eight to ten servings.

Watercress Salad

8	*tablespoons olive oil*
2	*tablespoons wine vinegar*
1	*tablespoon fresh lemon juice*
1	*tablespoon curry powder*
	Salt to taste
	Pepper to taste
6	*bunches watercress, washed, dried and chilled in a damp towel*
3	*oranges, peeled and sectioned*
2	*tablespoons chopped shallots*

In a small bowl or jar combine the oil, vinegar, lemon juice, curry powder, salt and pepper. Mix well. Place the watercress in a salad bowl and add the orange sections and shallots. Pour the dressing over and toss well. Serve immediately. Six servings.

Mary Snyder's Hearts of Palm Salad

1   14-ounce can hearts of
      palm, drained
½   cup salad oil
⅓   cup red wine vinegar
1   tablespoon lemon juice
1   clove garlic, finely minced
     Salt to taste
     Freshly ground pepper to
       taste
     Cayenne pepper to taste
1   head lettuce, torn into
      small pieces
¼   cup grated Parmesan cheese

Slice the hearts of palm into serving-size pieces. In a mixing bowl combine all of the other ingredients except the lettuce and cheese; pour the mixture over the hearts of palm and marinate overnight in the refrigerator. Just before serving, toss the salad with the lettuce and cheese and pile onto serving plates. Four servings.

Wilted Lettuce Salad

6   large heads leaf lettuce,
      well washed and
      drained
¼   pound bacon, diced
1   large onion, minced
1   tablespoon Dijon-style mustard
1   cup dry white wine

Squeeze the excess water out of the lettuce with your hands. Set the lettuce aside.

In a large, heavy skillet sauté the bacon for 2 minutes. Add the onion and stir over medium heat until the onion is golden and the bacon crisp; do not drain off the fat.

Stir in the mustard and wine; simmer for 5 minutes. Add the lettuce, cover, and steam for 10 minutes. Serve very hot. Twelve to eighteen servings.

Fresh Spinach Salad

¼   cup sugar
1   teaspoon salt
1   teaspoon dry mustard
1   teaspoon poppy seed
1   tablespoon onion juice
⅓   cup cider vinegar
1   cup salad oil
¾   cup cottage cheese
2   pounds fresh spinach,
      washed, heavy
      stems removed, and
      torn into serving
      pieces
½   pound bacon, fried crisp and
      crumbled
2–3   hard-cooked eggs, chopped
¼   pound fresh mushrooms, sliced

In a jar mix together the first 8 ingredients; refrigerate overnight (dressing will keep up to 1 week in refrigerator). When ready to serve, shake the dressing well and toss with spinach. Add the bacon, eggs and mushrooms and toss again. Serve immediately. Eight servings.

Orange and Red Onion Salad

2 tablespoons orange juice
2 tablespoons white wine vinegar
2 small garlic cloves, minced
1/2 teaspoon ground coriander seed
1/2 cup olive oil
1 head leaf lettuce,
    torn into bite-sized
    pieces, washed well
    and dried
4 navel oranges, peeled and sliced
2 red onions, thinly sliced

In a blender combine the orange juice, vinegar, garlic, coriander, salt and pepper. Add the oil in a steady stream, blending until the oil is incorporated.

Pile the lettuce on a serving platter and arrange the orange slices and onion slices, overlapping alternately, on top of the greens. Drizzle the dressing over the salad and serve immediately. Eight servings.

Rice Salad

1 tablespoon vinegar
2 tablespoons corn oil
3/4 cup homemade mayonnaise
1 teaspoon salt
1/2 teaspoon curry powder
2 cups hot cooked rice
2 tablespoons finely chopped onion
1 cup chopped celery
1 cup fresh small peas,
    steamed until just
    tender

In a mixing bowl beat together the vinegar, oil, mayonnaise, salt and curry powder. Add the cooked rice to the mixture, then add the chopped onion; cool. Add the celery and the peas. Six to eight servings.

NOTE: This is better if refrigerated overnight to let the flavors develop.

Fresh Mushroom Salad

1 1/2 cups vinegar
3 tablespoons sugar
   Salt to taste
1 1/2 teaspoons paprika
1 1/2 tablespoons Worcestershire
    sauce
1 teaspoon marjoram
1 teaspoon oregano
1 teaspoon chopped chives
1/2 cup salad oil
3 cloves garlic, finely
    chopped
3/4 pound fresh mushrooms,
    sliced and sprinkled
    with lemon juice
3 heads romaine lettuce,
    torn in pieces

In a medium saucepan blend the first 8 ingredients and cook over low heat for 8 minutes. Cool. Beat in the salad oil and garlic. Toss the mushrooms and lettuce with the dressing. Serve immediately. Eight to ten servings.

SEAFOOD MAIN DISHES

Broiled Swordfish with Sauce Dijon

2   *pounds swordfish steaks*
¼   *cup salad oil*
¼   *cup tarragon vinegar*
1   *teaspoon salt*
¼   *teaspoon paprika*
1   *clove garlic, sliced*
      Dash cayenne pepper
      Paprika for garnish
      Chopped parsley for garnish

SAUCE DIJON

2   *egg yolks, beaten*
¼   *cup water*
2   *tablespoons tarragon vinegar*
1   *tablespoon Dijon-style mustard*
1   *tablespoon sugar*
¼   *teaspoon salt*
½   *cup sour cream*

Place the swordfish in a shallow pan. In a small bowl combine the oil, vinegar, salt, paprika, garlic and cayenne; pour the mixture over the fish. Cover and refrigerate for at least 2 hours, turning several times. Preheat the broiler.

Place the steaks on a well-greased broiler pan; broil about 3 inches from the source of the heat for 6 to 8 minutes, basting with the marinade. Turn the steaks carefully; baste. Broil for 6 to 8 minutes more or until the fish flakes easily when tested with a fork, basting with the marinade several times.

To make the sauce, in a small saucepan combine all the ingredients except the sour cream and mix well. Cook over low heat, stirring constantly, until thickened. Do not boil. Stir in the sour cream; serve while still warm.

Place the broiled steaks on a serving platter; sprinkle with paprika and chopped parsley. Serve with Sauce Dijon. Six servings.

Trout Veronique

½   *pound fresh seedless green grapes, halved*
½   *cup white wine*
½   *cup (1 stick) butter*
6   *fresh trout fillets*
4   *teaspoons lemon juice*
2   *tablespoons chopped parsley*
      Salt to taste
      Freshly ground black pepper to taste

In a small saucepan poach the grapes in the wine for 5 minutes. In a large skillet melt the butter; sauté the trout fillets gently for 5 minutes on each side or a little longer if they are large. While the fillets are cooking add the lemon juice and chopped parsley to the skillet, then add the grapes and wine. Increase the heat and cook for about 2 minutes more. Serve on hot plates. Six servings.

Broiled Swordfish
with Sauce Dijon

Fried Marinated Perch

12 8–10-ounce whole perch
    or other fresh
    fish, with heads, cleaned
    and scaled
¾   cup corn flour
¾   cup cornmeal
    Pork lard or vegetable oil
    for pan frying

MARINADE

6   cups water
2   cups finely chopped onion
6   tablespoons red pepper sauce
2   tablespoons salt
2   teaspoons dried thyme leaves
4   bay leaves

SEASONING MIX

2   teaspoons salt
2   teaspoons cayenne pepper
2   teaspoons sweet paprika
1¾   teaspoons garlic powder
1¾   teaspoons black pepper
1   teaspoon onion powder
1   teaspoon dried oregano leaves
1   teaspoon dried thyme leaves

Score the fish across the width 3 or 4 times on each side (down to the bone but not through it). Set aside.

In a large bowl combine the ingredients for the marinade, stirring until the salt is dissolved.

Lay the fish in a pan in a single layer; pour the marinade over the fish. Cover the pan and refrigerate for 8 to 16 hours, turning the fish every few hours.

Combine the seasoning mix ingredients in a small bowl, mixing well. Drain the fish and sprinkle some of the mix on each, patting it with your hands (use about ¾ teaspoon on each fish). Combine the remaining mix with the corn flour and cornmeal in a pan (a loaf, cake or pie pan is fine), mixing until thoroughly blended. Set aside.

In a large skillet heat about ½ inch of oil to 350° F. (use just enough oil to come up the sides of the fish but not cover the top). Just before frying each fish, dredge it in the seasoned corn flour mixture, pressing the mixture firmly into the fish with your fingers; shake off excess. Fry the fish in the hot oil until cooked through and golden brown and crispy, about 1½ to 2 minutes per side (adjust heat as needed to maintain 350° F.). Drain on paper towels and serve immediately. Four servings.

NOTE: All-purpose flour may be substituted, but corn flour, available at many health food stores, is preferred.

Marinated Crawfish Tails

2   pounds cooked and peeled
    crawfish tails
1   onion, chopped
1   cup light olive oil
3   tablespoons white wine vinegar
1   teaspoon dry mustard

1   teaspoon salt
1/4 teaspoon pepper
2   teaspoons minced parsley
2   teaspoons minced chives
2   tablespoons drained capers

In a pyrex bowl layer the crawfish and onions. In a saucepan heat together the oil, vinegar, dry mustard, salt and pepper just to boiling. Stir in the parsley, chives and capers; pour the dressing over the crawfish mixture. Cover and refrigerate for at least 24 hours. Drain and serve.

NOTE: This recipe will provide six to eight luncheon main-course servings. As an appetizer it will provide twelve to eighteen servings.

Fish Mousse with Mustard Cucumber Dressing

2   pounds flounder fillets or other fillets of white fish
3   cups white fish stock or bottled clam juice
     Bouquet garni: 1 bay leaf, 2 branches fresh thyme or 1/2 teaspoon dried, 4 sprigs parsley
2   tablespoons unflavored gelatin
4   tablespoons dry white wine
3/4 cup heavy cream, chilled
1 1/2 teaspoons dried dill
1/4 teaspoon salt
     Freshly ground white pepper to taste
     Watercress leaves for garnish

MUSTARD CUCUMBER DRESSING

1   cucumber, peeled, seeded and grated
1   cup mayonnaise
1   tablespoon Dijon mustard
1   tablespoon fresh lemon juice

In a stainless steel or enamel saucepan or skillet combine the fish, stock or clam juice and bouquet garni. (The liquid should cover the fillets.) Bring the liquid to a boil and simmer the mixture, covered, for 10 minutes, or until the fish is just tender. Strain, reserving the liquid and discarding the bouquet garni. Flake the fish.

In a saucepan let the gelatin soften in the wine for 3 to 5 minutes. Over low heat stir in 2 cups of the reserved cooking liquid and stir the mixture until the gelatin dissolves completely. Do not let it boil. In a blender or food processor blend the mixture with the fish for 1 to 2 minutes. Pour the mixture into a bowl and chill until it is partially set.

In a chilled bowl whip the cream lightly and fold it into the fish mixture. Add the dill, salt and pepper and adjust the seasonings. Pour into a lightly oiled 1 1/2-quart ring mold or fish-shaped mold. Chill, covered, until firm.

To make the dressing, in a bowl combine the cucumber, mayonnaise, mustard, and lemon juice and blend thoroughly.

Before serving, unmold the mousse and garnish it with the watercress leaves. Serve the dressing separately. Six servings.

Paul Prudhomme's Redfish Courtbouillon

SEASONING MIX

2	*whole bay leaves*
¾	*teaspoon dried oregano leaves*
½	*teaspoon salt*
½	*teaspoon white pepper*
½	*teaspoon cayenne*
½	*teaspoon sweet paprika*
½	*teaspoon black pepper*
½	*teaspoon dried thyme leaves*
½	*teaspoon dried sweet basil leaves*

COURTBOUILLON

4	*tablespoons unsalted butter*
1	*cup peeled and chopped tomato*
1	*cup chopped onion*
1	*cup chopped celery*
1	*cup chopped green pepper*
1½	*teaspoons minced garlic*
3	*cups fish stock*
1¾	*cups tomato sauce*
1	*tablespoon plus 1 teaspoon sugar*
2½	*teaspoons Tabasco sauce*
7	*tablespoons salad oil*
¾	*cup flour*
	Salt to taste
2½	*pounds redfish (red drum) or red snapper fillets, skinned and cut into strips*
¼	*cup white wine*
	Cooked rice

To make the seasoning mix, in a small bowl thoroughly combine the ingredients; set aside.

In a 2-quart saucepan melt the butter over medium heat. Stir in the tomato and ¾ cup of *each of* the onion, celery and green pepper. Add the garlic and the seasoning mix, stirring well; sauté, stirring occasionally, until the onion is transparent, about 5 minutes.

Stir in the fish stock, tomato sauce, sugar and ½ teaspoon of the Tabasco sauce; bring to a boil. Reduce the heat to maintain a simmer and cook, stirring occasionally, until the vegetables are tender and the flavors have married, about 20 minutes. Remove the bay leaves and set the sauce aside.

In a small bowl combine the remain ¼ cup each of onion, celery and green pepper; set aside.

In a large cast-iron skillet heat the oil over high heat until it begins to smoke, about 4 minutes. With a long-handled metal whisk, gradually mix in the flour, stirring until smooth. Continue cooking, whisking constantly, until the roux is a dark red-brown, about 3 to 5 minutes (be careful not to let it scorch or splash on your skin). Remove the roux from the heat and immediately stir in the reserved vegetable mixture with a wooden spoon; continue stirring until the mixture is cooled, about 5 minutes.

Reheat the stock mixture to boiling over high heat. Add the roux by spoonfuls to the stock mixture and stir until thoroughly dissolved. Stir in the remaining 2 teaspoons of Tabasco sauce and salt to taste. Reduce the heat to low and cook, whisking almost constantly, until the flour taste is gone from the sauce, about 2 minutes.

Dip the fish in the white wine and add to the stock mixture, coating each piece well. Simmer, tightly covered, for 20 minutes, or until the fish flakes easily when touched gently with a fork. Serve at once from a heated serving bowl, accompanied by hot cooked rice. Six to eight servings.

Crisp Fried Catfish

6   small catfish, cleaned and filleted
1   teaspoon salt
$1/4$ teaspoon pepper
2   cups self-rising cornmeal or 2 cups cornmeal combined with 1 teaspoon baking powder
1   quart cooking oil (or more)

Lightly sprinkle the catfish with salt and pepper. Place the cornmeal in a brown paper bag; shake the catfish pieces in the bag of cornmeal to coat completely.

Half fill a deep kettle or skillet with the oil and heat until just under "smoking hot." Gently slide each piece of fish separately into the oil. Cook at high temperature until the fish floats to the top and turns golden brown. Drain well on paper towels. Serve hot. Six servings.

NOTE: This basic recipe and procedure will work well with any small fish, such as bream, that can be fried whole after cleaning.

Baked Stuffed Shrimp

24   jumbo shrimp
1   medium onion, minced
1   small green chili pepper, chopped
6   tablespoons butter
1   cup fresh crab meat or 1 $7^{1}/_2$-ounce can crab meat
1   teaspoon dry mustard
1   teaspoon Worcestershire sauce
$1/2$ teaspoon salt
2   tablespoons mayonnaise
2   tablespoons flour
1   cup milk
2   tablespoons sherry wine
    Red pepper sauce to taste
    Grated Parmesan cheese

Preheat oven to 350° F.

Clean and devein the shrimp, removing the heads and shells and leaving the tails. Split the shrimp and open them flat. In a medium skillet sauté the onion and pepper in 4 tablespoons of the butter until transparent. Add the crab meat, dry mustard, Worcestershire sauce, salt and mayonnaise. Toss the ingredients together and set aside.

Make a white sauce with the remaining 2 tablespoons butter, flour and milk. Add the sauce to the crab meat mixture along with the sherry and the red pepper sauce; mix well. Stuff the butterflied shrimp with the crab meat mixture, dot the shrimp with extra butter and sprinkle lightly with Parmesan cheese. Arrange the shrimp in a shallow baking pan and bake for 25 to 30 minutes. Four to six servings.

Antoine's Creole Gumbo

6   tablespoons butter
4   tablespoons flour
2   cups sliced fresh okra
3   bunches scallions, including green tops,
      sliced
1   large onion, chopped
6   cups chicken broth
2   pounds tomatoes, peeled, seeded and
      chopped
½   teaspoon ground black pepper
½   teaspoon ground red pepper
2   cups backfin lump crab meat, well
      picked over
2   cups peeled and deveined raw shrimp
1   pint raw oysters
    Salt to taste
1   tablespoon filé powder
4   cups hot cooked rice

In a small cast-iron skillet cook 3 tablespoons of the butter with the flour over low heat, stirring contantly, until the roux is dark brown, about 25 minutes. Remove from the heat.

In a 4-quart Dutch oven or saucepan sauté the okra in the remaining 3 tablespoons of butter until golden brown. Stir in the scallions and onions. Cook over medium heat until the onions are soft but not brown. Add the broth, tomatoes, black and red pepper and roux. Bring to a boil, reduce the heat, and simmer for 1 hour. Add the crab meat, shrimp and oysters; cook 10 minutes longer, or until the shrimp turn pink. Season with salt, then add the filé powder and stir until the mixture thickens slightly. *Do not boil.* Serve in individual soup plates topped with the cooked rice. Eight servings.

NOTE: See the Resource Guide for information on ordering filé powder.

Stuffed Crabs

¼   pound (1 stick) butter
1   medium onion, chopped
1   green pepper, finely chopped
3   cloves garlic, finely minced
½   cup chopped parsley
2   tablespoons sherry
    Salt to taste
    Freshly ground black pepper to taste
3   cups breadcrumbs
2   pounds lump crab meat, well
      picked over
    Melted butter (if necessary)

Preheat oven to 375° F. Butter well 12 crab shells.

In a skillet melt the butter and sauté the onion, green pepper, garlic and parsley until soft and transparent. Add the sherry, salt and pepper and stir to combine. Add the breadcrumbs and crab meat; mix well (if the mixture is too dry, add melted butter). Divide the mixture among the crab shells and bake for 15 minutes or until the mixture is hot and bubbly. Serve at once. Six to eight main-course servings or twelve appetizer servings.

NOTE: Scallop shells or gratin dishes can be substituted for the crab shells.

Stuffed Flounder

6   whole flounder (1–1½ pounds each)
1   medium onion, finely chopped
½   cup chopped celery
½   green pepper, finely diced
4   cloves garlic, minced
1   tablespoon butter
4   eggs, lightly beaten
1   tablespoon Worcestershire sauce
1   tablespoon prepared mustard
1   tablespoon sweet white wine
     Red pepper sauce to taste
¼   cup mayonnaise
½   cup dry breadcrumbs
2   cups fresh lump crab meat, well picked
         over
     Salt to taste
     Freshly ground black pepper to taste
     Sherry
     Parsley sprigs for garnish
     Lemon wedges for garnish

Preheat oven to 400° F.

Bone the fish carefully and set aside. In a small skillet cook the onion, celery green pepper and garlic in the butter until brown. In a mixing bowl beat the eggs with the Worcestershire sauce, mustard, wine and red pepper sauce until thoroughly combined. Beat in the mayonnaise. Pour the mixture over the breadcrumbs; add the cooked vegetables, crab meat, salt and pepper and mix well. Stuff the mixture lightly into the fish and bake for about 25 minutes, until golden brown. Just before serving sprinkle a few drops of sherry over each fish. Garnish with parsley sprigs and lemon wedges. Six servings.

The Stockpot's Seafood Diablo

1   onion, diced
8   tablespoons olive oil
4   cloves garlic, minced
¼   teaspoon cinnamon
¼   teaspoon cloves
1   teaspoon salt
1   cup tomato puree
½   pound bay scallops
½   pound bay shrimp
½   pound lump crab meat
½   cup black olives, drained and
         chopped
2   tablespoons capers, coarsely
         chopped
1   small jar diced pimiento, drained
3   serrano chilies, minced, or 2 jalapeño
         chilies, chopped with seeds
12   ounces cream cheese, room
         temperature
3   eggs, beaten
⅔   cup grated Monterey Jack cheese

In a large skillet sauté the onion in the olive oil until soft; add the garlic and cook until it begins to color. Blend in the next 4 ingredients and bring to a boil. Add the seafood, olives, capers, pimiento and chilies; let simmer for 5 minutes.

Cut the cream cheese into teaspoon-size pieces and add it to the hot seafood mixture; stir until melted. Add the beaten eggs, stirring well, and reheat to a simmer. Add the grated cheese and stir.

Serve very hot with tostada chips. Six to eight servings.

Cold Poached Red Snapper with Dill

1½ cups dry white wine
1½ cups water
½ teaspoon salt
½ teaspoon peppercorns
1 red snapper, cleaned
   Sprigs of fresh dill
   Prepared horseradish

In a fish poacher combine the wine, water, salt and peppercorns and bring to a boil. Add the snapper, cover and reduce the heat; simmer for 20 minutes or until the snapper flakes easily. Transfer the fish to a wire rack and place the rack in a jelly roll pan. Cover the pan and chill the fish thoroughly. Discard the cooking liquid.

Skin the chilled snapper and arrange on a serving platter. Garnish with sprigs of dill and serve with horseradish. Four to six servings.

Pickled Red Snapper

4 medium onions, very thinly
   sliced
2 large carrots, very thinly
   sliced
2 green peppers, seeded and
   cut into thin strips
1 lemon, seeded and very thinly
   sliced
3 bay leaves, crumbled
   Red pepper sauce to taste
½ cup white wine vinegar
6 tablespoons olive oil
2 pounds skinned, filleted red
   snapper
   Salt to taste
   Freshly ground black pepper
   to taste
⅛ teaspoon celery seed for
   garnish
¼ teaspoon chopped capers for
   garnish

In a big enameled or stainless steel pan combine the first 6 ingredients. Pour in the vinegar, 2 tablespoons of the olive oil and 2 cups of water. Bring to a boil over high heat, cover and simmer for about 20 minutes, until the vegetables are soft.

In a heavy skillet heat the remaining olive oil over medium heat; add the fish fillets a few at a time, cooking 2 or 3 minutes on each side until just golden brown. Drain and transfer to a deep serving dish. Pour the vinegar mixture over the fish, season with salt and pepper, and arrange the vegetables attractively in the dish. Cool to room temperature. Chill in the refrigerator for at least 24 hours before serving. Garnish with the celery seed and capers. Eight to ten servings.

VARIATION: Catfish prepared in this fashion is also very good.

Red Snapper

Broussard's Crawfish Cardinale with Rice Pilaf

RICE PILAF

- 2 tablespoons finely chopped onion
- 3 tablespoons butter
- 1 cup raw rice
- 1¾ cups chicken broth or water
  Salt to taste
  Ground white pepper to taste

- 2 shallots, minced
- ¼ cup tomato puree
- 2 tablespoons flour
- 1½ pounds peeled crawfish tails
- 1 tablespoon dry white wine
- 1 tablespoon dry sherry
- 1 cup heavy cream
- 2 tablespoons sour cream
- 1 tablespoon brandy
- 1 tablespoon chopped parsley or chives

Preheat oven to 350° F.

To make the rice pilaf, in an ovenproof skillet cook the onion in 1 tablespoon of butter until tender crisp. Add the rice, stirring to coat the rice grains with the butter. Add the broth and bring to a boil. Stir the mixture once or twice, cover and bake for 20 minutes or until the rice is tender and the liquid is absorbed. Fluff the rice with a fork and season with salt and pepper.

Meanwhile, in a large skillet cook the shallots in the remaining butter until tender crisp. Combine the tomato puree with the flour and stir the mixture into the shallots.

Add the crawfish tails and heat through. Add the wine, sherry, heavy cream and sour cream; simmer gently for 5 minutes. Stir in the brandy and the chopped parsley or chives. Season with additional salt and pepper if necessary. Serve immediately over the rice pilaf. Six servings.

Antoine's Crab Meat Étouffée with Rice

- ¾ cup chopped onions
- 2 tablespoons butter
- 2 tablespoons flour
- 2 cups chicken stock
- 1 pound tomatoes, peeled, seeded and chopped
- ½ cup chopped celery
- 1 clove garlic, minced
- ¼ cup chopped parsley
- ¼ teaspoon thyme leaves
- ¼ teaspoon ground white pepper
- ⅛ teaspoon ground red pepper
  Salt to taste
- 1 pound backfin lump crab meat, well picked over
- 3 cups hot cooked rice

In a large saucepan cook the onions in the butter until transparent. Add the flour and cook, stirring, until golden brown. Add the vegetables, garlic and seasonings; simmer for 30 minutes. Gently stir the crab meat into the sauce; heat through. Serve over rice. Six servings.

Creamed Crab Meat and Crawfish

2 scallions, chopped
4 tablespoons butter
1/4 cup white wine
1/4 cup tomato sauce

BÉCHAMEL SAUCE

2 tablespoons butter
2 tablespoons flour
  Salt to taste
1 1/2 cups hot milk

1/2 pound backfin lump crab meat, well picked over
1 pound cooked, peeled crawfish tails
1/4 cup crawfish fat
  Salt to taste
  Red pepper sauce to taste

In a skillet sauté the chopped scallions in the butter. Add the white wine and tomato sauce and reduce for 5 minutes.

Meanwhile, to make the béchamel sauce, in a small saucepan melt the butter; add the flour and cook over medium heat for 3 minutes. Add the salt and milk and cook until the mixture is very thick.

Add the béchamel sauce to the skillet and bring to a boil. Add the crab meat, crawfish and crawfish fat. Bring to a boil again, stirring very gently so as not to break up the crab lumps. Season with salt and red pepper sauce. Serve in small preheated individual casserole cups or individual pastry shells. Six servings.

Baked Sea Trout

1 4 1/2-pound sea trout or similar fish
  Juice of 2 lemons
1 teaspoon salt
1/2 teaspoon freshly ground white pepper
1 cup fresh orange juice
3 cloves garlic, finely minced
2 tablespoons olive oil
6 tablespoons finely chopped parsley
2 teaspoons Hungarian sweet paprika
1 green pepper, seeded and cut into rings
2 onions, thinly sliced
1/2 medium orange, thinly sliced
  Lemon wedges for garnish

Sprinkle both sides of the fish with the lemon juice; season the fish inside and out with the salt and pepper. In a food processor or blender combine the orange juice, garlic, olive oil, 4 tablespoons parsley and the paprika and blend until smooth. Slash the fish on both sides and place it in an ovenproof baking dish; cover with the orange juice mixture and marinate for 30 minutes. Preheat oven to 350° F.

Arrange the pepper, onion and orange slices over and around the fish; cover the dish tightly with foil and place it in the upper third of the oven. Bake for 1 hour or until fish flakes easily when tested with a fork. Transfer the fish to a serving platter, garnish with the remaining parsley and the lemon wedges and serve immediately. Six servings.

Conch Fritters

1½   pounds fresh or frozen
        conch meat,
        thawed if necessary
        and cleaned
1   large green pepper, seeded
1   large onion
1   rib celery
1   teaspoon salt
1   teaspoon oregano
2   cloves garlic, finely minced
¼   teaspoon paprika
        Red pepper sauce to taste
1½   cups flour, sifted
1   tablespoon baking powder
1½   cups cold milk
1   quart oil for deep frying
        (this amount of oil
        may include ½ cup olive
        oil, if desired)

Grind the conch fine. Grind the onions, green pepper and celery. In a bowl combine the vegetables and the conch. Add the seasonings and mix well; let stand in the refrigerator for about ½ hour. In a mixing bowl stir together the sifted flour and baking powder; beat in the cold milk, mixing thoroughly.

In a deep kettle heat the oil to 350° F. Dip a tablespoon into the hot oil, then use the heated tablespoon to drop a tablespoon of batter into the oil at a time (make about 1 dozen fritters at a time). Turn gently to brown on all sides, about 2 minutes. Remove the fritters from the oil, drain on paper towels and serve hot with cocktail sauce or mustard sauce. Makes about 2 dozen.

Crusty Conch or Clam Hash

3   large potatoes, peeled and cut into
        ½-inch cubes
2   medium onions, chopped
6   tablespoons butter
        Salt to taste
        Pepper to taste
¼   teaspoon marjoram or thyme
1–2 teaspoons chopped fresh dill
3   cups chopped or ground conch
        or clams
½   cup heavy cream
        Chopped parsley for garnish
        Lemon wedges for garnish

In a saucepan boil the potatoes in salted water until tender; drain. In a large skillet sauté the onion in 2 tablespoons butter until transparent. Add 2 tablespoons butter to the potatoes and add the potatoes to the skillet. Lower the heat and cook for 10 minutes. Spread the chopped conch or clams over the potatoes; pour the cream over the mixture in the skillet and continue to cook over low heat until the hash is crusty and brown on the bottom. Slide the hash onto a plate in 1 piece. Add the remaining butter to the skillet and invert the hash back into the skillet; brown the hash on the bottom until crunchy. Slide the hash onto a serving platter and sprinkle with the parsley. Garnish the platter with the lemon wedges. Four to six servings.

Sweetbreads with Crab

4 *fresh or frozen sweetbreads*
1 *cup dry white wine*
½ *cup chopped onions*
½ *cup chopped celery*
½ *cup chopped carrots*
2 *bay leaves*
   Salt to taste
   Freshly ground pepper to taste
   Flour for dredging
½ *cup (1 stick) butter*
2 *teaspoons drained capers*
   Juice of 2 lemons
2 *teaspoons Dijon-style mustard*
½ *teaspoon paprika*
6 *ounces lump crab meat, well*
      picked over
1 *teaspoon lemon juice*
   Red pepper sauce to taste
2 *tablespoons chopped fresh parsley*

Soak the sweetbreads in water to cover in the refrigerator for several hours, changing the water often. Drain.

Place the sweetbreads in a kettle, add fresh water to cover and the wine, onions, celery, carrots, bay leaves and salt. Bring to a boil and simmer for 5 minutes. Drain and weight the sweetbreads; press until cool, at least 2 hours.

Pick over the sweetbreads and remove all membranes, tubes, filaments or tendons. Cut each sweetbread into thin slices and season the slices with salt and pepper. Dredge in the flour and pat to remove the excess.

In a heavy skillet heat 1 tablespoon butter and add some of the sweetbread slices. Sauté the slices for about 1 minute per side. Repeat with the remaining sweetbreads, being careful not to burn the butter. Add butter as necessary. Discard any butter remaining in the pan.

Add 2 tablespoons of butter to the skillet and add the capers; cook, stirring, for about 30 seconds. Stir in the lemon juice. Spoon the lemon juice and capers over the sweetbreads.

Heat the remaining 2 tablespoons of butter in a heavy skillet and add the mustard and paprika. When the mixture bubbles add the crab meat. Sprinkle with 1 teaspoon of lemon juice; heat through but do not cook. Toss the sweetbreads with the hot crab mixture and season with red pepper sauce. Garnish with fresh parsley and serve. Four to six servings.

Crab Meat Norfolk

2 *cups lump crab meat, well*
      picked over
1 *cup homemade mayonnaise*
   Salt to taste
   Pepper to taste
   Dash nutmeg
¼ *cup sherry or vermouth*
   Paprika

Preheat oven to 375° F.

In a mixing bowl gently combine all of the ingredients except the paprika. Fill clean crab shells, scallop shells or small gratin dishes with the mixture. Sprinkle the tops lightly with paprika and heat for 20 minutes. Eight servings.

Pompano en Papillote

2 *cups fish stock*
8 *small pompano fillets*
4 *tablespoons butter*
2 *tablespoons flour*
4 *scallions, chopped*
2 *tablespoons freshly chopped parsley*
   Cayenne pepper to taste
   Nutmeg to taste
   Salt to taste
   Freshly ground black pepper to taste
¼ *cup dry white wine*
½ *cup heavy cream*
2 *egg yolks, beaten*
1 *cup raw shrimp, peeled, deveined and
      quartered*
1 *cup lump crab meat, well picked
      over*
4 *large sheets parchment paper*

Preheat oven to 400° F.

In a saucepan heat the fish stock to simmering. Poach the pompano fillets for 2 or 3 minutes. Remove the fish from the stock and set aside, reserving the stock.

In a heavy skillet melt the butter; add the flour and stir well. Add the scallions and parsley and cook for 5 mintues. Add the reserved fish stock and stir until the sauce thickens. Add the seasonings. In a small bowl beat together the wine, cream and egg yolks; stir the wine mixture into the skillet. Do not boil. Stir in the shrimp and crab meat. Cook over low heat, stirring very gently, for 5 minutes.

Cut each sheet of parchment paper into a large heart shape; fold each in half. Open the paper hearts and place 2 fillets on one side of each paper heart. Top the fillets on each paper heart with ¼ of the sauce and fold the paper over; crimp the edges well to seal each package.

Place the packages on a baking sheet and bake until the paper is golden and the packages are puffed, about 15 minutes. Serve at once. Four servings.

Beer Batter Fried Shrimp

1   *cup all-purpose flour*
1   *tablespoon paprika*
½   *teaspoon salt*
1½   *cups (12-ounce can or bottle) beer*
½   *teaspoon red pepper sauce*
2–3 *pounds raw shrimp, peeled and deveined*
     Flour for dredging
     Oil for deep frying

In a medium bowl stir together the flour, paprika and salt. Whisk in the beer, Worcestershire sauce and red pepper sauce. Let stand for at least 1 hour or cover and refrigerate until ready to use.

Fill a deep-fat fryer with oil about 3 inches deep; heat to 375° F. Dip the shrimp in the flour and then in the beer batter; fry for 1 to 2 minutes or until the shrimp are golden. Drain on paper towels. Serve with Spicy Pecans and Creole Tartar Sauce or seafood sauce. Eight servings.

NOTE: This recipe was originated by the late Albert Stockli.

Fried Shrimp

2 pounds medium shrimp, peeled and
    deveined
   Juice of 1 lemon
   Cayenne pepper to taste
   Flour for dredging
   Salt to taste
   Pepper to taste
2 eggs, beaten
1 cup cracker meal or cornmeal
   Oil for deep frying

Place the shrimp in a bowl and squeeze the lemon juice over them. Sprinkle with cayenne pepper and let stand for ½ hour. Season the flour with salt and pepper and dredge the shrimp in the seasoned flour. Let stand for ½ hour more. Dip the shrimp in the beaten egg and dredge them in the cracker meal, knocking off any excess.

In a large skillet heat the oil to frying temperature (350° F.); fry the shrimp until golden brown, 3 to 5 minutes depending on the size of the shrimp. Drain on paper towels. Serve hot with tartar sauce or seafood sauce, accompanied by Spicy Pecans (see Accompaniments section). Four to six servings.

Crawfish Pie

4 tablespoons butter
½ cup peanut oil
½ small onion, chopped
1 cup chopped celery
½ green pepper, chopped
½ bunch scallions, chopped
½ cup chopped parsley
2 cups sliced mushrooms
1 tablespoon butter
1 tablespoon flour
½ cup beef stock
¼ cup red wine
2 cups (1 pound) cooked and peeled
    crawfish tails
1 teaspoon Worcestershire sauce
½ teaspoon red pepper sauce or
    to taste
   Salt to taste
   Pepper to taste
2 teaspoons Beau Monde seasoning
    (optional)
1 baked 8-inch pie shell or
    6 individual shells,
    about 4 ounce capacity
    each

In a heavy skillet heat the butter and oil. Add the onion, celery and green pepper and sauté until the vegetables are limp and transparent. Add the scallions, parsley and mushrooms; sauté until the vegetables are wilted. Set aside and keep warm.

In a heavy pan melt the 1 tablespoon butter; add the flour and cook, stirring constantly, until golden. Add the beef stock and wine and stir until thickened.

Add the crawfish tails, thickened wine sauce and seasonings to the vegetables in the skillet, stirring and cooking just to blend. Pour the mixture into the pie shell or individual pastry shells and serve immediately. Six servings.

Crawfish Crêpes

1½   *cups cold milk*
1½   *cups cold water*
6   *eggs*
1½   *teaspoons salt*
3   *cups sifted flour*
6   *tablespoons melted butter*
   Butter to grease crêpe pan
¾   *cup (1½ sticks) butter*
3   *bunches scallions, finely chopped*
3   *pounds cooked crawfish tails*
   Salt to taste
   Pepper to taste
1   *clove garlic, minced*
1¾   *cups vermouth*
6   *tablespoons cornstarch*
½   *cup half and half cream*
   Salt to taste
   White pepper to taste
4½   *cups grated Gruyère cheese*
¼   *pound (1 stick) butter*

To make the crêpe batter, in a blender combine the first 6 ingredients at low speed. Chill the batter in the refrigerator for several hours.

Heat a crêpe pan or a 6- to 7-inch skillet and grease it well with butter. To make each crêpe, pour about ¼ cup of the batter into the pan and swirl. Cook the crêpe just until golden, lift the edges and flip it over. Cook only a few seconds more, then invert the pan to flip out the crêpe. To keep the pan from getting too hot, remove it from the heat for a second or two after making each crêpe. Stack the finished crêpes between layers of waxed paper. The crêpes may be refrigerated or frozen.

Preheat oven to 400° F.

In a skillet melt the ¾ cup butter and sauté the scallions. Add the crawfish, salt, pepper and minced garlic; toss lightly. Stir in ¾ cup of the vermouth and boil rapidly until the liquid is almost evaporated. Remove from the skillet and set aside.

Add the remaining vermouth to the skillet and boil rapidly until reduced to about 1½ tablespoons. In a small bowl beat together the cornstarch and cream. Remove the skillet from the heat and slowly stir in the cornstarch mixture; season with salt and pepper. Return to low heat and cook for several minutes until slightly thickened. Stir in 2¼ cups of the cheese and cook over low heat until the cheese is melted.

Blend ½ of the sauce with the crawfish mixture. Place a generous serving on each crêpe, roll up, and place, seam side down, in a buttered casserole. Spoon the remaining sauce over the crêpes and sprinkle them with the remaining cheese. Dot with the butter. Bake for 20 minutes or until hot and bubbly. Serve immediately. Sixteen servings.

NOTE: Crab meat or shrimp may be substituted for the crawfish.

Baked Crab

4   tablespoons butter
1   medium onion, finely
      chopped
2   tablespoons chopped
      parsley
6   ounces lump crab meat,
      drained well
1   clove garlic, minced
2   dashes red pepper sauce
¼   teaspoon Worcestershire
      sauce
    Salt to taste
    Pinch ground black pepper
2   tablespoons tomato paste
2   tablespoons fine
      breadcrumbs
4   lemon slices for garnish

Preheat oven to 350° F. Butter well 4 scallop
or crab shells.

   In a heavy skillet melt the butter; sauté the
onion and parsley for 2 minutes. Add all the
other ingredients except the breadcrumbs and
lemon slices; sauté over medium heat, stirring
frequently, until the mixture starts to dry.

   Spoon the mixture onto the buttered scallop
or crab shells and bake for 15 minutes.
Remove from the oven, sprinkle with the
breadcrumbs, return to the oven and bake
until the breadcrumbs are lightly browned.
Serve hot, garnished with the lemon slices.
Four servings.

Vietnamese Mackerel in Tomato Sauce

3   tablespoons safflower oil
1   pound fresh mackerel
      fillets
2   cloves garlic, sliced very
      thin
2   shallots, sliced very thin
2   ripe tomatoes, seeded and
      chopped
3   tablespoons **Nuoc Maam**
      or Oriental
      fish sauce
1   tablespoon sugar
    Red pepper sauce to taste

In a heavy skillet heat the oil; add the fish in
one layer. Reduce the heat and brown the fish
quickly on both sides. Remove the fish to a
serving platter and keep warm.

   Remove all but 1 tablespoon of the oil from
the skillet. Add garlic and shallot and sauté
just until golden, stirring constantly. Add the
tomatoes and cook for 2 minutes. Add the fish
sauce, sugar and red pepper sauce.

   Boil the sauce for 2 to 3 minutes, stirring
constantly. Pour the hot sauce over the fish.
Serve at once with rice or rice pilaf. Four
servings.

NOTE: Catfish fillets may be substituted for
the mackerel.

Mary Snyder's Jewels from the Sea (Seafood Kebabs)

MARINADE

1¼ *cups peanut oil*
¼   *cup lime juice*
¼   *cup dry white wine*
2   *cloves garlic, crushed*
    Dash white pepper
¼   *teaspoon salt*
3   *tablespoons capers*

2   *lobster tails*
16 *shrimp, peeled and deveined*
16 *sea scallops*
16 *cherry tomatoes*
6   *green pepper wedges*
    Lemon wedges for garnish
    Parsley sprigs for garnish

Preheat oven to 375° F.

To make the marinade, place in the blender all of the ingredients except the capers and blend until smooth. Stir in the capers and set aside.

Remove the lobster from the shells and cut into 16 pieces. In a large shallow baking dish combine the lobster meat with the shrimp, scallops, tomatoes, and green pepper. Pour the marinade over all and let stand for 2 hours, turning the ingredients frequently in the marinade. Thread the ingredients alternately onto 8 skewers; bake the kebabs for 20 to 25 minutes, brushing them often with the marinade until all of the marinade has been used. Garnish with the lemon wedges and parsley and serve over rice. Eight servings.

Shrimp and Feta Cheese

⅓   *cup olive oil*
¼   *cup finely chopped onion*
4   *ripe medium tomatoes,*
    peeled, seeded
    and coarsely chopped
½   *cup dry white wine*
½   *teaspoon oregano*
3   *tablespoons finely chopped*
    parsley
1   *teaspoon salt*
    Freshly ground pepper to taste
2½ *pounds raw medium shrimp,*
    peeled
4   *ounces feta cheese, cut in*
    ¼-inch cubes

In a large skillet heat the oil. Add the onion and cook for 5 minutes; stir in the tomatoes, wine, oregano, 2 tablespoons parsley, salt and pepper. Cook, stirring constantly, until the mixture becomes a light puree. Add the shrimp and cook for 5 minutes more, or until shrimp are pink. Stir in the cheese. Taste for seasoning and correct if necessary. Sprinkle with the remaining parsley and serve. Six servings.

Greek Fish Plaki

1/3   cup olive oil
2   large onions, chopped
2   cloves garlic, minced
3   ribs celery, sliced
3   carrots, peeled and sliced
    1/4 inch thick
4   tomatoes, sliced
1 1/2   pounds potatoes, sliced
    1/4 inch thick
1   teaspoon salt
    Freshly ground black pepper
2   cups boiling water
3   pounds fish fillets (snapper,
    grouper, catfish, etc.)
3   tablespoons lemon juice
1/2   cup sliced black olives
3   tablespoons chopped parsley

Preheat oven to 350° F.

In a large ovenproof casserole heat the olive oil and sauté the onions until golden; add the garlic, celery, carrots, tomatoes, potatoes, 1/2 teaspoon salt and the pepper. Add the boiling water. Heat the mixture to boiling and simmer over low heat for 15 minutes.

Arrange the fish fillets on top of the vegetables in the casserole and add the remaining salt, additional pepper and the lemon juice. Cover and bake for 10 minutes. Remove the cover, add the olives and parsley and cook for 10 minutes more. Serve in soup bowls accompanied by hot bread. Eight servings.

Mme Huger's Oyster Omelette

6   eggs, separated,
    yolks beaten, whites
    beaten until stiff peaks form
30   small oysters, chopped and
    drained
    Salt to taste
    Freshly ground black pepper
    to taste
1   teaspoon grated onion
1   teaspoon chopped fresh dill
    Red pepper sauce to taste
1   tablespoon butter
1   tablespoon lard
1   tablespoon melted butter
2   tomatoes, sliced
2   tablespoons lemon juice
1   teaspoon horseradish

In a mixing bowl combine the egg yolks with the oysters. Add the salt, pepper, onion, dill and red pepper sauce; mix well. Fold in the beaten egg whites.

In a heavy skillet melt the butter and lard. Pour the omelet mixture into the hot pan and cook until puffy and golden on the bottom. Slip the omelet onto a plate and invert the plate back over the skillet. Continue cooking until the omelet is golden on the second side.

Arrange the omelet on a serving plate and drizzle with the melted butter. Serve with sliced tomatoes that have been dressed with 2 tablespoons of lemon juice and 1 teaspoon horseradish. Four servings.

Baked Catfish

1   egg, well-beaten
1   tablespoon water
1/2 cup finely crushed cracker
       crumbs
1/4 cup grated Parmesan
       cheese
       Salt to taste
       Pepper to taste
2   tablespoons butter, melted
4   fresh catfish, cleaned, heads
       removed

BUTTER SAUCE

1/2 cup (1 stick) butter
2   tablespoons chopped scallions
2   tablespoons lemon juice
2   tablespoons chopped parsley
1/2 teaspoon salt
1/2 teaspoon white pepper
       Red pepper sauce to taste
       Worcestershire sauce to taste

Preheat oven to 375° F. Grease well a 15- x 9- x 2-inch baking dish.

In a small bowl combine the egg with the water. In a separate bowl combine the cracker crumbs, cheese, salt and pepper. Dip the catfish in the egg mixture and roll in the crumb mixture. Place the catfish in the baking dish and drizzle with the melted butter. Bake for 20 to 25 minutes or until the fish flakes easily when tested with a fork.

To make the butter sauce, in a small saucepan combine all the ingredients; simmer over low heat for 2 to 3 minutes. Spoon a small portion of the sauce onto the baked fish and serve the remaining sauce separately. Four servings.

Shark Kebabs

1/2 cup lemon juice
3   tablespoons Dijon-style mustard
1/2 cup olive oil
3   tablespoons dry white wine
2   teaspoons minced fresh thyme
       Salt to taste
       Freshly ground black pepper
         to taste
2   pounds fresh shark steak, cut into
       1 1/2-inch cubes
1/2 pound small white onions,
       parboiled
18   medium mushroom caps

In a small bowl beat together the lemon juice, mustard, 3 tablespoons of the olive oil, the white wine, thyme, salt and pepper. Place the fish pieces in a shallow pan and pour the mixture over them; refrigerate for 2 hours to marinate.

Prepare a charcoal fire in your outdoor grill. When the fire is ready thread the shark cubes on skewers alternately with the onions and mushroom caps; reserve the marinade. Combine the remaining olive oil with the marinade and brush the mixture over the kebabs. Grill for 10 to 15 minutes, turning the skewers so that the shark is completely cooked. Four to six servings.

Fillet of Sole with Shrimp

2   tablespoons butter
4   tablespoons minced
      shallots
6   medium fillets lemon
      or gray sole
      (about 6 ounces each)
    Salt to taste
    Freshly ground pepper
      to taste
1   pound very small shrimp,
      peeled and
      deveined
½   cup dry white wine
½   cup crème fraiche or
      heavy cream

Preheat oven to 425° F. Lightly butter a 1-quart ovenproof baking dish.

In a large, heavy skillet melt the remaining butter and sauté the shallots until transparent. Spread half the shallots in the baking dish. Season the fillets with salt and pepper and sprinkle them with the remaining shallots. Place a spoonful of shrimp in the center of each fillet and roll the fillets around the shrimp.

Place the rolled fillets seam side down in the baking dish. Pour the wine over and around the fish. Cover the dish loosely with foil and bake for 15 minutes. Remove the fish fillets from the pan and keep warm.

Pour the cooking liquid into a large skillet and reduce the liquid until only about 3 tablespoons remain. Stir in the crème fraiche and simmer until the sauce is thickened and smooth. Season to taste with salt and pepper. Transfer the rolled fillets to a warm serving platter, cover with the sauce and serve. Six servings.

Steamed Crabs

⅓   cup Old Bay seasoning
¼   cup coarse salt
3   tablespoons pickling
      spice
2   tablespoons celery seed
    Vinegar
12 live blue crabs

In a small bowl combine the Old Bay seasoning, coarse salt, pickling spice and celery seed; set aside.

In a very large pot with a lid, combine water and vinegar in equal amounts to a depth of 1 inch; bring to a boil. Place a rack over the boiling liquid and arrange ½ the crabs on the rack. Sprinkle with ½ the seasoning mixture, top with the remaining crabs and sprinkle with the remaining seasoning. Cover the pot tightly and steam the crabs for 20 to 25 minutes or until they turn bright red. Serve hot or cold. Four servings.

Crab Patties

¼ cup salad oil
5 scallions, finely chopped
4 ribs celery, finely chopped
    Red pepper sauce to taste
¼ teaspoon ground nutmeg
    or mace
¼ teaspoon ground thyme
    Pinch ground allspice
    Pinch ground cloves
    Pinch salt
1 cup fresh breadcrumbs
¼ cup beef broth or milk
1 pound fresh lump crab
    meat, well picked
    over
2 hard-cooked eggs, finely
    chopped
1 tablespoon cornstarch
    Flour for dredging
¼ cup (½ stick) butter

In a heavy skillet heat 2 tablespoons of the oil; sauté the scallions and celery until transparent. Add the red pepper sauce, nutmeg, thyme, allspice, clove and salt. Moisten the breadcrumbs with enough broth to make a thick paste. Add the breadcrumb paste to the skillet; mix well. Reduce the heat and add the crab meat, chopped eggs and cornstarch; stir to combine. Remove the mixture from the skillet and shape into patties approximately 1½ inches in diameter and ¾ inch thick. Dredge each patty in the flour, coating well. In the skillet melt the butter with the remaining 2 tablespoons of oil. Fry each patty until well browned and crisp. Six servings (18 patties).

Charcoal Baked Redfish

3 pounds redfish, filleted
½ cup fresh lemon juice or
    lime juice
6 tablespoons butter,
    softened
2 small cloves garlic, finely
    chopped
5 scallions, finely chopped
¾ teaspoon salt
½ teaspoon cracked pepper

Build a hot fire in a barbecue grill that has a cover, placing the rack 4 to 6 inches above the coals.

Place the fish in a glass dish in a single layer. Pour the lemon or lime juice over the fish and let stand for 30 minutes, turning frequently. Drain the fish and arrange in a metal baking pan.

Meanwhile, blend together the butter and garlic. Sprinkle the scallions over the fish and add the salt and pepper. Spread the garlic butter over the fillets.

Place the fish on the grill rack; cover and bake for 20 minutes or until the fish flakes easily when tested with a fork. Serve immediately, pouring the pan juices over the fish; it will not be browned, but the juices will be golden. Six servings.

Crab Meat in Avocado

¼ cup (½ stick) butter
¼ cup flour
¾ teaspoon salt
   Freshly ground pepper
      to taste
   Pinch nutmeg
2 cups milk
1 teaspoon grated onion
2 cups crab meat, well
      picked over
2 hard-cooked eggs,
      chopped
½ cup sliced mushrooms
3 tablespoons sherry
4 avocados
½ cup grated Monterey
      Jack cheese
⅓ cup cracker crumbs

Preheat oven to 350° F.

In the top of a double boiler over direct heat melt the butter. Stir in the flour, salt, pepper and nutmeg and cook until bubbly. Place the top of the double boiler over boiling water and gradually add the milk to the butter mixture. Add the onion, stirring until the mixture is smooth. Add the crab meat, eggs and mushrooms and mix well. Stir in the sherry and keep the mixture warm over hot water.

Cut the avocados in half and place them in a baking dish; fill each avocado ¾ full with the crab meat mixture. Spread the cheese over the top. Sprinkle with the cracker crumbs and bake for about 20 minutes or until the crumbs are golden. Eight servings.

Baked Catfish Continental

6 whole catfish, cleaned
1 teaspoon salt
   Dash pepper
1 cup chopped parsley
¼ cup (½ stick) butter,
      softened
1 egg, beaten
¼ cup milk
1 teaspoon salt
¾ cup dry breadcrumbs
½ cup grated Swiss cheese
3 tablespoons melted butter

Preheat oven to 450° F.

Sprinkle the catfish inside and out with the salt and pepper. In a small bowl add the parsley to the softened butter and mix well. Spread the inside of each catfish with about 1 tablespoon of the parsley butter. In a shallow bowl combine the egg, milk and salt. In another shallow bowl combine the bread-crumbs and cheese. Dip the catfish in the egg mixture and roll in the cheese mixture. Place on a well-greased 15½- x 12-inch cookie sheet. Sprinkle the remaining crumb mixture on top of the catfish. Drizzle with the melted butter and bake for 15 to 20 minutes or until the catfish flakes easily when tested with a fork. Six servings.

Catfish Baked in Foil

6   ¾-pound catfish, cleaned, heads
      removed
1   teaspoon pressed garlic
4   tablespoons melted butter
⅓   cup soy sauce
½   teaspoon salt

Preheat oven to 400° F.

Place the dressed catfish in foil. In a small bowl combine the remaining ingredients; brush the mixture very generously over the catfish. Wrap the foil tightly around the catfish and bake for about 30 minutes. Six servings.

Catfish with Artichoke Sauce

2   pounds catfish fillets
½   cup butter
¼   cup sliced scallions
2   tablespoons chopped parsley
3   cloves garlic, minced
1   14-ounce can artichoke hearts, drained
      and sliced
½   pound fresh mushrooms, sliced
2   tablespoons diced pimiento
1   tablespoon lemon juice
1   teaspoon salt
½   teaspoon pepper
      Parsley sprigs for garnish

Preheat oven to 350° F.

Place the fillets in a well-greased baking dish approximately 12- x 8- x 2 inches. In a medium skilllet melt the butter and sauté the scallions, parsley and garlic until soft. Add the artichokes, mushrooms, pimiento, lemon juice, salt and pepper; stir until the vegetables are well coated and combined. Pour this sauce over the fillets and bake for 30 to 35 minutes or until the fish flakes easily when tested with a fork. Garnish with the parsley sprigs. Six servings.

Crab Ravigote

1   teaspoon Dijon-style mustard
1   tablespoon finely chopped parsley
1   hard-cooked egg, finely chopped
3   tablespoons cider vinegar
1   tablespoon olive oil
      Salt to taste
      Cayenne pepper to taste

2   cups lump crab meat, well picked over
1½–2 cups Sauce Verte (see Accompaniments
      section)

In a bowl combine all the ingredients except the crab meat and Sauce Verte; season with the salt and cayenne. Add the crab meat and toss gently to combine. Spoon the mixture into scallop shells or divide it among serving plates. Garnish each serving with a little Sauce Verte and serve the remaining sauce on the side. Four servings.

POULTRY AND GAME MAIN DISHES

Chicken Mole Poblano

1   *large chicken*
1   *onion, quartered*
    Salt to taste
½   *cup olive oil*
1   *onion, chopped*
3   *green poblano chilies*
4   *whole tomatoes, peeled,*
      seeded and chopped
3   *cloves garlic*
¼   *cup breadcrumbs*
¼   *cup ground peanuts*
¼   *cup ground almonds*
½   *teaspoon cinnamon*
6   *peppercorns, cracked*
2   *squares unsweetened*
      chocolate, grated
2   *cups well-seasoned chicken*
      stock (from poaching chicken)
1   *tablespoon sesame seeds,*
      toasted

Place the chicken in a large pot; add the quartered onion, salt and water to cover. Bring to a boil, reduce the heat and simmer until tender, about 1 hour. Remove the chicken and reserve 2 cups of the liquid. (Remaining stock can be reserved for another use.)

Preheat oven to 400° F.

Brush the chicken with the olive oil and place it in a roasting pan. Roast until golden (or chicken can be cut up, patted dry and browned in 3 tablespoons oil). When golden, return the chicken to the empty pot. Pour the reserved stock around the chicken.

In the bowl of a food processor process the chopped onion, chilies, tomatoes, garlic, breadcrumbs and nuts until just blended and still a little grainy. Beat in the spices and chocolate. Heat 4 tablespoons olive oil in a small pan. Add the chocolate mixture to the oil and cook, stirring, for 5 minutes.

Spread the chocolate mixture over the chicken, cover and simmer for 2 hours, basting every 15 minutes. To serve, spoon the sauce over the chicken and sprinkle with sesame seeds. Four to six servings.

Grilled Pigeon

8   *whole pigeon, split*
      and flattened
2–4 *cups milk*
8   *slices bacon*

Soak the pigeon overnight in milk to cover.

Prepare a mesquite and charcoal fire in your outdoor grill. Wrap each pigeon with a slice of bacon and secure with a toothpick. Grill the pigeon 4 to 6 inches from the heat until the bacon is crisp and the birds are browned and tender, about 20 minutes. Four servings.

Partridge or Game Pie

12 partridges (doves,
       snipe, etc.), split in
       half
    Salt to taste
    Pepper to taste
1   bunch parsley
1–2 onions, finely chopped
3   whole cloves
½   pound salt pork, diced
2   tablespoons flour
1   tablespoon butter
    Rich pastry for a
       2-crust pie
2   cups finely diced potatoes

Place the birds in a heavy kettle with about 2 quarts of water. Bring to a boil and skim off all scum that arises. Add the salt, pepper, parsley, onion, cloves and salt pork. Simmer until the birds are tender, adding water to cover as needed. *Do not boil the birds; they will become tough.*

Dissolve the flour in ¼ cup lukewarm water, stirring the mixture until it is smooth. Add the flour mixture to the sauce and simmer for 10 to 15 minutes. Stir in the butter. Remove from the heat and let cool. Preheat oven to 450° F.

Roll out ⅔ of the pastry to a thickness of about ⅛ inch and line the bottom and sides of a buttered soufflé dish or casserole. Place some of the birds in the crust, follow with some of the potatoes and repeat the layers until the dish is full. Pour the gravy over the top.

Roll out the remaining pastry and cover the filled dish. Cut a slit in the center to allow steam to escape while baking; crimp the edges of the pastry closed. Bake for 15 to 20 minutes. Twelve servings.

Chicken Mole

1   5–6 pound roasting chicken,
       cut in serving pieces
6   tablespoons vinegar
1½ teaspoons black pepper
1½ teaspoons salt
1   teaspoon sugar
3   cloves garlic, crushed
8   tablespoons oil

SAUCE

2   ounces sesame seeds
       (reserve a few for
       garnish)
2   ounces ground almonds
2   corn tortillas
6   ounces canned green chilies,
       drained
3   cloves garlic, crushed
6   black peppercorns
12 whole cloves
½   teaspoon anise seed
½   teaspoon ground cinnamon
3   onions, quartered
¼   cup tomato puree
1   ounce bitter chocolate, grated
½   cup sour cream

Wash and trim the chicken pieces and sprinkle them with the vinegar, pepper, salt, sugar and garlic. Marinate overnight in the refrigerator.

In the morning heat the oil in a heavy skillet. Add the chicken to the skillet, reserving the marinade, and fry until golden. Drain, and reserve the oil. Place the chicken and the marinade in a casserole, add 2 cups of water and simmer for about 1½ hours, until the meat is very tender. Cool the chicken; remove the skin and bones if you wish.

To make the sauce, roast the sesame seeds and almonds in a dry frying pan by tossing them over moderate heat for about 4 minutes. Remove and reserve. Place the tortillas in the same pan for about 5 minutes, turning them occasionally until they become hard and brittle. Break them into small pieces.

In a food processor blend the green chilies, crushed garlic cloves, spices and quartered onions into a smooth paste.

Place 2 tablespoons of the reserved oil in a heavy skillet, add the green chili mixture, sesame seeds, almonds and tortilla pieces and fry for about 5 minutes. Add the tomato puree, chocolate, sour cream and the cooked chicken with its liquid; simmer gently over low heat until the sauce is thick and creamy, stirring occasionally to prevent the sauce from sticking to the bottom of the skillet.

Serve the chicken garnished with the reserved sesame seeds and accompanied by white rice, cooked beans and warm soft tortillas. Twelve servings.

Mrs. Smith's Baked Duck

4	wild ducks
	Salt
4	onions
2	apples, halved
6	ribs celery
4	tablespoons shortening for browning the ducks
8–10	ounces catsup
1	cup chopped celery
1	large onion, chopped
2	tablespoons Worcestershire sauce
1	tablespoon salt
1	teaspoon pepper

When the ducks have been picked and cleaned, sprinkle the cavities with salt. Stuff each duck with an onion, half an apple and some of the celery ribs, including the leaves. (The quantity of ingredients you need may vary slightly; canvass back or mallard ducks may require a bit more of each ingredient to fill the cavities.) Sew up the ducks or pin the flaps with poultry skewers. Brown the ducks in the shortening in a large skillet or Dutch oven.

In a mixing bowl combine the catsup, celery, onion, Worcestershire sauce, salt and pepper to make a sauce. Pour the mixture over the ducks, cover the skillet or Dutch oven tightly and cook over medium heat on top of the stove for about 1½ hours. Remove the celery, onion and apple from the ducks before serving. Serve with currant jelly. Eight servings.

Paul Prudhomme's Chicken and Andouille Smoked Sausage Gumbo

1   *chicken (2–3 pounds), cut up*
    Salt
1   *clove garlic, minced*
    Tabasco sauce
1   *cup finely chopped onion*
1   *cup finely chopped green*
     pepper
¾   *cup finely chopped celery*
1¼ *cups flour*
½   *teaspoon salt*
½   *teaspoon minced garlic*
    Oil for deep frying
1   *teaspoon Tabasco sauce*
7   *cups chicken stock*
     (approximately)
½   *pound andouille smoked*
     sausage, cut
     into ¼-inch cubes
1   *teaspoon minced garlic*
    Hot cooked rice

Remove the excess fat from the chicken pieces. Rub a generous amount of salt, minced garlic and Tabasco sauce on both sides of each piece, making sure each is evenly covered. Let stand at room temperature for 30 minutes.

Meanwhile, in a medium bowl combine the onion, green pepper and celery; set aside.

In a paper or plastic bag combine the flour, ½ teaspoon salt and ½ teaspoon minced garlic. Add the chicken pieces and shake until the chicken is well coated. Reserve ½ cup of the seasoned flour.

In a large skillet heat 1½ inches of oil until very hot (375° to 400° F.). Fry the chicken until the crust is brown on both sides and the meat is cooked, about 5 to 8 minutes per side; drain on paper towels. Carefully pour the hot oil into a glass measuring cup, leaving as many of the browned particles in the pan as possible. Scrape the skillet bottom with a metal whisk to loosen any stuck particles, then return ½ cup of the hot oil to the skillet.

Place the skillet over high heat. Using a long-handled metal whisk, gradually stir in the reserved ½ cup of seasoned flour. Cook, whisking constantly, until the roux is a dark red-brown to black, about 3½ to 4 minutes (be careful not to let the roux scorch or splash on your skin). Remove the skillet from the heat and immediately add the reserved vegetable mixture and the 1 teaspoon of Tabasco sauce, stirring constantly until the roux stops getting darker. Return the skillet to low heat and cook, stirring constantly and scraping the skillet bottom well, until the vegetables are soft, about 5 minutes.

Meanwhile, place the stock in a 5½-quart saucepan or large Dutch oven; bring it to a boil. Add the roux mixture by spoonfuls to the boiling stock, stirring until dissolved between additions. Return to a boil, stirring and scraping the pan bottom often. Reduce the heat to a simmer and stir in the andouille and minced garlic. Simmer uncovered for about 45 minutes, stirring often toward the end of the cooking time.

While the gumbo is simmering, debone the cooked chicken and dice the meat into ½-inch pieces. When the gumbo is cooked, stir in the chicken and adjust the seasoning with salt and pepper. Serve immediately. To serve as a main course, mound ⅓ cup cooked rice in the center of each soup bowl; ladle about 1¼ cups gumbo around the rice. For an appetizer, place 1 heaping teaspoon of cooked rice in a cup and ladle about ¾ cup gumbo on top. Six main-course or ten appetizer servings.

NOTE: See the Resource Guide for information on ordering andouille smoked sausage. If it is not available, Polish sausage (Kielbasa) is a good substitute.

Chicken Pie

1   *fowl (5–6 pounds) or*
     2 frying chickens,
        cut up
1   *rib celery, diced*
1   *carrot, diced*
1   *onion, sliced*
1   *bay leaf*
     Salt to taste
     Freshly ground black pepper
        to taste
6   *cups chicken broth*
½   *cup chicken fat or butter*
½   *cup flour*
½   *teaspoon sage*
3   *hard-cooked eggs,*
        halved

CRUST

3   *cups flour*
1   *teaspoon salt*
4   *teaspoons baking powder*
½   *teaspoon baking soda*
1½   *cups crème fraiche*
2   *eggs, beaten*
     Light cream

Place the cut up fowl or chickens in a heavy casserole. Add the celery, carrot, onion, bay leaf, salt, pepper and broth. Bring to a boil, cover and simmer until tender, about 1 hour for fowl and 35 minutes for fryers. Remove the chicken pieces and take the meat off the bones. Discard the skin. Strain the cooking liquid and measure 4½ cups, adding milk if necessary. Preheat oven to 350° F.

In a skillet melt the chicken fat or butter; blend in the flour and cook for 3 minutes. Gradually stir in the broth and bring to a boil, stirring. Season with salt, pepper and sage. Add the chicken pieces and pour in a shallow baking pan about 12- x 8- x 3-inches. Arrange the hard-cooked egg halves on the filling.

To make the crust, into a large bowl sift together the dry ingredients. Combine the crème fraiche and the beaten eggs and stir into the dry ingredients. Spoon the mixture over the chicken in the baking dish and spread evenly. Brush with light cream and bake for 35 minutes or until golden brown. Six to eight servings.

Rabbit with Red Wine Sauce

4   slices bacon, finely chopped
1   2-pound rabbit, cut up, washed and dried
½   teaspoon salt
¼   teaspoon green peppercorns, crushed
¼   cup flour
1   large onion, finely chopped
2   cloves garlic, finely chopped
1   teaspoon Dijon-style mustard
¾   cup dry red wine
¾   cup chicken stock
¼   teaspoon dried thyme
¼   teaspoon dried rosemary
1   bay leaf

In a large, heavy casserole fry the bacon until crisp. Drain and set aside, reserving the fat. Combine the salt and peppercorns with the flour and dredge the rabbit pieces in the seasoned flour. Brown the rabbit pieces over high heat in the bacon fat. Remove the rabbit pieces and set aside.

Sauté the onion and garlic in the remaining bacon fat for about 4 minutes. Add the mustard, wine, stock and herbs; stir to combine. Return the rabbit pieces to the pot. Add the reserved bacon, cover and simmer over low heat for 2 to 3 hours or until the rabbit is tender. Check for liquid and add stock as needed. Adjust the seasonings, if necessary, before serving. Two servings.

Roast Pheasant with Horseradish Sauce

3   pheasants
6   slices bacon
¼   cup (½ stick) butter
8   shallots, thinly sliced
1   garlic clove, crushed
½   cup brandy
2   cups chicken stock
½   teaspoon freshly ground black pepper
1   teaspoon salt
2   cups heavy cream
¼   cup horseradish

Preheat oven to 375° F.

Cover the breasts of the pheasants with bacon slices and wrap the pheasants with string to secure the bacon. In a cast iron skillet brown the pheasants with the butter, shallots and garlic. When the pheasants are browned, place them in a baking dish and cover them with the pan juices. In a small saucepan heat the brandy; pour the brandy over the pheasants and ignite. When the flame dies, add the chicken stock, pepper and salt. Roast, uncovered, for ½ hour, basting frequently. Stir the cream and horseradish into the sauce in the roasting pan; continue roasting for 15 minutes more, basting frequently. Serve the pheasants on a heated platter with a little sauce around them and serve the remaining sauce separately. Six servings.

Wild Duck with Sauce Piquante

2   wild ducks
2   small onions
     Salt to taste
     Pepper to taste

SAUCE PIQUANTE

2   duck livers
1   tablespoon finely chopped
        parsley
2   teaspoons grated lemon
        peel (yellow part
        only)
3   teaspoons chopped shallots
1½   cups good red wine
⅓   cup tomato paste
2   teaspoons Dijon-style mustard
2   teaspoons lemon juice
     Salt to taste
     Pepper to taste

Preheat oven to 400° F.

Feather, singe and wash the ducks; insert a small onion inside each to absorb the wild taste. Season with salt and pepper and place in a roasting pan. Cook at 400° F. for 15 to 20 minutes or until the ducks absorb the seasonings. Add a small amount of water to the pan and lower the temperature to 350° F. Cover and cook until thoroughly done, about 1 hour. Baste the ducks often with sauce during the last 30 minutes of roasting.

To make the sauce, in a bowl mash the duck livers to a paste and mix with the parsley, lemon peel and shallots. Take the juices from the roasting pan and add the wine, tomato paste, salt, pepper, mustard and lemon juice; mix well. Four to six servings.

Mississippi Fried Chicken

2   fryers, cut up
     Salt
2   cups flour for dredging
     Bacon drippings
¼   cup (½ stick) butter
4   tablespoons salad oil or
        solid shortening

Soak the chicken pieces in cold salted water for ½ hour. Drain, dry and sprinkle salt over each piece. Place the flour in a large brown-paper bag and shake a few pieces of chicken at a time in the bag to coat them with flour. Coat each piece of chicken twice (this is the secret to crispy fried chicken).

In a heavy skillet melt the bacon drippings, butter and oil or shortening and bring to frying temperature (350 ° F.). Add the chicken pieces, skin side up. Reduce the heat. When the chicken is golden on the under side turn the pieces and continue cooking until tender, about 15 minutes (time will vary depending on the size of the chickens). Drain on paper towels. Serve hot. Six servings.

NOTE: The chicken can be fried ahead of time and run under a broiler just before serving to heat and regain crispness.

Chicken Breasts with Tarragon

3   *whole chicken breasts, skinned, boned and halved*
    Salt
    Freshly ground pepper
1/4 *cup flour*
4   *tablespoons butter*
1   *tablespoon chopped shallots*
1/4 *cup dry white wine*
1   *tablespoon freshly chopped tarragon*
1/4 *cup chicken broth*
1/4 *cup heavy cream*

Sprinkle the chicken breasts with salt and pepper and dredge them in the flour. Reserve the flour.

In a large skillet heat 3 tablespoons of the butter, add the chicken and brown on both sides. Set aside the chicken and keep warm. Add the shallots to the skillet and sauté for 2 minutes. Add the wine. Cook the liquid over high heat until only 3 tablespoons remain, scraping up all the brown particles. Add the reserved flour and stir to make a thick paste. Sprinkle with the tarragon and stir in the chicken broth.

Return the chicken to the skillet, cover and cook until tender, about 25 minutes. Transfer the chicken to a heated platter and keep warm. Add the remaining butter and the cream to the skillet and heat, whisking constantly. Test for seasoning and correct if necessary. Pour the sauce over the chicken and serve. Six servings.

Chicken Okra Gumbo

4   *tablespoons butter*
1   *3 1/2- to 4-pound chicken, cut up*
1   *large onion, chopped*
1/2 *cup chopped celery*
1/2 *teaspoon thyme*
1   *cup chopped smoked sausage, such as andouille or Kielbasa*
6   *tomatoes, peeled, seeded and chopped*
1/2 *pound small okra, sliced*
1/4 *cup chopped parsley*
6   *cups hot water*
1 1/2 *teaspoons red pepper sauce*
    Salt to taste

In a 3-quart saucepan heat the butter; brown the chicken pieces in the butter over medium heat. Remove the chicken. Lower the heat, add the onions, celery, thyme and sausage to the pan and stir to combine. Sauté for 5 minutes. Add the tomatoes, okra and parsley. Cook over medium heat, stirring constantly, until the okra is golden. Stir in the hot water, red pepper sauce, salt and chicken pieces. Cover and simmer for 1 hour.

Remove the chicken pieces from the pan, separate the meat from the bones and return the meat to the gumbo. Heat through and serve with cooked rice. Six servings.

Braised Pheasant

4   tablespoons butter
    Salt to taste
    Pepper to taste
1   pheasant, cleaned and
        quartered
½   cup chicken broth
½   cup bourbon whiskey
½   cup heavy cream

Preheat oven to 350° F.

In a heavy skillet melt the butter over low heat. Sprinkle the pheasant quarters with salt and pepper and add them to the skillet. Increase the heat and sauté, uncovered, turning frequently until golden brown on all sides. Transfer the sautéed pheasant to a small roasting pan. Add enough water to cover the meat about halfway. Add the chicken broth. Add the whiskey at this point, or pour it over the birds about 30 minutes before the end of the cooking period if a stronger taste is desired. Seal the pan tightly with foil. Braise in the oven for about 3 hours. Remove the pheasant to a serving platter and keep warm.

Pour the pan juices into a saucepan, scraping up any brown bits. Add the cream and boil until reduced and slightly thick. Serve with the pheasant. Three to four servings.

NOTES: If desired, an equal amount of any game bird except duck can be substituted for the pheasant. To serve the pheasant, use tongs or a large serving spoon; the meat is very moist and tender and easily falls off the bone. Wild rice is an excellent accompaniment to this dish.

Mrs. Smith's Escalloped Chicken

1   large stewing hen
¼   cup (½ stick) butter
1   pound fresh mushrooms
2   medium onions, chopped
3–4 ribs celery, chopped
¼   cup sherry or vermouth
    Salt to taste
    Pepper to taste
    Parsley sprigs for garnish

In a large pot or kettle stew the whole hen in six cups of water until tender, about 1 hour. Remove the hen from the broth and cut the meat away from the bones; discard the bones. If the broth seems greasy, strain the fat by pouring the broth over ice cubes. The fat will congeal on the ice; throw the fat and ice cubes away and use the remaining broth as the base for the stew.

In a skillet melt the butter and brown the mushrooms, onions and celery. Add the shredded chicken, then add 4 or 5 cups of the broth. If the broth needs thickening, combine ¼ cup cornstarch with a little cold water or milk and add the cornstarch mixture to the pan, stirring to combine. Add the sherry or vermouth and season with salt and pepper. Garnish with parsley and serve over cornbread squares. Six servings.

Broussard's Quail in Red Wine with Dirty Rice

BROWN SAUCE

2	tablespoons butter
2	tablespoons flour
2½	cups beef stock
½	cup red wine
1	teaspoon tomato paste
6	large quail, cleaned (reserve giblets)
	Salt to taste
	Freshly ground black pepper to taste
	Flour
6	tablespoons butter
22	cloves garlic
3	cups brown sauce
1	cup dry red wine
1	teaspoon cracked black pepper
⅛	teaspoon dried thyme leaves, crushed
1	pound quail and chicken gizzards, hearts and kidneys, finely chopped
3	tablespoons salad oil
1	large onion, chopped
½	large green pepper, chopped
¼	cup chopped celery
	Red pepper sauce to taste
¼	pound quail and chicken livers
3	cups cooked rice
¼	cup chopped parsley

Preheat oven to 450° F.

To make the brown sauce, in a heavy pan melt the butter; add the flour and cook, stirring constantly, until golden brown. Add the beef stock, wine and tomato paste and stir until thickened. Set aside.

Season the quail inside and out with the salt and pepper. Dust lightly with the flour.

In a large, ovenproof skillet melt 3 tablespoons of the butter over medium-high heat. Brown the quail on all sides. Roast the quail in the oven for 20 minutes, or until done. Keep warm, reserving the drippings for the wine sauce.

Meanwhile, heat the remaining butter in a medium skillet until it turns slightly brown. Add 19 garlic cloves and cook over medium heat, stirring frequently, until the garlic is soft.

Combine the brown sauce, wine, pepper and thyme in a medium saucepan. Simmer over medium-high heat to reduce the volume by one-third. Add the cooked garlic and reserved pan drippings to the sauce; keep warm.

In a large skillet cook the giblets in the oil until brown, stirring frequently. Chop the remaining garlic and add it to the skillet along with 2 tablespoons flour, the onions, pepper, celery, 1½ teaspoons salt, ¼ teaspoon black pepper and red pepper sauce. Simmer until the vegetables are crisply tender. Add the livers and cook until brown. Stir in the rice and heat through. Top with the parsley. Serve the quail and wine sauce over beds of the rice mixture. Six servings.

Spicy Fiesta Chicken

3   eggs, beaten
1/3   cup bottled green chili salsa
1/4   teaspoon salt
2   cups fine dry breadcrumbs
2   teaspoons chili powder
1   teaspoon dried oregano
6   chicken breast halves, boned
      and skinned
3   tablespoons butter or
      margarine
      Shredded lettuce
1   cup sour cream for garnish
1/4   cup chopped scallions for
      garnish
1   avocado, peeled and sliced,
      for garnish
6   lime wedges for garnish

Preheat oven to 375° F.

In a shallow bowl combine the eggs, salsa and salt; set aside. Combine the breadcrumbs, chili powder and oregano in a shallow pan and mix well.

Dip the chicken pieces in the egg mixture and dredge them in the breadcrumb mixture; repeat and set aside.

Melt the butter in a 13- x 9- x 2-inch pan. Place the chicken in the pan, turning once to coat with butter. Bake, uncovered, for 30 to 35 minutes.

To serve, arrange the chicken on a bed of shredded lettuce. Garnish with the sour cream, scallions, avocado slices and lime wedges. Six servings.

Herb-Smoked Turkey

3   cups hickory chips
6   slices bacon, chopped
2   large garlic cloves, minced
6   tablespoons melted butter
1/2   cup chopped fresh parsley
2   tablespoons rubbed sage
2   tablespoons dried thyme
1   15-pound turkey
1   teaspoon freshly ground
      black pepper
4   slices bacon

Soak the hickory chips in water overnight. About 4 hours before you wish to serve, light a charcoal fire in a large barbecue grill with a domed cover. When the fire is ready, place a pan of water in the center of evenly distributed charcoal and adjust the grill about 6 inches above the coals.

In a medium bowl combine the chopped bacon, garlic, parsley, 4 tablespoons of the butter and the herbs. Stuff the turkey with the bacon mixture and truss. Baste the turkey with the remaining 2 tablespoons of melted butter, sprinkle with the pepper, and place the slices of bacon over the skin. Secure the bacon by wrapping the turkey with string.

Place the turkey on the prepared grill and cook, covered, for 1½ hours. Begin adding the hickory chips to the fire a few at a time and replace the charcoal and water as needed.

Continue cooking and adding hickory chips for 2 hours more. Remove the bacon slices and continue cooking until the turkey is browned and the thigh meat springs back when pressed with a fork, about ½ hour more. (Total cooking time is approximately 4 hours.) Eight to ten servings.

Chicken with Turnip Greens

1 tablespoon butter
1 bunch scallions, sliced
2 cloves garlic, minced
1 3-pound chicken, cut up
2 small hot peppers
3 quarts chopped turnip
    greens
   Salt to taste
   Pepper to taste

In a 3-quart kettle melt the butter; sauté the onion and garlic until the onion is transparent. Brown the chicken quickly on both sides in the kettle. Add the hot peppers and water to cover. Cover the kettle with a lid and simmer until the chicken is tender. Remove the chicken; cool. Bring the chicken broth to a boil and add half the greens. Reduce the heat to low and cook, covered, for about 5 minutes, until the greens cook down. Add the rest of the greens and simmer, uncovered, just until the greens are tender.

Remove the chicken from the bones and cut the meat into bite-sized pieces. Serve in individual bowls with the greens and some of the broth. Serve with pepper vinegar as an accompaniment. Four to six servings.

Dove Pie

12 whole doves or dove breasts
 1 tablespoon salt
 1 small onion, quartered
 1 rib celery, sliced
 1 bay leaf
3–4 peppercorns
   Pastry for a 2-crust pie
 4 tablespoons butter,
    sliced, plus enough
    butter to dot the pastry
   Salt to taste
   Pepper to taste
 2 tablespoons flour
¼ cup minced parsley
   Paprika

Preheat oven to 350° F.

In a large saucepan or Dutch oven cover the doves with water. Add the salt, onion, celery, bay leaf and peppercorns and bring to a boil. Cover and simmer until the doves are tender, about 45 to 50 minutes. Cool in the broth.

Roll out ⅔ of the pastry and line a greased, deep 1½-quart casserole; dot the pastry with butter. Drain the doves. Strain and reserve the broth. Place the doves in the pastry-lined baking dish and sprinkle generously with salt and pepper. Blend 2 cups of the reserved broth with the flour and pour the flour mixture over the doves. Add the parsley and the 4 tablespoons sliced butter. Bake for 45 minutes. Four servings.

Roast Duckling Bigarade

2   *4½- to 5-pound Long Island ducklings*
2   *large onions, sliced*
2   *large apples, sliced*
2   *cloves garlic, minced*
    Dash red pepper sauce
    Salt to taste
    Pepper to taste

BIGARADE SAUCE

4   *tablespoons butter*
1   *small onion, chopped*
¼   *cup flour*
1½ *cups beef stock*
2   *tablespoons tomato paste*
½   *cup dry red wine*

    Bouquet garni:
      ½ teaspoon thyme,
      6 sprigs parsley tied in cheesecloth
½   *cup bitter orange marmalade*
⅔   *cup fresh orange juice*
¼   *cup brandy*
    Juice of ½ lemon
3   *large navel oranges*
¼   *cup Grand Marnier, Cointreau or other orange liqueur*

1   *tablespoon chopped fresh parsley for garnish*

Preheat oven to 400° F.

Prick the skin of the ducks with a fork. Stuff the duck cavities with the onion slices and apple slices. Place the ducks in a roasting pan and sprinkle them with the garlic, red pepper sauce, salt and pepper. Roast for 1 hour and 15 minutes.

To make the sauce, melt the butter in a skillet and sauté the onion until transparent. Add the flour; stir and cook until light brown. Add the stock, tomato paste, wine and the bouquet garni; bring to a boil, stirring. Simmer for 25 to 30 minutes. Remove the bouquet garni, strain the sauce through a sieve, and return it to the skillet. Add the remaining ingredients except the oranges and the liqueur. Bring the sauce to a boil, then simmer for 20 to 30 more minutes. Coarsely grate the orange peels and blanch in water to cover for 10 minutes; drain well and add to the sauce. Section the oranges and add ⅔ of the orange sections and the liqueur to the sauce.

Remove the ducks from the oven and increase the oven temperature to 500° F.

Split the ducks in half with a cleaver or poultry shears. Arrange the duck halves on a roasting rack and cook them in the oven for 10 minutes to crisp the skin.

Arrange the duck halves on a serving platter. Garnish with the reserved orange sections and parsley. Pour a little sauce over all, and serve the remaining sauce in a separate dish. Six to eight servings.

Chicken Ranch Style

2 *frying chickens*
   (about 3 pounds each),
   quartered

BASTING SAUCE

½ *cup white vinegar*
1½ *teaspoons Worcestershire sauce*
3 *teaspoons salt*
2 *tablespoons barbecue sauce*
⅓ *cup salad oil*
3 *tablespoons chopped white onion*
10 *drops or more red pepper sauce*
¼ *teaspoon dry mustard*

Prepare the basting sauce 24 hours in advance. In a small bowl combine all ingredients and beat by hand until thoroughly blended. Refrigerate overnight.

Wash the chicken and pat dry. Place the chicken, skin side down, in a 9- x 12-inch ovenproof dish. Pour the prepared sauce over the chicken and cover with foil. Refrigerate overnight.

Prepare a good bed of coals on your outdoor grill. When the fire is ready, remove the chicken from the marinade and reserve the marinade. Place the chicken on the grill, skin side down. In a small saucepan heat the marinade to boiling and simmer for 5 minutes. Baste the chicken with the hot marinade and turn every 10 to 15 minutes. Grill until done, 45 to 60 minutes. Serve the chicken immediately or keep it warm in a 200° F. oven, basting from time to time. Six servings.

Baked Chicken Garibaldi

1 *large frying chicken*
½ *cup Spanish olive oil*
2 *cloves garlic, minced*
1 *onion, sliced*
1 *green pepper, seeded and*
   sliced
1 *cup chicken broth*
1 *tablespoon salt*
¼ *cup red wine*
20 *mushroom buttons or slices*
¼ *cup grated Parmesan cheese*
¼ *cup grated toasted almonds*
   for garnish
   Chopped fresh parsley for garnish

Preheat oven to 350° F.

Roast the chicken for 40 minutes; set aside (do not turn off the oven). In a skillet heat the olive oil and sauté the garlic, onion and green pepper. Add the chicken broth and salt. Bring to a boil, add the red wine and mushrooms and stir to combine; set aside.

Remove the chicken meat from the bones and place the meat in an ovenproof casserole. Cover the chicken with the sauce and sprinkle with the Parmesan cheese. Place the casserole in the oven and bake for 30 minutes or until the cheese is well browned. Garnish with the toasted almonds and parsley. Four servings.

Brunswick Stew

1	3-pound chicken or 2 squirrels
1½	pounds lean beef
1	pound lean pork
2	quarts cold water
2	tablespoons salt
½	teaspoon whole black peppercorns
2	tablespoons dried red pepper
1	cup diced potatoes
1	cup green beans
3	ribs celery, chopped
2	large onions, chopped
2	cups sliced okra
2	cups lima beans
2	cups fresh corn cut from the cob
12	large tomatoes, peeled, seeded and chopped
1	teaspoon black pepper
⅓	cup butter
	Red pepper sauce to taste

Into a large kettle place the chicken, beef and pork along with the water, salt, peppercorns and red pepper. Cover and cook slowly for 2 hours or until the meat falls from the bones. Discard the bones.

Cut the meat into large cubes and return it to the stock. Add the remaining ingredients, cover and cook gently for 2 hours more, stirring frequently to prevent scorching. Serve hot. Makes 1½ gallons or about 25 servings.

NOTE: Brunswick stew never tastes as good when made in a smaller quantity.

Chicken Jambalaya

1	3-pound frying chicken, boiled until tender and deboned (reserve the stock)
¾	pound country-style ham, cubed
3	cloves garlic, minced
1	large onion, chopped
2	green peppers, chopped
½	cup chopped celery
½	cup (1 stick) butter
1	bunch scallions, sliced, including green tops
¼	cup chopped parsley
1	large tomato, peeled, seeded and chopped
2	cups reserved stock from cooking the chicken
	Salt to taste
	Pepper to taste
	Red pepper sauce to taste
1½	cups raw rice

In a large skillet sauté the chicken, ham, garlic, onion, green pepper and celery in the butter until the vegetables are golden. Stir in the scallions, parsley, tomato and chicken stock. Season with salt, pepper and red pepper sauce and simmer for 20 minutes. Stir in the rice and cook until the rice is tender, about 20 minutes. Serve hot with more red pepper sauce. Eight servings.

Ginger Chicken

3   tablespoons flour
      seasoned with salt and
      pepper to taste
2   teaspoons ground ginger
1   3¹/₂-pound chicken,
      cut up and patted
      dry
4   tablespoons butter
1   tablespoon peanut oil
1¹/₂   cups chicken stock
¹/₂   cup heavy cream
      Preserved ginger for garnish

In a paper bag mix together the seasoned flour and ground ginger and dredge the chicken in the mixture. Reserve the flour.

In a large skillet melt the butter with the oil and sauté the chicken until golden brown. Remove the chicken from the skillet. Add the reserved flour to the skillet and blend well with the butter and oil. Gradually beat in the chicken stock and bring it to a boil, stirring constantly. Return the chicken to the skillet, cover, reduce the heat and simmer for about 25 minutes. Transfer the chicken to a serving platter.

Add the cream to the sauce in the skillet and heat through; do not boil. Pour the sauce over the chicken and chill for at least 2 hours. Remove from the refrigerator 15 minutes before serving and garnish with thin slices of preserved ginger. Four to six servings.

Fried Chicken and Pan Gravy

1   3-pound frying chicken,
      cut up
1   cup flour
¹/₂   teaspoon salt
¹/₄   teaspoon pepper
      Fat for deep frying
1   cup milk, scalded

Chill the chicken in the refrigerator overnight if possible. Mix the flour with the salt and pepper and place the mixture in a brown paper bag. Add several pieces of chicken at a time and shake to coat the chicken with the seasoned flour. Reserve the flour.

In a large frying pan heat about 2 inches of oil or melted lard. Arrange the chicken in the hot fat, cover and cook for 5 to 7 minutes. Uncover and turn the chicken when the underside is golden brown. Cover again and cook for 5 to 7 minutes more; remove the cover and cook until the bottom side of the chicken is brown. Reduce the heat and cook for 20 minutes more, turning the chicken pieces only once.

To make the gravy, pour off most of the fat from the skillet, leaving the brown bits. Add a little of the reserved seasoned flour and cook until brown. Add the milk and stir until smooth and thickened. Season with salt and pepper and serve with the Fried Chicken. Four servings.

Creole Fried Quail

8	quail, whole or split
2–4	cups milk
	Oil for frying
1	cup flour
½	teaspoon salt
¼	teaspoon pepper
2–3	tablespoons chili powder
1–1½	cups light cream
	Red pepper sauce to taste

Cover quail with milk and let stand overnight.

In a heavy skillet heat ½ inch of oil to 350° F. In a shallow bowl combine the flour, salt, pepper and chili powder. Drain the quail and toss in the flour mixture. Fry for 10 to 15 minutes until browned and tender. Set aside.

Pour off all but 2 tablespoons of the oil in the skillet. Add 2 tablespoons of the flour mixture and blend well, scraping the sides and bottom of the skillet. Slowly stir in the cream and cook over low heat until the gravy is of desired consistency. Adjust the seasonings, adding red pepper sauce to taste. Pour the gravy over the quail and serve. Four servings.

Fried Chicken Breasts

6	chicken breast halves
	Salt to taste
	Pepper to taste
1	cup flour
½	teaspoon salt
½	teaspoon black pepper
1	teaspoon baking powder
	Oil for deep frying

Wash the chicken breasts and dry them well; sprinkle with salt and pepper. In a brown paper bag combine the flour, salt, pepper and baking powder. Shake the chicken in the flour mixture until well coated. Place the coated chicken pieces in the refrigerator for at least ½ hour and up to 6 hours.

In a large, heavy skillet heat oil to a depth of 1 inch to frying temperature (350° F.). Place the chicken pieces in the hot oil and turn the heat down to medium low. Cook the chicken pieces in the oil for 7 to 10 minutes on each side or until well browned and crisp. Six servings.

Chicken Divan

5	pounds broccoli, trimmed and steamed until just tender
1	medium chicken, boiled, cooled, and the meat sliced

SAUCE

½	cup melted butter
½	cup all-purpose flour
2	cups scalded milk
1	cup heavy cream, whipped
½	teaspoon Worcestershire sauce
1½	tablespoons grated Parmesan cheese
¼	cup sherry
½	cup hollandaise sauce
	Salt to taste
	Pepper to taste

Preheat oven to 525° F.

In an ovenproof casserole arrange the

broccoli in a layer and cover it with the chicken slices. In a large saucepan combine the butter, flour and milk and stir over low heat until thickened. Add the cream, Worcestershire sauce, cheese and sherry; stir until blended. Add the hollandaise sauce and season with salt and pepper. Pour the sauce over the chicken in the casserole and sprinkle with additional Parmesan cheese. Bake for 10 minutes or until brown. Eight servings.

Arroz con Pollo

3   tablespoons olive oil
1   onion, chopped
2   cloves garlic, minced
1   medium roasting chicken, cut up
1/4 pound ham, cut up
1   teaspoon salt
    Pepper to taste
    Paprika to taste
2   tablespoons minced parsley
    Pinch saffron
2   large tomatoes, peeled, seeded and
       chopped
2   cups boiling water
1   cup raw rice
    Grated Parmesan cheese

In a large kettle heat the olive oil; add the onion and garlic and sauté until golden brown. Add the chicken, ham, salt, pepper, paprika, parsley and saffron. Cook about 30 minutes, turning the chicken occasionally. Add the tomatoes and the boiling water, cover and simmer for 1½ hours. Remove the chicken from the pot and keep warm; strain the broth.

Return the broth to the pot, add the rice, cover and simmer for about 30 minutes. To serve, mound the rice on a platter and place the chicken over the rice. Sprinkle with the grated cheese. Four servings.

Chicken with Artichokes

1   3-pound chicken, cut up
1   large onion, thinly sliced
1   green pepper, seeded and sliced
1/2 cup olive oil
    Juice of 1 lemon
1   cup raw rice, washed
2   cups hot chicken broth
1/4 pound fresh mushrooms, sliced and
       sautéed in butter
4   cooked artichoke hearts, sliced
    Salt to taste
    Pepper to taste
24 toasted almonds

Preheat oven to 350° F.

In a large skillet sauté the chicken, onion and green pepper in the olive oil. Remove the chicken and pour the lemon juice over it. Add the rice and the chicken broth to the skillet and stir gently. Cover and cook for about 20 minutes. Remove the skillet from the heat and add the mushrooms, artichoke hearts, salt and pepper; stir.

Pile ⅔ of the rice mixture into a large ovenproof casserole and arrange the chicken in a single layer over the rice. Top with the remaining rice, cover and bake for 1 hour. Sprinkle with the toasted almonds just before serving. Four to six servings.

MEAT MAIN DISHES

Roast Pork Fillets with Prunes

24   large dried pitted prunes, soaked
       in 1 cup white wine
 2   pork tenderloins, cut into medallions
       1½ inches thick
      Salt to taste
      Freshly ground black pepper
       to taste
      Flour
 3   tablespoons butter
 ½   cup chicken broth
 ½   cup heavy cream
 2   teaspoons red currant jelly

In a saucepan simmer the prunes for 10 minutes in the wine. Drain, reserving the liquid. Sprinkle the pork medallions with salt, pepper and flour. In a skillet melt the butter and sauté the pork slices until brown on both sides; remove and set aside. Pour out almost all the fat from the pan and add the prune-flavored wine. Reduce until only 2 tablespoons of liquid remains. Add the chicken broth and bring to a boil; add the pork medallions and simmer gently for 30 to 40 minutes or until tender. Remove the meat, add the cream to the pan and bring to a boil, scraping up all the browned bits. Cook, stirring, until slightly thickened. Add the jelly and stir to dissolve. Add the prunes, heat through and taste for seasoning; adjust if necessary with salt and

pepper. Arrange the tenderloins on a serving platter with the prunes around them; spoon the sauce over all. Four to six servings.

Grilled Steaks with Green Chilies

 3   1½-inch-thick New York cut
       strip steaks
 1   teaspoon oregano
      Salt
      Pepper
 ⅔   cup teriyaki sauce
 2   tablespoons Worcestershire sauce
 1   4-ounce can whole green chilies,
       sliced into strips

Soak mesquite wood chips in water for at least 1 hour.

Place the steaks in a shallow dish and sprinkle one side of each with the oregano and salt and pepper. In a small bowl combine the teriyaki sauce and Worcestershire sauce; pour the mixture over the meat and marinate for 1 hour.

Prepare a charcoal fire in your grill; let it burn for 15 to 20 minutes, then cover the coals with the soaked mesquite chips. Remove the steaks from the marinade and grill them over medium-hot coals for 6 to 8 minutes. Turn the steaks and place several strips of green chilies on each. Grill an additional 6 to 8 minutes or until done as desired. Three servings.

Beef en Daube Gélée

1   3-pound of boneless rump or bottom
      round roast, trimmed of fat
½   pound veal steak, trimmed of fat
2   pig's feet, well cleaned
2   tablespoons chopped fresh parsley
3   onions, coarsely chopped
2   ribs celery with leaves, coarsely chopped
1   clove garlic, finely chopped
1   teaspoon dried thyme or 1 tablespoon
      fresh thyme
2   whole cloves, pounded
      Red pepper sauce to taste
      Salt to taste
½   cup sherry

Place the beef in a heavy kettle and add cold water to cover. Bring to a boil, skim the fat from the top, reduce the heat and simmer for 3 hours until the meat is very tender.

In another large saucepan place the veal and the pig's feet, add 2½ quarts of water and all the other ingredients except the sherry. Bring to a boil, reduce the heat and simmer for 4 hours or until the meat on the pig's feet falls from the bones. Transfer the veal and pig's feet to a chopping board and chop the meat.

Strain the veal stock and remove the bones; stir in the sherry. Remove the beef from the kettle and place it in a deep bowl. Pour the stock over the beef, add the chopped meats and stir to distribute the ingredients evenly. Cool the mixture to room temperature, then chill for at least 6 hours, preferably overnight, to set.

To serve, turn out onto a serving platter and carve into thin slices. Ten to twelve servings.

Veal Kidneys Flambes à la Eugene

6   veal kidneys
4   tablespoons butter
3   shallots, minced
½   pound mushrooms, quartered
¼   cup cognac
¼   cup dry white wine
¼   cup heavy cream
      Salt to taste
      Pepper to taste
3   tablespoons chopped parsley for garnish

Carefully remove the fat capsules and membranes from the kidneys; do not wash or soak. Slice crosswise in ¼ inch slices. In a heavy skillet heat the butter and sauté the shallots until just transparent. Add the mushrooms and kidneys to the skillet and cook until lightly browned. Add the cognac, heat slightly and ignite. When the flame dies down add the wine; simmer gently for a few minutes to reduce slightly. Remove the kidneys and mushrooms from the sauce and keep warm in a serving dish. Stir the cream into the sauce and season with salt and pepper. Reduce the sauce until slightly thickened; pour over the kidneys, garnish with parsley and serve with boiled rice. Six servings.

Highlands Bar and Grill's Lamb with Cognac and Mint

12 lamb medallions, cut from rib chops, each 1 inch thick
1 teaspoon salt
Freshly ground pepper
1/2 cup flour
1/2 cup plus 1 tablespoon unsalted butter
1 tablespoon peanut oil
1/4 cup chopped shallots
1/2 cup cognac or brandy
1/2 cup heavy cream
1 teaspoon concentrated beef bouillon
1/4 cup chopped fresh mint

Pat the lamb dry and season with the salt and pepper. Dredge in the flour, shaking off any excess.

In a large heavy skillet heat 1 tablespoon butter with the oil almost to the smoking point. Add the lamb and sauté over high heat for 1½ minutes on each side for medium rare. Transfer to a serving platter and keep warm.

Pour off the fat from the skillet. Add the shallots and cook over medium-high heat until transparent. Remove from the heat; add cognac, ignite and return to the heat, scraping up any brown bits from the bottom of the skillet. Reduce the contents of the skillet by half; add the cream, bouillon and mint and cook over high heat until thickened, about 3 minutes.

Pour any lamb juices into the skillet, remove from the heat and whisk in the remaining ½ cup butter, a little at a time. Season with ½ teaspoon pepper, strain and spoon over the lamb. Four servings.

Lamb in Crust

2 pounds leg of lamb, boned
1/2 cup butter
1 lamb kidney, sliced
1/4 cup Madeira wine
1/2 pound mushrooms, sliced
1/2 teaspoon thyme
1/2 teaspoon rosemary
1/2 teaspoon tarragon
Butter
1/2 pound puff pastry, rolled to 1/8-inch thickness
1 egg, slightly beaten

Preheat oven to 450° F.

In a skillet brown the boned lamb leg with the butter and the sliced kidney. Remove the boned lamb. Deglaze the pan with the Madeira and add the mushrooms and the seasonings. Stuff the hollow of the boned lamb leg with the kidney mixture. Roll the lamb leg and sew or tie it together. Rub the surface of the lamb with butter and roast in preheated oven for 25 minutes.

Remove the lamb from the oven and cover it with the puff pastry. Glaze the pastry with the beaten egg and return the lamb to the oven for 15 to 20 minutes more or until the pastry is puffed and golden. Six to eight servings.

Paul Prudhomme's Seven Steak, Tasso and Okra Gumbo

2½ *pounds seven steak (seven bone steak) or beef neck chops*

SEASONING MIX

2 *tablespoons salt*
1 *tablespoon sweet paprika*
2 *teaspoons white pepper*
2 *teaspoons onion powder*
1½ *teaspoons dried thyme leaves*
1¼ *teaspoons garlic powder*
1 *teaspoon dry mustard*
1 *teaspoon dried sweet basil*
¾ *teaspoon black pepper*

½ *cup pork lard, bacon fat, shortening or salad oil*
½ *cup flour*
2 *pounds okra, sliced into ¼-inch pieces (8 cups sliced)*
¾ *pound tasso or other smoked ham, cut into ¼-inch cubes*
3 *cups chopped onion*
2 *tablespoons unsalted butter*
4 *bay leaves*
1 *teaspoon Tabasco sauce*
7½ *cups beef stock or water*
2 *cups chopped celery*
2 *cups chopped green pepper*
2 *cups peeled and chopped tomato*
2 *tablespoons chopped jalapeño pepper (optional)*
1 *tablespoon minced garlic*
¾ *pound peeled medium shrimp (optional)*
3 *cups hot cooked rice*

Cut the meat into 8 equal pieces. In a small bowl thoroughly combine the seasoning mix ingredients; sprinkle some of the seasoning mix on the meat, rubbing it into both sides. Reserve the leftover seasoning mix.

In a large, heavy skillet heat the pork lard. Meanwhile, combine *1½ teaspoons* of the seasoning mix with the flour in a shallow pan; dredge the meat in the flour. Brown the meat on both sides in the hot lard. Remove the meat from the skillet and set it aside.

Add *4 cups* of the okra to the skillet. Fry the okra over high heat until dark brown, about 8 minutes, stirring occasionally. Add the tasso, *1 cup* of the onion, the butter and *2 teaspoons* of the seasoning mix. Cook over high heat for 4 minutes, stirring frequently. Add the bay leaves, *½ cup* of the beef stock and the Tabasco sauce; continue cooking for 4 minutes, stirring often. Add *½ cup* more of the stock and continue cooking for 3 minutes, stirring occasionally. Add the remaining 2 cups onion, the celery, green pepper and the seasoning mix; stir well. Stir in the tomato, jalapeño pepper, and garlic. Cook for 5 minutes, stirring occasionally.

Transfer the mixture to a gumbo or large soup pot. Add the remaining 6 cups of the stock and the meat. Cover and cook over high heat for 10 minutes. Add the remaining 4 cups of okra and lower the heat to a simmer. Cook, covered, until the meat is tender, about 20 minutes, being careful not to let the gumbo scorch. Add the shrimp, cover and remove from the heat; let stand for 10 minutes. Serve immediately in bowls, allowing for each person about ⅓ cup of rice, a portion of meat and 1½ cups gumbo poured on top. Eight main-course servings.

NOTE: Seven steak, or seven-bone steak, is a cut of chuck steak.

Veal Cordon Bleu

8   *thin veal cutlets*
4   *slices salty Virginia-style ham*
4   *slices Gruyère cheese*
1   *egg*
2   *tablespoons water*
    Salt to taste
    Pepper to taste
2   *tablespoons flour*
½   *cup cracker crumbs*
3   *tablespoons butter*
¼   *cup salad oil*
    Horseradish mustard

Place 1 slice of ham and 1 slice of cheese in between 2 of the veal cutlets. Press down the edges on all sides to enclose the ham and cheese completely. Repeat the process until you have 4 packages.

Beat the egg lightly with the water. Season the cutlet packages with the salt and pepper, dip them in the flour, then in the egg mixture and then in the cracker crumbs.

In a heavy skillet melt the butter; add the oil and heat the mixture. Place the cutlet packages in the skillet with the hot oil mixture and cook over medium heat until golden brown. Serve with a good horseradish mustard. Four servings.

Stuffed Ham with Clove and Mustard Seed Dressing

1   *12-pound ham, hock removed*
1   *tablespoon vinegar*
2   *tablespoons brown sugar*
1   *pound crackers, toasted and ground*
1   *1-pound loaf of bread, toasted and ground*
2   *tablespoons sugar*
1   *teaspoon mustard seed*
2   *teaspoons Dijon-style mustard*
1   *rib celery, finely chopped*
2   *onions, finely chopped*
3   *tablespoons minced parsley*
4   *eggs, beaten*
1   *cup sherry*
    Red pepper sauce to taste
    Vinegar to combine dressing ingredients

In a heavy kettle simmer the ham in water to cover with the vinegar and brown sugar until the meat is tender enough to feel loose at the bone, about 2 hours. Cool the ham and remove the bone and fat. Preheat oven to 300° F.

Reserve 1 cup of the fat and grind coarsely. In a large bowl combine the ground fat with all of the remaining ingredients, using enough vinegar to give the dressing a pastelike consistency; mix well. Stuff the cavity of the ham with part of the dressing and coat the outside of the ham with the remainder. Wrap the ham securely in cheesecloth and tie tightly with cord. Bake for 30 minutes. Chill for 24 hours. To serve, slice very thinly. Twenty servings.

Fajitas

½   *cup olive oil*
¼   *cup red wine vinegar*
⅓   *cup fresh lime juice*
⅓   *cup finely chopped onion*
1   *teaspoon sugar*
1   *teaspoon dried whole oregano*
½   *teaspoon salt*
½   *teaspoon pepper*
¼   *teaspoon ground cumin*
3   *cloves garlic, minced*
2–2½   *pounds skirt steak or flank steak*
6–8   *flour tortillas*
    Fresh Salsa Verde
      (See Accompaniments Section)
    Guacamole
    Onion slices
    Sour cream
    Refried beans

In a bowl combine the first 10 ingredients to make a marinade.

Pound the steak between sheets of waxed paper to tenderize it. Arrange the tenderized steak in a shallow pan and pour over the marinade. Marinate for 6 to 8 hours or overnight.

Prepare a charcoal fire in your outdoor grill, using mesquite if available. Drain the meat carefully and dry it well before placing it on the grill. Grill the meat on a rack 4 to 6 inches from the flame for 3 to 4 minutes on each side if you like it rare or 6 to 7 minutes for medium. While the meat is grilling, warm the tortillas in a 300° F. oven wrapped in a towel, napkin or aluminum foil.

To serve, cut the meat across the grain in strips and place several strips in the middle of each warmed tortilla. Add salsa and some or all of the accompaniments suggested above; roll up the tortillas around the fillings. Six to eight servings.

NOTES: If you do not wrap the tortillas before you heat them they will dry out and you will not be able to roll them up around the fillings.

If you wish, strips of chicken can be substituted for the beef. Use 2 pounds of chicken breasts and adjust the cooking time accordingly. Pound the chicken breasts between sheets of waxed paper in exactly the same way, so that the marinade will penetrate the meat to flavor it.

Natchitoches Meat Pies

2   *pounds ground lean beef*
1   *pound ground pork*
2   *teaspoons butter or lard*
5   *scallions, finely chopped*
3   *medium onions, very finely chopped*
2   *green peppers, seeded and finely chopped*
2   *tablespoons finely chopped parsley*
1   *clove garlic, minced*
1   *teaspoon thyme*
    Red pepper sauce to taste
    Black pepper to taste
    Salt to taste
¼   *teaspoon paprika*
2   *tablespoons all-purpose flour*
2   *tablespoons water, if needed*

PASTRY

    4   cups all-purpose flour
    1   teaspoon salt
    4   teaspoons baking powder
  ½   cup butter or lard
    2   eggs
    1   cup milk
       Fat for deep frying

In a heavy skillet cook the meat in the butter over medium heat, stirring often until it is crumbled. Add the scallions, onions, green pepper, parsley, garlic, thyme and seasonings and cook for 10 minutes more. The mixture should be highly seasoned. Remove the skillet from the heat and stir in the flour and water; blend the ingredients together. Cool, then freeze for 30 minutes or refrigerate for 2 hours.

To prepare the pastry, in a large bowl stir together the dry ingredients. Cut in the butter or lard with a pastry blender until the mixture resembles coarse meal. Beat the eggs and add them to the milk. Add the egg mixture to the dry ingredients gradually and knead the dough until it reaches a consistency to roll out. On a floured board roll out the pastry as thin as possible; cut into rounds about 4 inches in diameter.

Place 1 tablespoon of the meat mixture in the center of each pastry round. Fold over in half, dampen the edges with water, and press with a fork to seal the edges well. In a heavy skillet heat the oil to 350° F.; fry the meat pies until golden brown. Makes 24 pies.

Empanadas

    2   tablespoons butter or margarine
    1   medium onion, finely chopped
    1   green pepper, finely chopped
1½   pounds ground meat
  ½   teaspoon salt
    1   teaspoon ground cumin
  ½   teaspoon cayenne pepper or to taste
    1   teaspoon sugar
    2   hard-cooked eggs, finely chopped
  ½   cup golden raisins
  12   large stuffed green olives, thinly sliced
       Pastry sufficient for 3 pie crusts

Preheat oven to 400° F.

In a large skillet melt the butter; sauté the onion and green pepper until slightly soft; remove and set aside.

In the same skillet, brown the meat. Add the remaining ingredients and the reserved onion and green pepper; stir to combine all ingredients.

On a floured board roll out the pastry in thirds as for pie crust. Using a 3- to 4-inch biscuit cutter, cut the pastry into circles. Cover one half of each circle with some of the meat mixture; wet the edges with water, fold over and crimp the edges of the pastry with a fork. Continue the process until all of the meat mixture has been used.

Place the empanadas on a lightly oiled cookie sheet and bake for 20 minutes or until brown. Six servings.

Venison Stew

2   pounds venison loin, cut in 2-inch
     chunks
     Red wine for marinade
     Flour for dredging
2   tablespoons olive oil
2   tablespoons butter
1   tablespoon salt
4   large tomatoes, peeled, seeded and
     chopped
1   small yellow onion, chopped
½   cup chopped celery
2   cloves garlic, crushed
     Pinch cayenne pepper
½   teaspoon black pepper
4   tablespoons flour
3–4 cups beef stock
2   tablespoons Calvados or Apple Jack
8–10 whole new potatoes, peeled in a strip
     around the middle
6   carrots, sliced into strips
10 whole pearl onions
1   pound whole mushrooms, washed
     Chopped parsley for garnish

Marinate the venison overnight in red wine to cover. Pour off the marinade, dry the venison and dredge in flour, knocking off any excess.

In a heavy kettle melt 1 tablespoon butter in the olive oil and brown the venison. Add the tomatoes, chopped onion, celery, and garlic; season with cayenne and black pepper. In a separate saucepan stir 3 tablespoons of flour into the stock and beat well to combine; heat until thickened. Pour the stock over the meat and vegetables in the kettle and simmer, covered, for 2 hours. Add the brandy, potatoes, carrots, pearl onions and mushrooms; simmer for 20 minutes more or until the vegetables are tender. Serve garnished with the chopped parsley. Six servings.

Zesty Pork Chops and Rice

8   thick pork chops
4   tomatoes, thickly sliced
1   large onion, sliced
1   green pepper, seeded and coarsely
     chopped
1   pound mushrooms, sliced
     Salt to taste
     Pepper to taste
½   teaspoon thyme
½   teaspoon sage
2   cups chicken broth
1   cup white wine
1⅓ cups raw rice

Preheat oven to 350° F.

In a heavy skillet brown the chops on both sides; transfer to a buttered 3-quart casserole. Arrange the tomatoes, onion, green pepper and mushrooms over the chops and season with the salt, pepper, thyme and sage. In a saucepan heat together the chicken broth and wine. Sprinkle the rice into the casserole and pour the wine and broth mixture over all of the ingredients. Cover and bake for 45 minutes or until the liquid has been absorbed and the rice is tender. Eight servings.

Tamale Pie

2 pounds chuck steak
3 cloves garlic, minced
   Salt to taste
   Pepper to taste
2 tablespoons shortening
1 medium onion, chopped
6 large tomatoes, peeled, seeded and
      chopped
   Red pepper sauce to taste
¾ cup cornmeal
1 cup beef stock
2 teaspoons chili powder
½ teaspoon ground cumin (optional)

Preheat oven to 400° F.

In a saucepan boil the meat with water to cover, 1 clove garlic and salt and pepper until tender. Cool, remove the meat from the broth and shred the meat with 2 forks. In a heavy skillet melt the shortening; add the chopped onion and the remaining garlic cloves, the shredded meat and ½ of the tomatoes. Season with red pepper sauce and set aside.

In a saucepan combine the beef stock with about 1½ cups of the cooking broth; bring to a boil. Add the remaining tomatoes. Gradually pour in the cornmeal, stirring constantly with a whisk. Continue stirring until the meal thickens into a cornmeal mush.

Line a 1-quart casserole with most of the cornmeal mixture. Place the meat mixture on top and cover with a final thin layer of the cornmeal mixture. Bake for 30 to 40 minutes or until the top is light and bubbly. Six to eight servings.

NOTE: This can be prepared the day before and reheated for serving.

Barbecued Pork Ribs

6 pounds country-style pork ribs
3 cloves garlic, minced, sautéed in
      2 tablespoons butter
1½ cups water
¾ cup chili sauce
1 cup catsup
¼ cup brown sugar
2 tablespoons Worcestershire sauce
2 tablespoons soy sauce
2 tablespoons Dijon-style mustard
2 teaspoons chili powder
1 tablespoon celery seed
½ teaspoon salt
   Red pepper sauce to taste
1 large onion, sliced
1 lemon, thinly sliced

Preheat oven to 450° F.

Place the ribs in a shallow roasting pan, cover and bake for 45 minutes. Meanwhile, in a saucepan combine the remaining ingredients except the onion and lemon slices and heat to boiling.

Remove the ribs from the roasting pan and drain off all fat. Arrange the ribs in the pan, placing a slice of onion and a slice of lemon on each piece. Reduce the heat to 350° F., pour the sauce over the ribs and continue baking, uncovered, for about 1½ hours more, basting the ribs with the sauce about every 15 minutes. Six servings.

Baked Fresh Ham with Port Wine Sauce

1   *fresh ham (12–14 pounds)*
3   *large garlic cloves, sliced*
1   *tablespoon rosemary*
1   *tablespoon sage*
    Salt to taste
    Freshly ground pepper
        to taste
2   *medium onions, peeled*
        and sliced
½   *cup port wine*
2   *cups chicken stock*
1   *tablespoon tomato paste*
½   *cup white wine*

Preheat oven to 375° F.

Using the tip of a very sharp knife make deep cuts in the surface of the ham; insert a slice of garlic into each cut.

In a small bowl blend together well the rosemary, sage, salt and pepper; rub the surface of the ham with the mixture. Place the ham, fat side up, in a roasting pan and bake, basting occasionally, for 2½ hours. Remove the fat from the roasting pan and add the onions. Reduce the oven temperature to 350° F. and cover the pan. Continue baking and basting for 30 minutes more. Remove the fat from the pan.

In a small bowl blend together the port wine, chicken stock and tomato paste. Add the mixture to the roasting pan, cover and bake for 1½ hours more, adding water to the pan if the sauce reduces too much. (The total cooking time is 4½ hours.)

Remove the ham from the roasting pan and let stand at least 20 minutes before carving. Skim the fat from the sauce in the roasting pan, add the white wine and bring the sauce to a boil. Slice the ham, arrange the slices on a platter and cover with the sauce. Eighteen to twenty servings.

Sweetbreads and Mushrooms in Cream

2   *pairs sweetbreads*
¼   *pound mushrooms, sliced*
2   *tablespoons butter*
    Salt to taste
    Pepper to taste
2   *tablespoons flour*
2   *cups heavy cream*
¼   *cup white wine*
4   *individual pastry shells*

Clean the sweetbreads, place them in a saucepan of boiling water to cover and parboil for 20 minutes. Drain the sweetbreads, remove all tubes, fibers and membranes and chop the meat into 2-inch pieces. In a saucepan melt the butter, add the flour and stir until the mixture is smooth. Add the cream to the sauce and stir until it comes to a boil. Add the mushrooms and let it simmer for about 10 minutes. Add the sweetbreads, wine, salt and pepper to the sauce and cook for 5 minutes longer. Pour over pastry shells and serve immediately. Four servings.

Roast Leg of Venison

SAUCE

4 tablespoons seedless white raisins
1 cup port wine
½ cup currant jelly

1 3-pound roast of venison, larded with
   salt pork
   Salt to taste
   Pepper to taste
2 tablespoons Worcestershire sauce
2 tablespoons flour

Soak the raisins for the sauce overnight, or at least 2 hours, in the port.

Preheat oven to 325° F.

Rub the roast with the salt, pepper and Worcestershire sauce. Place the roast on a rack in a roasting pan and roast for about 1½ hours. Remove the roast from the oven and keep it warm. Pour the drippings from the roasting pan into a measuring cup, scraping up all the brown bits. Stir the flour into the pan drippings and add enough hot water to make 1½ cups. Stir the mixture until thickened.

To make the sauce, place the raisins in a small saucepan with the port and cook for 5 minutes. Add the currant jelly and continue to cook over low heat until the jelly is melted. As soon as the jelly is melted add the flour mixture to the sauce and serve at once. Eight servings.

Venison Chili

½ pound dry pinto beans
1 teaspoon salt
10 large tomatoes, peeled, seeded and
   chopped
3 large onions, chopped
3 green peppers, seeded and chopped
2 tablespoons olive oil
½ cup chopped parsley
2 cloves garlic, crushed
3 tablespoons butter
2½ pounds ground venison
1 pound ground pork
   Chili powder to taste
1½ teaspoons pepper
1½ teaspoons cumin seed

Wash the beans thoroughly and soak them overnight in water 2 inches above the beans. Wash them again and simmer them with the salt until tender, about 4 hours.

In a large saucepan or cast-iron pot simmer the tomatoes with ½ cup water for 5 minutes. In a small skillet sauté the onions and green pepper in the olive oil; add to the tomatoes and cook until the vegetables are tender. Add the parsley and garlic.

In a large skillet melt the butter and sauté the venison and pork for 15 minutes. Drain off the grease and add the meat to the tomato and onion mixture. Stir in the chili powder and cook for 10 minutes. Add the beans, pepper and cumin seeds and simmer, covered, for 1 hour. Uncover and simmer for 30 minutes more. Serve with tortillas or rice. Six servings.

Spicy Pork Stew

4   tablespoon salad oil
3½–4 pounds boneless pork shoulder, cubed
1   large onion, finely chopped
3   cloves garlic, finely chopped
1   tablespoon chili powder
1   tablespoon finely chopped jalapeño
      chilies
2   teaspoons finely chopped fresh oregano
      or 1 teaspoon dried
1   teaspoon cumin seed
2   quarts beef stock
1   cup dried pinto beans
4   large carrots, thinly sliced
3   ears fresh corn, cut from the cob
    Salt to taste
    Pepper to taste
    Cooked brown rice
    Halved cherry tomatoes
    Chopped scallions, including green tops
    Chopped fresh coriander
    Sour cream
    Lime wedges
    Chopped fresh jalapeño chilies
    Chopped avocado

In a heavy saucepan heat the oil over medium-high heat. Add the meat to the skillet and brown it well on all sides. Remove the meat and set aside.

Add the onion and garlic to the saucepan and sauté until transparent. Stir in the chili powder, jalapeño, oregano, cumin seed, beef stock and beans. Add the meat, cover and simmer for about 1½ hours or until the meat and the beans are very tender. Cover and refrigerate. When chilled, skim the fat from the broth and discard.

Heat the stew to boiling. Add the carrots, cover and simmer for 30 minutes or until the carrots are tender. Stir in the corn and add the salt and pepper; simmer just until the corn is tender. Serve over cooked brown rice with the accompaniments in separate dishes. Twelve servings.

NOTE: Always use rubber gloves when working with fresh hot chili peppers, such as the jalapeños in this recipe.

Pork Chop Casserole

4   pork chops cut 1 inch thick
4   cups soft breadcrumbs
½   cup melted butter
½   teaspoon salt
    Freshly ground black pepper to taste
4   tablespoons chopped onion
4   tablespoons chopped green pepper
2   tablespoons chopped parsley
1   apple, cored and sliced

Preheat oven to 350° F.

In a skillet over low heat brown the pork chops. Place the breadcrumbs in an ovenproof casserole and stir in the melted butter with a fork; stir in the salt and pepper, then stir in the onion, green pepper and parsley. Arrange the browned pork chops on top of the dressing. Arrange the apple slices over the chops and sprinkle with salt to taste. Bake, uncovered, for 1 hour. Four servings.

Sweet and Sour Stuffed Collard Rolls

1   dozen large collard leaves

FILLING

2   tablespoons salad oil
1   onion, diced
2   large turnips, diced
1   large rutabaga, diced
1/4   pound mushrooms, sliced
1   teaspoon basil
1   teaspoon thyme
1   teaspoon marjoram
1   cup cooked lentils
1   cup cooked barley
1   pound cooked lean ground sausage
    Salt to taste
    Pepper to taste

SWEET AND SOUR SAUCE

2   tablespoons salad oil
4   cloves garlic, minced
2   cups diced onion
6   large tomatoes, peeled, seeded and diced
2   tablespoons honey
2   tablespoons cider vinegar
2   cups tomato sauce
    Red pepper sauce to taste

Wash the collard leaves and cut off the stem ends. In a large Dutch oven steam the leaves over boiling water until they are pliable. Set aside to cool.

To make the filling, heat the oil in a deep kettle and sauté the onion, turnip and rutabaga until tender. Add the mushrooms and herbs and simmer for 2 minutes. Stir in the cooked lentils and barley. Add the salt and pepper and mix well. Transfer the mixture to a large bowl and let cool.

To make the sauce, in a large skillet heat the oil; cook the garlic and onion until golden. Add the tomatoes, honey, vinegar and tomato sauce; simmer for 15 minutes. Preheat oven to 350° F.

To make the collard rolls, place 1/4- to 1/2-cup of the filling mixture in each collard leaf. Roll into a bundle, tucking in the sides while rolling. Layer the rolls in the kettle and cover them with the sweet and sour sauce. Cover and bake for 40 to 50 minutes until the collard rolls are tender. Serve immediately. Four to five servings.

Baked Sesame Veal Cutlets

1   egg, beaten
1/2   pint sour cream
1   cup flour
1   teaspoon baking powder
2   teaspoons salt
1/4   teaspoon pepper
2   teaspoons paprika
1/4   cup finely chopped pecans
2   tablespoons sesame seeds
6   veal cutlets
1/2   cup (1 stick) butter

Preheat oven to 400° F.

In a shallow bowl beat together the egg and sour cream. In another shallow bowl combine the flour, baking powder, salt, pepper, paprika, pecans and sesame seeds. Dip the veal cutlets into the egg mixture and then into the flour mixture. Melt the butter in a shallow pan in the oven. Remove the pan from the oven and place the cutlets in the pan, turning each one to coat them all with the butter. Bake for 30 minutes, turn the cutlets and bake for 20 minutes more. Serve immediately. Six servings.

Cuban Sandwich

1½ loaves Cuban bread or
    French bread
    Mustard to taste
    Butter to taste
¾ pound thinly sliced Virginia-style
    baked ham
½ pound very thinly sliced barbecued or
    roast pork
¼ pound thinly sliced Swiss cheese
¼ pound thinly sliced Genoa-style
    salami
1 dill pickle, thinly sliced

Preheat oven to 350° F.

Cut the bread in six 8-inch slices; split the slices lengthwise and spread mustard on 1 side and butter on the other. Divide the ham, pork, Swiss cheese, salami and pickle among the 6 sandwiches, arranging the ingredients on the bread in layers. Wrap each sandwich in a paper napkin and secure with a toothpick. Warm the sandwiches in the oven for 15 minutes before serving. Six servings.

Chilies Rellenos

1   pound ground beef
1   small onion, chopped
    Salt to taste
    Pepper to taste
2   4-ounce cans whole green
    chilies, cut in half
    lengthwise and seeded
1½ cups shredded medium
    Cheddar cheese
¼   cup all-purpose flour
1½ cups milk
4   eggs, beaten
    Red pepper sauce to taste
½   teaspoon salt
    Dash pepper

Preheat oven to 350° F.

In a heavy skillet brown the ground beef and onion, stirring to crumble beef; drain well. Season with the salt and pepper.

Arrange half of the chilies in a lightly greased 10- x 1½-inch baking dish. Sprinkle with half of the cheese and top with the meat mixture. Arrange the remaining chilies over the meat.

In a medium bowl combine the flour and ¼ cup milk, blending until smooth. Add the eggs, remaining 1¼ cups milk, red pepper sauce, salt and pepper and mix well. Pour over the meat mixture and top with the remaining cheese. Bake for 45 to 50 minutes. Let stand 5 minutes; cut into squares. Six servings.

Feijoada Completa

1	*pound black beans*
2	*large onions, chopped*
2	*ounces salt pork, diced*
1	*pound beef chuck, cubed*
1½	*pounds boneless smoked pork butt*
2	*tablespoons light rum*
4	*cups chopped onion*
3	*tablespoons olive oil*
4	*cloves garlic, minced*
3	*ripe tomatoes, peeled, seeded and chopped*
2	*tablespoons chili powder*
1	*tablespoon ground cumin*
2	*tablespoons chopped parsley*
1	*pound chorizo or other spicy pork sausage, cut in ½-inch slices*
	Hot cooked rice
	Peeled orange slices
	Banana chunks
	Stir-fried spinach
	Salsa Forte (see Accompaniments section)

Wash the beans in cold water and soak them in water to cover for 6 to 8 hours or overnight; drain. Place the beans in a heavy kettle with at least 8 cups of water and bring to a boil. Boil for 5 minutes, remove from the heat, cover tightly and let stand for 1 hour until cool. Drain and set the beans aside.

In the same kettle sauté the onion with the salt pork. Add the beef cubes and cook until they are lightly browned. Add the beans, 4 cups water, the smoked pork butt and the rum. Simmer for 2 hours.

In a saucepan or skillet brown the 4 cups of chopped onion in the olive oil. Add the minced garlic, tomatoes, chili powder, cumin and parsley. Remove 2 cups of the cooked beans from the Dutch oven and mash them; add the mashed beans to the chopped onion and tomato mixture. Puree the mixture in a blender or food processor and add the puree to the Dutch oven; stir to combine. Simmer for 30 minutes. Cut the cooked pork butt into pieces and return it to the Dutch oven.

In a separate skillet brown the sausage slices. Add these to the Dutch oven and cook until heated through, about 5 minutes. Taste for seasoning and adjust if necessary.

Serve the bean and meat mixture over the hot cooked rice on a large platter, surrounded with sliced oranges, banana chunks tossed with rum and spinach that has been lightly sautéed with garlic in olive oil. Serve with Salsa Forte. Fifteen servings.

Roulades of Beef

2	*pounds beef sirloin tip in 1 piece, thinly sliced*

MARINADE

3	*cups dry red wine*
1	*onion, sliced*
1	*small carrot, sliced*
2	*tablespoons olive oil*
2	*tablespoons red wine vinegar*
1	*teaspoon whole peppercorns*
2	*tablespoons butter*

STUFFING

    2   *cloves garlic, finely minced*
  1/4   *pound very lean slab bacon, diced and*
          browned
    4   *large shallots, finely minced*
  1/3   *cup finely chopped parsley*
        Freshly ground black pepper to taste

SAUCE

    2   *tablespoons butter*
    2   *tablespoons flour*
 1 1/2 *cups hot beef broth*
    1   *tablespoon tomato paste*
        Bouquet garni: parsley, bay leaf and
          thyme tied in cheesecloth
        Salt to taste

To prepare the marinade, in a mixing bowl combine all the ingredients. Place the meat slices in a large ovenproof dish; add the marinade and cover with waxed paper. Refrigerate for 6 hours or overnight, turning the meat several times.

To prepare the stuffing, in a small bowl combine the ingredients.

To prepare the brown sauce, melt the butter in a skillet over low heat. Blend in the flour and cook slowly, stirring, for 2 minutes, but do not brown. Remove the roux from the heat; pour in the hot broth all at once. Beat vigorously with a wire whisk to blend. Cook over moderate heat, stirring; add the tomato paste and the bouquet garni. Season with salt if needed.

Remove the meat from the marinade and set aside. Simmer the reserved marinade for 1/2 hour, reducing it to approximately 2 cups. Strain and stir it into the brown sauce.

Dry the meat with paper towels. Place 1 teaspoon of stuffing on each piece. Roll the meat, using a toothpick to hold it together.

In a large skillet heat the butter; sear the roulades on all sides. Allow the meat to simmer in its own juice for 10 minutes. Strain the grease from the pan. Cover the roulades with the brown sauce. Season lightly with salt and generously with pepper or red pepper sauce. Cook on low heat for 40 to 50 minutes. Remove the bouquet garni before serving. Eight servings.

Orange-Glazed Spareribs

    4   *pounds spareribs, cut into serving pieces*
  1/2   *cup fresh orange juice*
  1/2   *cup orange marmalade*
 1 1/2 *teaspoons Worcestershire sauce*
    1   *clove garlic, minced*
        Salt to taste
        Pepper to taste

Place the ribs in a large Dutch oven or heavy kettle, add water to cover and bring to a boil. Cover, reduce the heat and simmer for 1 hour. Drain the ribs and place them in a shallow roasting pan. Preheat oven to 325° F.

In a small bowl combine the remaining ingredients; mix well and simmer over low heat until the marmalade is dissolved. Brush the ribs with the sauce. Bake the ribs, uncovered, for 30 to 40 minutes, basting and turning occasionally. Four servings.

VEGETABLES

Hopping John

1   cup raw black-eyed peas, or lima beans,
      or green peas
4   cups water
2   teaspoons salt
1   cup raw rice
4   slices bacon fried with 1 medium
      chopped onion

In a saucepan boil the peas in the water with
the salt until the peas are tender; drain. In a
double boiler over boiling water combine the
peas and 1 cup of their liquid with the rice.
Add the bacon, the chopped onions, and the
bacon grease. Steam for 1 hour or until the
rice is tender. Eight servings.

Stewed Tomatoes

¼   cup (½ stick) butter
½   green pepper, seeded and finely chopped
2   bunches scallions, white parts only,
      thinly sliced
1   clove garlic, minced
6   large tomatoes, peeled, seeded and
      chopped
¼   cup sugar
½   cup dry white wine
      Salt to taste
      Freshly ground black pepper to taste
½   teaspoon thyme
½   cup soft breadcrumbs

In a heavy saucepan melt the butter and sauté
the pepper, scallions and garlic until
transparent. Add the tomatoes, sugar, wine,
salt, pepper and thyme and simmer for 15
minutes. Stir in the breadcrumbs and cook for
5 minutes more. Serve immediately. Six
servings.

NOTE: Stewed Tomatoes and Garlic Grits are
a wonderful combination. Stir them together
and serve.

Garlic Grits

1   cup grits
½   cup (1 stick) butter
1½   tablespoons Worcestershire sauce
¾   pound sharp Cheddar cheese, grated
½   clove garlic, minced
       Red pepper sauce to taste
2   egg whites, beaten until stiff peaks form

Cook the grits according to the package
directions. Add to the hot grits all the
remaining ingredients except the egg whites.
Let cool. Preheat oven to 400° F.

   Fold the egg whites into the grits, pour the
mixture into an ovenproof casserole and bake
for 20 minutes. Serve immediately. Six
servings.

NOTE: Garlic Grits and Stewed Tomatoes are
a wonderful combination. Stir them together
and serve.

Stewed Tomatoes and
Garlic Grits

Zucchini and Mushrooms

4   zucchini, cut in ¼-inch slices
1   large onion, thinly sliced
1   small chocho, peeled and chopped
2   tablespoons butter or margarine
2   tablespoons all-purpose flour
1½ cups milk, warmed
1   teaspoon salt
    White pepper to taste
1   cup grated Monterey Jack cheese
½   pound fresh mushrooms, sliced and
      sautéed in 2 tablespoons butter
    Cracker crumbs
    Grated Monterey Jack cheese

Preheat oven to 350° F.

In a large saucepan cook the zucchini, onion and chocho in boiling, salted water until tender, about 10 to 15 minutes. Drain. In a saucepan melt the butter; stir in the flour and blend well. Add the milk all at once and stir until thickened. Season with the salt and pepper. Remove from the heat and stir in 1 cup of the cheese until melted. Arrange the zucchini, onion, chocho, and mushrooms in a 7- x 11-inch casserole. Pour the cheese sauce over the vegetables and sprinkle with the cracker crumbs and grated Monterey Jack cheese. Bake for 20 minutes or until bubbly. Eight servings.

NOTE: *Chocho* is also referred to as *mirliton* or *chayote* and is sometimes called a "vegetable pear." It is frequently used in South American cooking as a starch and can be prepared almost every way potatoes are prepared. It is generally peeled before cooking.

Stuffed Mirlitons

8   small mirlitons (chocho)
1   medium onion, chopped
2   cloves garlic, minced
2   tablespoons butter or lard
2   tablespoons butter or lard
⅓   cup chopped celery
¼   cup chopped green pepper
⅓   cup chopped mushrooms
⅓   cup chopped parsley
    Dash thyme
¼   pound cooked shrimp
½   pound bulk hot sausage, browned and
      drained
¼   cup breadcrumbs
    Salt to taste
    Pepper to taste
1   cup grated sharp Cheddar cheese
½   cup breadcrumbs tossed with
      2 tablespoons butter

Preheat oven to 350° F.

In a large saucepan parboil the mirlitons for about 20 minutes or until tender. Cut them in half and scoop out the pulp. Set the pulp and the shells aside.

In a heavy skillet sauté the onions and garlic in butter until transparent; add the celery, green pepper, mushrooms, parsley and thyme and cook until tender.

Cut up the mirliton pulp and mix it with the shrimp, sausage and ¼ cup breadcrumbs. Add to the vegetables in the skillet and combine; add salt and pepper. Fill the mirliton shells with the mixture, top with the cheese and the buttered breadcrumbs and bake until the crumbs are browned, about 15 minutes. Eight vegetable servings or four luncheon main-course servings.

Broccoli and Horseradish

1/4	cup (1/2 stick) butter, melted
3/4	cup mayonnaise
1	tablespoon horseradish
1	tablespoon grated onion
1/4	teaspoon salt
1/4	teaspoon dry mustard
	Dash red pepper
1	head fresh broccoli
	Salt to taste

In a small bowl combine the first 7 ingredients and refrigerate until ready to use. Cut the broccoli into spears, scrape the ends, and steam it until just tender. Do not overcook; broccoli should be crisp. Drain the broccoli spears and season them lightly with salt. Serve the broccoli with a spoonful of sauce over each serving. Six servings.

NOTE: For an excellent summer vegetable, cool the broccoli to room temperature before serving.

Southwest Broccoli

1	head broccoli, washed and cut into flowerets
3	tablespoons olive oil
3	cloves garlic, minced
1	bunch scallions, thinly sliced
3	large ripe tomatoes, peeled, seeded and chopped
1	tablespoon dried oregano
	Salt to taste
	Red pepper sauce to taste

Steam the broccoli until just crisply tender and still very green.

In a heavy skillet heat the olive oil; sauté the garlic and scallions until golden but do not brown. Add the tomatoes, oregano and salt; simmer for 10 minutes. Add the broccoli and simmer for 2 to 3 minutes more. Season with red pepper sauce. Four servings.

Wild Rice Pilaf

1/2	onion, finely chopped
2	tablespoons butter
1	cup wild rice, rinsed well and thoroughly drained
2	teaspoons fresh thyme
	Salt to taste
	Pepper to taste
2	cups chicken stock
1/2	cup slivered almonds

Preheat oven to 350° F.

In an ovenproof skillet sauté the onion in the butter until transparent. Add the wild rice and simmer, stirring, for 5 minutes. Add the thyme, salt and pepper; cook for 1 minute more, stirring constantly. Stir in the stock. Cover and bake for 1 hour or until the rice is tender. Just before serving add the almonds and toss lightly to combine. Four servings.

Green Beans with Tomatoes

1   *pound fresh green beans, washed and*
     stringed
1   *small onion, chopped*
1/2 *cup chopped celery*
1/4 *cup chopped green pepper*
1/2 *teaspoon dried basil or 1 tablespoon*
     chopped fresh basil
     Pepper to taste
3   *large tomatoes, peeled, seeded and*
     chopped

Cut the beans into 1½-inch pieces. In a
saucepan bring ½ cup water to a boil and add
the beans, onion, celery, green pepper, basil
and pepper. Simmer until the beans are
tender, about 10 minutes. Add the tomatoes
and simmer for 10 minutes more. Serve
immediately. Eight servings.

Green Beans with Almonds

2   *pounds very thin green beans*
2   *tablespoons butter*
2   *tablespoons lemon juice*
1/2 *teaspoon white pepper*
1/4 *cup slivered almonds*
1   *teaspoon Beau Monde*
     seasoning

In a saucepan simmer the green beans in
lightly salted boiling water until tender. Drain
the beans, season with the remaining
ingredients and serve. Six to eight servings.

Potatoes in Cheese Sauce

8   *medium potatoes*
1   *large onion, chopped*
1/2 *green pepper, chopped*
6   *tablespoons butter*
6   *tablespoons flour*
3   *cups milk*
1½   *cups grated sharp cheese*
     (such as Cheddar)
     Salt to taste
     Pepper to taste
2   *tablespoons chopped parsley*
     Thin slices of cheese
     Paprika

In a large saucepan boil the potatoes in water
to cover until barely fork-tender; Drain and
cool. Peel and slice the potatoes and set aside.
In a saucepan simmer the onion and green
pepper in a little water until tender. Drain and
set aside. Preheat oven to 300° F.

In a large saucepan melt the butter, add the
flour, stirring well, then add the milk and stir
to combine. Add the grated cheese and cook
over low heat, stirring, until the cheese is
melted. Add the onions, green pepper, salt
and pepper to the cheese sauce and stir to
combine. Add the parsley, then add the
potatoes and mix well. Transfer the potato
mixture to a baking dish, cover the mixture
with the sliced cheese, sprinkle with the
paprika and bake for 30 minutes. Ten
servings.

Spicy Black-Eyed Peas

4   cups shelled fresh black-eyed peas
2   cups beef broth
1   medium onion, finely chopped
    Red pepper sauce to taste

In a saucepan combine the peas, broth, onion and red pepper sauce. Bring to a boil, cover and reduce the heat. Simmer for 30 minutes or until the peas are tender, adding water if necessary. Eight servings.

Smothered Cotton-Eyed Peas

1   pound fresh black-eyed peas
1/4 pound bacon, fried until crisp and
    crumbled
3   tablespoons grease from frying bacon
1   cup chopped celery
1   cup chopped green pepper
1   cup chopped onions
6   large tomatoes, peeled, seeded and
    chopped
    Salt to taste
    Pepper to taste
1   teaspoon sugar (optional)

In a large saucepan simmer the black-eyed peas in water to cover until tender, at least 40 minutes. In the skillet used for frying the bacon sauté the celery, pepper and onion until the onion is transparent. Add the tomatoes, black-eyed peas, salt, pepper, sugar if desired and crumbled bacon. Simmer for 30 minutes and serve hot. Twelve servings.

NOTE: Cooking time will vary depending on the freshness of the peas. Peas harvested late in the season with require more water and more cooking time.

Texas Black-Eyed Peas

4   cups shelled fresh black-eyed peas
1/2 pound thick-sliced breakfast bacon, cut
    into 3/4-inch pieces
2   large onions, finely chopped
3   large cloves garlic, finely chopped
4   tablespoons Worcestershire sauce
1   tablespoon plus 1 teaspoon salt
    Red pepper sauce to taste

Rinse the peas and clean them.
   In a large kettle sauté the bacon pieces until crisp; set aside.
   Sauté the onions and garlic in 1/2 cup of the bacon fat until soft but not browned. Add the peas and stir. Add water to cover the peas by 1 inch. Cover and simmer for 1 hour, stirring and checking occasionally to see if additional water is needed.
   Add the Worcestershire sauce, salt and red pepper sauce to the peas and simmer for an additional 30 minutes, uncovered, stirring occasionally and checking the moisture. Add water if necessary. Taste to correct seasoning. Add the cooked bacon and serve. Six servings.

NOTE: Cooking time for black-eyed peas varies with freshness and maturity. Late in the season they will take longer to cook and will absorb more water.

Spinach Casserole

1½	*pounds fresh spinach, washed and steamed until just tender*
¾	*cup cottage cheese or ricotta cheese, drained*
1	*clove garlic, minced*
¼	*teaspoon nutmeg*
	Salt to taste
	Pepper to taste
2	*tomatoes, thinly sliced*
½	*cup grated mozzarella cheese*
1	*tablespoon grated Parmesan cheese*

Preheat oven to 350° F.

Drain the spinach well. In a medium bowl combine the drained spinach with the cottage cheese, garlic, nutmeg, salt and pepper; blend well. Spread ½ the mixture in a lightly greased 1-quart casserole. Cover with ½ the tomato slices and ½ the mozzarella. Repeat the layers and sprinkle the top with the Parmesan cheese. Bake for 25 minutes or until the cheese is melted and the casserole is heated through. Four servings.

Mary Snyder's Seasoned Rice

4½	*cups chicken broth*
2	*cups raw rice*
½	*teaspoon salt*
2	*tablespoons butter*
2	*tablespoons chopped parsley*

In a saucepan bring the chicken broth to a boil; add the rice and the salt and cook over medium heat for 15 to 18 minutes until all the broth is absorbed. Add the butter and the chopped parsley. Serve warm. Eight servings.

Roast Green Chilies

12	*fresh green chilies*

FILLING

2	*ripe avocados, mashed*
	Salt to taste
2	*teaspoons lemon juice*
½	*cup sour cream (approximately)*
8	*ounces fresh crab meat, well picked over*
1	*teaspoon minced onion (optional)*

SAUCE

1½	*cups sour cream*
1	*clove garlic, minced*
½	*teaspoon coriander leaves*
⅛	*teaspoon cayenne*
½	*teaspoon oregano*

Wear rubber gloves when handling the chilies. Split the chilies lengthwise, removing the seeds and veins. Broil the chilies on a large baking sheet in your oven or grill them over charcoal, turning them frequently to prevent burning. Allow the chilies to blister on all sides, remove them from the heat and place them in a plastic bag for 10 to 15 minutes. Peel them from the stem end.

To make the filling, mash the avocados and season with salt. Add the lemon juice to prevent darkening. Add enough sour cream to blend the avocado mixture easily. Add the crab meat to the mixture and the minced onion, if desired. Fill the prepared green chilies and chill.

To make the sauce, in a small bowl mix together the sour cream, garlic, coriander, cayenne and oregano. Cover with aluminum foil and refrigerate overnight.

To serve, pour a small amount of the sauce over the tops of the cold chilies, or serve the sauce separately. Twelve servings.

Creole Tomatoes

4   large tomatoes, cut in half crosswise
2   green peppers, seeded and chopped
1   small onion, chopped
    Salt to taste
    Red pepper sauce to taste
3/4 cup chicken broth
1   clove garlic, minced (optional)
    Chopped parsley for garnish

Preheat oven to 350° F.

Lay the tomatoes, cut side up, in a baking pan; sprinkle the chopped pepper and onion over them. Season with the salt, red pepper sauce and garlic, if desired. Pour 1/2 cup of the chicken broth around the tomatoes and bake for 15 minutes. Check to see if the tomatoes are tender; if not, add the remaining 1/4 cup broth and continue cooking for a few minutes more. Garnish with the chopped parsley. Four to six servings.

Cheddar Grits Pudding

1 1/2 teaspoons salt
1   cup hominy grits
1/2 cup yellow cornmeal
3   tablespoons unsalted butter, cut up
1   teaspoon sugar
     Red pepper sauce to taste
2   teaspoons baking powder
1/2 cup milk
4   large eggs, slightly beaten
1/4 pound sharp Cheddar cheese, grated
1   clove garlic, finely minced
1   bunch scallions, thinly sliced

In a large, heavy saucepan bring 4 cups of water to a boil, add the salt and whisk in the grits and cornmeal gradually. Bring the mixture to a boil, whisking constantly; cover and cook over very low heat, stirring occasionally, for 25 minutes or until the mixture is very thick.

Remove the pan from the heat, beat in the butter, sugar and red pepper sauce and stir until the butter is melted. Preheat oven to 325° F.

In a large bowl dissolve the baking powder in the milk, add the eggs and beat the mixture until it is combined. Add the grits mixture and stir well; add 1 cup of the grated Cheddar cheese and the garlic and scallions, mixing well. Spoon the mixture into a buttered 2-quart baking dish and bake for 1 hour. Sprinkle the remaining cheese over the top and bake for 15 to 20 minutes more or until the pudding is puffed and golden. Eight servings.

Squash Soufflé

1½   tablespoons butter
½   teaspoon minced onion
½   teaspoon Worcestershire sauce
1   tablespoon flour
    Salt to taste
    Pepper to taste
2   eggs, separated, yolks beaten, whites
       beaten until stiff peaks form
2   pounds winter squash, cooked until
       tender, drained and mashed

Preheat oven to 375° F.

In a skillet melt the butter and add the onion and Worcestershire sauce. Blend in the flour, salt and pepper; add the egg yolks and beat well. Add the mixture to the mashed squash. Gently fold in the beaten egg whites and pour the mixture into a greased soufflé dish. Bake for 30 to 40 minutes. Six or more servings.

NOTE: Any winter squash, including pumpkin, can be used for this dish.

Spicy Cabbage

3   tablespoons olive oil
1   medium head Savoy cabbage, sliced
1   green chili, seeded and chopped
½   cup white wine or rice wine vinegar
1   tablespoon sugar
1   teaspoon whole cloves
1   teaspoon whole peppercorns
    Salt to taste
    Red pepper sauce to taste

In a large skillet heat the olive oil; sauté the cabbage and green chili in the oil for 2 minutes. Stir in the vinegar, sugar, cloves, peppercorns and salt. Simmer gently for 15 to 20 minutes, or until tender. Stir in red pepper sauce; heat through and serve. Four to six servings.

NOTE: Be sure to wear rubber gloves when handling the chili pepper.

Chili Squash Bake

1   tablespoon salad oil
1   small onion, chopped
2   cloves garlic, minced
2   cups sliced yellow summer squash
6   green chilies, peeled, seeded and cut into
       strips
1   cup corn cut from the cob
    Salt to taste
    Red pepper sauce to taste
½   cup dry white wine
½   cup grated Monterey Jack cheese

Preheat oven to 400° F.

In a heavy skillet heat the oil; sauté the onion and garlic until transparent. Add the squash, cover, reduce the heat and cook until the squash is tender, about 10 minutes. Add the green chilies, corn, salt and red pepper sauce; stir in the wine. Simmer for about 15 minutes. Pour the mixture into an ovenproof casserole, top with the cheese and bake until the cheese is melted. Serve very hot. Six servings.

Squash Casserole

1½–2 pounds (about 6) squash, sliced
1 medium onion, chopped
½ cup (1 stick) butter
   Salt to taste
   Pepper to taste
½ cup heavy cream
1 medium carrot, grated
1 cup sour cream
2 cups herbed breadcrumbs

Preheat oven to 325° F.

In a saucepan cook the squash with the onion in a small amount of water until tender; drain. Add ½ the butter and the salt and pepper. Add the cream, carrots and sour cream and set aside. In a medium saucepan melt the remaining butter, add the breadcrumbs and stir to combine. Add about ¾ of the breadcrumbs to the squash and pour the mixture into a buttered 2-quart ovenproof casserole. Top with the remaining breadcrumbs and bake for 30 minutes. Four to six servings.

Pecan Rice

1 bunch scallions, thinly sliced
2 tablespoons butter, melted
2½ cups cooked brown rice
½ cup pecans, finely chopped
2 tablespoons minced fresh parsley
   Salt to taste
   Pepper to taste
1 teaspoon chopped fresh basil

In a skillet sauté the scallions in the butter until they are tender. Stir in the remaining ingredients; reduce the heat and simmer until heated through. Four servings.

Eggplant Creole

1 onion, chopped
1 green pepper, chopped
½ cup butter
½ cup raw rice
1 large eggplant, peeled and chopped
4 large tomatoes, peeled, seeded and chopped
¼ teaspoon basil
¼ teaspoon oregano
1 cup beef stock
½ teaspoon salt
½ teaspoon pepper
   Red pepper sauce to taste
1 cup grated sharp Cheddar cheese

Preheat oven to 350° F.

In a heavy skillet sauté the onion and green pepper in the butter. Add the rice and sauté until golden. Add all the other ingredients except the cheese. Bake in a greased 2-quart casserole for 30 minutes. Remove from the oven, sprinkle the cheese over the top and bake for 30 minutes longer. Serve hot. Six to eight servings.

NOTE: To peel eggplant easily, roast at 450° F. until the skin begins to bubble; place the hot eggplant in a paper bag for 10 minutes; remove and peel.

Sesame Asparagus

1½ pounds asparagus, washed and cut into
     1½-inch lengths
3   tablespoons olive oil
3   tablespoons toasted sesame seeds
     Salt to taste
     Freshly ground pepper to taste

Steam the asparagus over boiling water until just tender. In a skillet or wok heat the olive oil; toss the steamed asparagus in the hot oil until heated through. Sprinkle with sesame seeds and season with salt and pepper. Toss well and serve very hot. Four servings.

Fried Okra

1   pound okra
8   cups water
½   cup salt
½   cup cornmeal
     Salad oil or vegetable oil for frying

Wash the okra and drain it well; cut off the tips and stems, and cut into ½-inch slices. Combine the water and salt and pour over the okra in a large saucepan. Bring the water to a boil, reduce the heat and simmer the okra for about 15 minutes; drain, rinse well and drain again. Dry the okra slices well.

In a large skillet bring the oil to frying temperature, about 350° F. Roll the okra in the cornmeal and fry it in the hot oil. Drain and serve immediately. Six servings.

Spicy Rice

4   ounces wild rice, cooked
1½   cups cooked white rice
½   cup (1 stick) butter, melted
½   cup slivered almonds
½   cup chopped celery
3   tablespoons chopped green chili pepper
½   cup chopped onion
½   cup sliced ripe olives
½   cup sliced water chestnuts
1   teaspoon ground tumeric
1   teaspoon marjoram
     Salt to taste
     Freshly ground pepper to taste

In a 2-quart saucepan with a lid combine all the ingredients. Cover and simmer for 5 to 10 minutes, stirring frequently. Six to eight servings.

Creamed Spinach

3   pounds raw spinach, well washed, stems
     removed, chopped
4   tablespoons butter
1   tablespoon grated onion
¼   pint heavy cream

Place the spinach in boiling water for 3 minutes; drain. Heat the butter in an iron pan or skillet; when bubbling, stir in the onion and brown it, being careful not to let it burn. Add the chopped spinach and heavy cream, heat and serve. Ten servings.

Eggplant Pie

Pastry for a 2-crust pie
1 *eggplant, peeled, cut into ½-inch slices*
⅓ *cup olive oil or salad oil*
1 *large onion, thinly sliced*
1 *green pepper, halved, seeded and cut into thin strips*
1 *zucchini, very thinly sliced*
3 *cloves garlic, minced*
¾ *teaspoon oregano*
¾ *teaspoon basil*
½ *teaspoon salt*
Freshly ground black pepper to taste
½ *cup grated Parmesan cheese*
Red pepper sauce to taste
3 *large tomatoes, sliced*
8 *ounces mozzarella cheese, grated*
Heavy cream

Preheat oven to 425° F.

Roll out ½ of the pastry and line a 10-inch pie plate. Refrigerate the pastry-lined pie plate and the remaining pastry.

Brush the eggplant slices on both sides with the olive oil. In a shallow ovenproof pan bake the eggplant until it is golden and tender. Cut the cooked eggplant into small cubes.

In a skillet heat the remaining olive oil (¼ cup). Add the onion, green pepper, zucchini and garlic; cook, stirring, until the vegetables are transparent, about 5 minutes. Remove from the heat. In a small bowl combine the oregano, basil, salt, pepper and red pepper sauce; set aside.

Dust the bottom of the pastry in the pie plate with ½ of the Parmesan cheese. Spread ½ of the eggplant mixture over the cheese; add ½ of the onion mixture. Arrange ½ of the tomato slices over the onions and sprinkle with ½ the herbs, 1 tablespoon Parmesan cheese and ½ the mozzarella cheese. Repeat the layers with the remaining ingredients, reserving 1 tablespoon of the Parmesan cheese.

Roll out the remaining pastry, cut it into ½-inch strips and arrange the strips in lattice fashion over the pie. Make a fluted crust by pinching the pastry around the edge of the pie plate. Brush the top of the pie with the cream and sprinkle with the remaining Parmesan cheese. Bake for 25 to 30 minutes or until the pastry is golden brown. Let cool for 10 minutes or so before cutting. Eight servings.

Green Peas Sautéed with Jicama

1 *medium jicama, cut into small cubes*
¼ *cup (½ stick) butter*
2½ *pounds fresh green peas, shelled*
Salt to taste
Freshly ground pepper to taste
Red pepper sauce to taste

Blanch the jicama in boiling water for 1 minute; drain. In a saucepan melt the butter; add the green peas and stir until they are coated with the butter. Add the jicama and the seasonings and simmer over medium heat, stirring, until the jicama and peas are very tender. Serve immediately. Six to eight servings.

Mexican Tomatoes

4   *large tomatoes*
     Salt to taste
     Pepper to taste
2   *small garlic cloves, peeled and pressed*
2   *tablespoons minced shallot*
1/2 *cup minced fresh oregano*
1/2 *cup grated Monterey Jack cheese*
1/2 *cup fine dry breadcrumbs*
1   *tablespoon lemon juice*
2   *tablespoons olive oil*

Preheat oven to 400° F.

Core the tomatoes, cut each in half crosswise and remove the seeds. Season each tomato half with salt and pepper. Combine the remaining ingredients except the olive oil in a bowl; spread the mixture on top of the tomato halves. Place the tomato halves close together in a buttered baking dish and drizzle a little olive oil over each one. Bake for 15 minutes. Four servings.

Ginger Stir-Fry

2   *tablespoons cornstarch*
3/4 *cup water*
1/4 *cup soy sauce*
2   *tablespoons cooking oil*
1   *large yellow onion, halved and sliced*
2   *medium carrots, sliced*
1   *medium zucchini, cut into chunks*
1   *cup fresh broccoli flowerets*
2   *cups fresh spinach leaves, washed and stemmed*
2   *tablespoons chopped fresh ginger*
1   *cake tofu (bean curd) cut in cubes*

In a small bowl mix the cornstarch with the water and soy sauce; set aside.

In a large skillet or wok heat the oil over high heat for 30 seconds. Add the onion and carrots and cook, stirring constantly, for 3 minutes. Add the zucchini and cook for 2 minutes more. Add the broccoli and cook for 2 minutes more. Add the spinach and cook for 1 minute or until just softened. Add the ginger and stir to combine.

Push the ingredients to one side of the skillet. Pour the cornstarch mixture into the pan, stir it until it thickens and clears, then stir all the ingredients in the skillet together with the sauce. Gently fold in the tofu cubes, heat through and serve over hot cooked rice. Four servings.

Okra and Tomatoes with Corn

2   *medium onions, chopped*
2   *tablespoons salad oil*
1 1/2 *cups okra*
4   *large tomatoes, peeled, seeded and chopped*
2   *cups corn cut from the cob*
     Salt to taste
     Freshly ground black pepper to taste
1   *clove garlic, minced*

In a skillet sauté the onions in the oil until just transparent. Add the okra and cook over very low heat for 5 minutes. Add the tomatoes, corn, salt and pepper. Cook, covered, over very low heat for 30 to 45 minutes. Six servings.

Mexican Bean Pot

2 *pounds dried pinto beans*
4 *cups water*
¾ *pound salt pork*
6 *cloves garlic, minced*
2 *teaspoons oregano*
8–9 *chili pequins (small, very hot red chili peppers)*
2 *tablespoons salt*

Wash and pick over the beans, then soak them in water overnight in a 3-quart saucepan.

Add the salt pork and simmer the beans in the same water, covered, over low heat. Cook, covered, for a total of 5 hours, adding the garlic for the second hour, the oregano the third, the red chilies the fourth and the salt the fifth. Serve with cornbread. Eighteen to twenty-four servings.

Dixie Fried Corn

1 *tablespoon bacon grease*
1 *tablespoon peanut oil*
2 *cups corn cut from the cob*
½ *cup boiling water*
  Salt to taste
  Pepper to taste

In an iron skillet heat the bacon grease and the peanut oil; add the corn and fry over medium-high heat, stirring well as corn begins to brown and to stick to the pan. When about half the corn is browned lower the heat and add boiling water and salt and pepper. Cover and simmer to desired thickness, adding more water if necessary. Four servings.

Refried Beans

8 *ounces small, dried red pinto beans*
5–6 *cups water*
1 *large onion, finely chopped*
2 *cloves garlic, finely minced*
1 *tablespoon bacon drippings*
1½ *teaspoons salt*
2 *tablespoons lard or bacon drippings*

In a large saucepan combine the beans, water, ½ cup onion, garlic and 1 tablespoon bacon drippings. Bring to a boil, cover and simmer for 1½ to 2 hours or until the beans are very tender. Add the salt and cook 15 minutes more. Drain, reserving the liquid.

In a large, heavy skillet heat the lard or bacon drippings. Add the remaining onion and cook until soft. Add enough beans to cover the bottom of the skillet. Turn the heat to high. Mash the beans, adding the cooking liquid as needed. Continue until all the beans are mashed and the mixture has become a paste. Cook 15 to 20 minutes more, or until the beans are semi-dry and the edges are crispy. Serve immediately. Six servings.

Red Beans and Rice

2 *cups dried red beans (kidney beans are fine), washed*
1 *cup rice*
2 *cups water*
  Salt to taste
1 *tablespoon butter*
8 *thin slices salt pork, fried until crisp, fat reserved*

1 *onion, chopped*
2 *cloves garlic, minced*
   Salt to taste
   Pepper to taste

Soak the beans overnight in water to cover by 2 inches. Do not drain, but bring the beans to a boil in their own liquid. Simmer for 3 to 4 hours until the beans are soft and the juice is very thick.

Boil the rice in the 2 cups of water with the salt and butter. When all the liquid has been absorbed remove the pan from the heat, cover it with a towel and metal lid and let it stand for 15 minutes.

While the rice is cooking, in a skillet sauté the onion and garlic in the salt pork drippings until golden. Stir the vegetables, including the pan drippings, into the beans. Stir in the salt pork and simmer until the rice is ready.

To serve, mound the rice in individual bowls or a serving bowl and top with the bean mixture. Six to eight servings.

Corn, Lima Beans and Tomatoes

8 *slices bacon*
2 *cups fresh lima beans*
5 *large tomatoes, peeled, seeded and chopped*
1 *medium onion, chopped*
1 *green pepper, seeded and chopped*
2 *cups corn cut from the cob*
   Salt to taste
   Pepper to taste

Preheat oven to 350° F.

Cover the bottom of a casserole with 4 bacon strips. Cover the bacon with the lima beans, follow with half of the tomatoes, then the chopped onion and green pepper, then the corn, a second layer of tomatoes and the remaining bacon strips, sprinkling salt and pepper to taste between the layers. Cover and bake for at least 1 hour or until the lima beans are done. Six servings.

Green Beans Vinaigrette

2 *pounds string beans, steamed until just tender*
   Bacon strips, cut in half

VINAIGRETTE SAUCE

3 *tablespoons butter*
2 *tablespoons vinegar*
1 *tablespoon tarragon vinegar*
1 *teaspoon salt*
½ *teaspoon taragon*
1 *tablespoon chopped parsley*
1 *teaspoon grated onion*

Preheat broiler.

Wrap 6 or 7 string beans in a half-strip of bacon and secure with a toothpick. Repeat with the remaining string beans and bacon strips. Broil until the bacon is crisp.

Meanwhile, to make the vinaigrette sauce, in a saucepan combine all the ingredients and bring to a boil. Pour the hot vinaigrette sauce over the green beans and bacon and serve immediately. Eight servings.

Vidalia Onions with Leeks

½	cup tarragon vinegar
1½	tablespoons grated onion
	Creole mustard or Dijon-style mustard to taste
1	teaspoon sugar
1	cup olive oil
1	head leaf lettuce, washed and drained
4	Vidalia onions, steamed until tender, drained, cooled and sliced
6	leeks, well washed, trimmed, steamed and sliced lengthwise
2	medium tomatoes, peeled, seeded and chopped, for garnish
2	hard-cooked eggs, cut into wedges, for garnish
½	cup minced fresh herbs for garnish (parsley, tarragon, chervil, dill, etc.)

In a bowl beat together the vinegar, grated onion, mustard and sugar. Add the oil slowly, beating until the dressing is thick.

Arrange the lettuce on serving plates. Top with the onions and leeks and some of the dressing. Garnish with the chopped tomato and the egg wedges and sprinkle with the fresh herbs. Serve additional dressing in a separate bowl. Four to six servings.

Turnip Greens

2	large bunches young turnip greens, well washed
½	pound lean salt pork, sliced ¼ inch thick
2	tablespoons bacon drippings

Strip the larger leaves from the turnip green stems. In a large saucepan boil the salt pork in 1 quart of water with the bacon dripppings; simmer for 30 minutes and add the washed greens. Cover the pot and heat again to a boil, stirring the greens from time to time. Reduce the heat to low and cook for about 2 hours. To keep the leaves covered, add boiling water as needed. Eight to ten servings.

NOTES: Actual cooking time will depend on the age and tenderness of the greens. If desired, small turnips can be cut up and cooked along with the greens.

Creole Zucchini

2	onions, chopped
3	ribs celery, chopped
1	small green pepper, chopped
1	clove garlic, minced
¼	cup salad oil
6	large tomatoes, peeled, seeded and coarsely chopped
	Salt to taste
	pepper to taste
1	teaspoon thyme
3–4	medium zucchini, sliced thin

In a heavy skillet brown the onions, celery, garlic and green pepper in the oil. Add the tomatoes and the seasonings; simmer, covered, for 1 hour. Add the zucchini and simmer for 15 minutes. Remove the cover and simmer for a few more minutes if there is too much liquid. Six to eight servings.

Corn Pudding

3   cups corn cut from the cob
½   cup milk
1   tablespoon butter
1   tablespoon sugar
3   eggs, separated, yolks beaten, whites
       beaten until stiff peaks form

Preheat oven to 350° F.

In a baking dish mix together the corn, milk, butter, sugar and beaten egg yolks. Fold the beaten egg whites into the corn mixture and bake, uncovered, for 35 minutes. Four to six servings.

Onion Casserole

9–10   medium onions, thinly sliced
   1   tablespoon salt
   2   small green chilies, seeded
          and chopped
4–5   slices buttered toast, crusts
          removed
   ½   pound Cheddar cheese,
          grated
   1   egg
   1   cup milk
   1   teaspoon salt
   ¼   teaspoon pepper
   1   teaspoon celery seed

Preheat oven to 375° F. Butter a flat 2-quart baking dish.

Boil the onions in salted water to cover until just tender, about 10 minutes; drain. Line the baking dish with the toast. Cover with a layer of onions, a layer of chilies and a layer of cheese. Repeat layers of toast, onions and cheese. Beat the egg slightly and add the milk, salt, pepper and celery seed. Pour the egg mixture over the casserole. Bake for 40 minutes and serve at once. Eight servings.

NOTE: The casserole can be prepared ahead, covered with plastic wrap and stored in the refrigerator for up to 8 hours.

Potato Casserole

   5   cups freshly cooked mashed potatoes
          (6 medium potatoes cooked until
          tender with salt to taste)
   3   cups cream-style cottage cheese
   1   cup sour cream
   2   eggs, beaten
   2   tablespoons finely grated onion
2½   teaspoons salt
       Melted butter
   ½   cup toasted almonds

Preheat oven to 350° F.

Prepare the mashed potatoes without using milk or butter. In a blender puree the cottage cheese. In a mixing bowl combine the warm mashed potatoes with the cottage cheese puree. Add the sour cream, beaten eggs, onion, salt and pepper. Spoon the mixture into a shallow buttered 2-quart casserole. Brush the surface with melted butter. Bake for 30 minutes, then place under a broiler for a few minutes until lightly brown. Sprinkle with the toasted almonds and serve. Eight servings.

Texas Hot German Potato Salad

- 1/4 **pound bacon**
- 1 **tablespoon flour**
- 1/2 **cup water**
- 1/2 **cup white wine vinegar**
   Salt to taste
- 1 **teaspoon sugar**
- 1 **bunch scallions, sliced, including some green tops**
- 1 **4-ounce can chopped green chilies, drained**
- 8 **medium potatoes, unpeeled, well-washed and simmered until just tender**
- 2 **teaspoons chopped parsley**

In a skillet fry the bacon until crisp; remove from skillet, crumble and set aside. Stir the flour into the bacon drippings in the skillet, then stir in the water and vinegar. Simmer until the mixture begins to thicken. Stir in the salt, sugar, scallions and chilies.

While they are still hot, dice the potatoes and toss them in a serving bowl with the crumbled bacon. Pour the cooked dressing over the potatoes and toss gently. Garnish with the parsley and serve hot. Four to six servings.

Turnip Pudding

- 8 **medium white turnips, peeled and sliced**
- 1/2 **large onion, chopped**
- 2 **tablespoons butter**
- 1/2 **cup heavy cream, scalded**
   Salt to taste
   Freshly ground black pepper to taste
- 2 **egg whites, beaten until stiff peaks form**

Preheat oven to 350° F.

Steam the turnips and onion over boiling water until tender; drain. Puree in a blender or food processor.

Add the puree and the butter to the scalded cream and cook over low heat until the cream is absorbed; cool. Season with salt and pepper. Fold the beaten egg whites gently into the turnip puree and pour the mixture into a buttered 1½-quart baking dish. Bake until puffed and lightly browned, about 30 to 40 minutes. Serve immediately. Eight to ten servings.

Quick Spinach Soufflé

- 4 **tablespoons butter**
- 4 **tablespoons flour**
- 1 **teaspoon salt**
- 1/2 **teaspoon pepper**
- 1 **cup milk**
- 1/2 **cup grated cheese**
- 2 **eggs, lightly beaten**
- 1 **cup cooked spinach**

Preheat oven to 350° F.

In a skillet melt the butter; remove from the heat and blend in the flour and seasonings. Mix until smooth, gradually stirring in the milk and mixing until well blended. Cook over low heat, stirring constantly, until thick and smooth. Stir in the cheese and the eggs and continue stirring until the cheese is dissolved. Add the spinach, mixing well. Pour into a greased casserole dish and bake for 45 minutes. Four servings.

Ratatouille

2   cups peeled sliced eggplant
2   cups sliced yellow squash or zucchini
3   tomatoes, peeled and sliced
3   medium onions, sliced
2   green peppers, seeded and sliced
2   cloves garlic
1   teaspoon salt
1/3   cup olive oil
1/2   teaspoon ground cumin
1/2   teaspoon dill leaves
1/2   teaspoon oregano

Preheat oven to 350° F.

Arrange the vegetables in a shallow baking dish. Crush the garlic with the salt and add it to the oil; add the cumin, dill and oregano. Pour the seasoned oil over the vegetables. Cover the dish and bake for 1 hour or until the vegetables are tender. Eight to ten servings.

Souffléed Carrot Ring

12   medium carrots, cooked and mashed
1   tablespoon prepared horseradish
1/2   cup mayonnaise
2   tablespoons finely minced onion
3   eggs, well beaten
1/2   teaspoon salt

Preheat oven to 350° F. Lightly oil a medium-sized ring mold.

In a large bowl combine all of the ingredients and mix well. Pour the mixture into the prepared ring mold. Place the filled mold in a pan of hot water and bake for 40 minutes. Turn the ring out onto a serving platter and fill as desired. Serve immediately. Eight servings.

NOTE: Suggested fillings include creamed peas, sautéed zucchini, or any other appropriate green vegetable.

Baked Cream Peas

2   cups fresh cream peas, boiled until tender, drained
3   fresh tomatoes, peeled, seeded and chopped
4   strips bacon, cut into 1/2-inch pieces, cooked until transparent
1/2   green pepper, seeded and chopped
1/2   small yellow onion, chopped
1/4   cup milk
1/4   cup cream
1   tablespoon brown sugar
    Freshly ground black pepper to taste
    Pinch salt
1/2   cup breadcrumbs
2   tablespoons butter, melted

Preheat oven to 325° F.

In a large bowl combine the peas, tomatoes, bacon, green pepper and onion. In a medium bowl beat together the milk, cream, brown sugar, pepper and salt. Stir the mixture into the vegetables. Butter a 1-quart baking dish and pour in the vegetable mixture.

Mix the breadcrumbs with the melted butter and spread over the vegetables. Bake for 1 hour. Four servings.

Corn and Chilies

2 cups fresh corn cut from the cob
1 cup sour cream
   Salt to taste
   Pepper to taste
3 small zucchini, sliced thin, steamed 3
      minutes and drained well
1 4-ounce can chopped green chilies
½ cup grated Monterey Jack cheese

Preheat oven to 350° F.

In a large bowl combine the corn, sour cream, salt and pepper, zucchini and chilies. Spoon the mixture into an ovenproof 1½-quart casserole. Bake for 30 minutes. Remove the casserole from the oven and sprinkle with the grated cheese. Return the casserole to the oven and bake until the cheese is melted and bubbling. Serve very hot. Six servings.

Turnip Casserole

2 pounds white turnips, peeled
      and cut up
1 tablespoon butter
1 large onion, minced
1 tablespoon flour
1 teaspoon sugar
1 tablespoon oregano
   Salt to taste
   Pepper to taste
½ cup chicken broth
⅓ cup dry white wine
¼ pound bacon, fried until crisp,
      crumbled
3 tablespoons freshly chopped parsley

Preheat oven to 400° F.

Parboil the turnips in salted water for 5 minutes; drain. In a heavy skillet melt the butter and sauté the onion until golden. Add the flour and stir well. Add the sugar, oregano, salt, pepper and chicken broth; stir until smooth. Stir in the wine.

Arrange the turnips in an ovenproof casserole and pour the sauce over them. Cover and bake for 30 minutes. Remove the cover and brown the casserole in the oven for 2 to 3 minutes more. Garnish with the crumbled bacon and chopped parsley and serve. Six servings.

Texas Barbecued Beans

4 cups plain pork and beans
⅓ cup catsup
⅓ cup brown sugar
2 tablespoons prepared mustard
½ teaspoon hot chili powder
½ cup hot Texas Barbecue Sauce
2 onions, chopped and fried in bacon fat
      until limp
8 slices salt pork or bacon

Preheat oven to 350° F.

In a large bowl mix together well all the ingredients except the salt pork or bacon. Spread the mixture in a flat, ovenproof dish, top with the sliced salt pork or bacon and bake for 1 hour. Serve very hot. Eight servings.

NOTE: For outdoor barbecuing, spread the mixture in a baking pan, cover with aluminum foil and place on a grid over the coals for at least 1 hour.

Yams with Rum Glaze

6   yams, cooked, peeled and sliced
3   tablespoons cornstarch
¾   cup brown sugar, packed
¼   teaspoon salt
1½   cups orange juice
⅓   cup seedless raisins
¼   cup chopped walnuts
1   teaspoon grated orange peel
½   cup dark rum
6   tablespoons butter
1   orange, thinly sliced, for garnish

Preheat oven to 350° F.

Arrange the sliced yams in overlapping rows in a buttered 9- x 13-inch casserole. In a saucepan combine the cornstarch, brown sugar and salt; beat in the orange juice and bring to a boil, stirring. Remove from the heat, add the remaining ingredients and stir well to combine. Return the pan to the heat and bring to a boil; when clear, spoon the glaze over the yams. Bake, uncovered, for 20 minutes or until the yams are well glazed. Garnish with orange slices and serve immediately. Eight servings.

Asparagus Custard

4   eggs, lightly beaten
1   pound asparagus, trimmed and steamed
        until tender
1   cup shredded cheese
1   cup mayonnaise
1   cup heavy cream
¼   pound mushrooms, sautéed in butter
        until golden and drained

Preheat oven to 350° F.

In a food processor combine all of the ingredients and blend well. Pour the mixture into a lightly greased 1½-quart soufflé dish. Place the soufflé dish in a second pan and add 2 inches of water. Bake for 55 minutes to 1 hour or until a knife inserted in the center comes out clean. Serve immediately. Six servings.

Eggplant Casserole

1   medium eggplant, peeled, boiled, drained
        and mashed
½   onion, finely chopped
1   egg, lightly beaten
1   cup heavy cream
2   teaspoons melted butter
1   teaspoon Worcestershire
        sauce
     Salt to taste
     Pepper to taste
½   cup breadcrumbs tossed
        with 1 tablespoon melted
        butter

Preheat oven to 300° F.

In a mixing bowl combine the eggplant, onion, egg, ½ cup of the cream, the butter, Worcestershire sauce and seasonings. Pour the mixture into a greased 1-quart casserole. Pour the remaining cream over the top and bake for 15 to 20 minutes. Remove the casserole from the oven, sprinkle with the buttered breadcrumbs and bake for 10 to 15 minutes more. Six servings.

Green Rice

3/4 cup thinly sliced scallions, including
      green tops
1/2 cup finely chopped green pepper
2   tablespoons olive oil
1   cup raw rice
1/4 cup chopped parsley
1   teaspoon salt
1/4 teaspoon pepper
2   cups boiling chicken broth

Preheat oven to 350° F.

In a skillet sauté the scallions and green pepper in the olive oil until soft but not brown. Place the rice in a 2-quart baking dish and add the sautéed vegetables, parsley, seasonings and broth. Stir. Cover with a tight-fitting lid or heavy-duty foil. Bake for 25 minutes or until the rice is tender and the liquid is absorbed. Toss lightly with a fork before serving. Six servings.

Maque Choux

2   tablespoons lard or bacon drippings
1   onion, chopped
1   green pepper, chopped
5–6 cups corn cut from the cob
     Salt to taste
     Pepper to taste
1/4 teaspoon dried thyme
1/4 teaspoon dried basil
3   tomatoes, peeled, seeded and chopped
1   teaspoon sugar
1/2 cup cream
1   tablespoon minced parsley

In a heavy skillet melt the lard and sauté the onion and green pepper. Add the corn and the seasonings and stir to combine. Add the tomatoes and the remaining ingredients. Stir to combine and simmer, covered, over low heat for 5 to 10 minutes or until creamy. Six to eight servings.

Brussels Sprouts with Bacon Dressing

2   eggs
1/4   cup sugar
2/3   cup white vinegar
1/3   cup water
1/2   teaspoon dry mustard
      Salt to taste
      Freshly ground black pepper to taste
12   strips bacon, halved
1   tablespoon salt
1 1/2 pounds Brussels sprouts

In a small bowl beat the eggs lightly with a fork. Add the sugar, vinegar, water, dry mustard, salt and pepper; beat well. Cover and refrigerate for at least 1 hour.

About 1 hour before serving fry the bacon in a heavy skillet; drain and crumble. Remove all but 4 tablespoons of the bacon fat, reduce the heat to low, beat the egg mixture again and add the mixture to the skillet; stir until the sauce is thick and set aside. Do not boil. Cook the Brussels sprouts in boiling, salted water for about 8 minutes or until tender; drain. Serve the Brussels sprouts hot with the warm sauce over them, garnished with crumbled bacon. Eight to ten servings.

Hot Cabbage Creole

2   *slices bacon, chopped*
1   *large onion, chopped*
1   *large green pepper, seeded and chopped*
10 *large tomatoes, peeled, seeded and chopped*
1   *head cabbage, shredded*
2   *teaspoons salt*
1/4 *teaspoon pepper*
    Cayenne pepper to taste
1/3 *cup vinegar*

In a large skillet fry the bacon until nearly crisp. Add the onion and green pepper and sauté until they are tender. Add the tomatoes and stir to combine. Add the cabbage, salt and pepper; sprinkle lightly with the cayenne. Add the vinegar, bring to a boil and cover; simmer for 30 minutes. Eight servings.

Hot Cabbage Slaw

2   *tablespoons butter*
1/2 *cup chopped onion*
1/3 *cup water*
1/4 *cup dry white wine*
    Salt to taste
1/4 *teaspoon red pepper sauce*
8   *cups shredded cabbage (1/2 medium head)*

In a large skillet melt the butter; add the onion and sauté for 5 minutes or until the onion is tender. Stir in the water, wine, salt and red pepper sauce. Add the cabbage and mix well; cover and simmer for 15 minutes or until the cabbage is crisp-tender. Four to six servings.

Consommé Rice

2   *onions, chopped*
1/2 *pound fresh mushrooms, thinly sliced*
3   *tablespoons butter*
1   *cup raw rice*
2 1/2 *cups consommé*

Preheat oven to 350° F.

In an ovenproof pan sauté the onion and mushrooms in the butter until transparent. Add the rice and cook, stirring, until the rice is browned. Add the consommé and stir well to combine. Cover tightly and bake for 30 to 45 minutes, stirring occasionally, until all the liquid has been absorbed. If liquid remains after 45 minutes, uncover and bake for 10 minutes more. Four servings.

NOTES: This is delicious with fowl or game. Wild rice or brown rice may also be used to prepare this dish.

SAUCES AND ACCOMPANIMENTS

Bread and Butter Pickles

4   *quarts thinly sliced, unpeeled medium cucumbers*
6   *medium white onions, thinly sliced*
1   *green pepper, seeded and sliced*
3   *cloves garlic*
1/3 *cup salt*
5   *cups sugar*
3   *cups cider vinegar*
1 1/2 *teaspooons turmeric*
1 1/2 *teaspoons celery seed*
2   *teaspoons mustard seed*

In a large pan gently combine the cucumbers, onions, pepper, garlic cloves and salt. Cover the mixture with cracked ice, mix thoroughly and let stand for at least 5 hours. Drain well. In a large saucepan combine the remaining ingredients and bring the mixture to a boil. Pour the sugar mixture over the cucumbers and heat just to a boil. Pack into hot sterilized jars and seal with sterilized lids. Makes 8 pints.

Pickled Okra

7   *cloves garlic*
7   *hot peppers*
3   *pounds small okra (1 to 3 inches long), scrubbed*
7   *sprigs fresh dill*
1   *quart distilled white vinegar*
1   *cup water*
1/2 *teaspoon coarse (kosher) salt*

Sterilize 7 pint jars. While the jars are still hot, place 1 clove garlic, 1 sprig dill and 1 hot pepper into the bottom of each jar. Pack the jars with the okra.

In a medium saucepan bring the vinegar, water and salt to a boil and simmer for 5 minutes; pour immediately over the okra. Seal with warm, sterilized lids and process in a boiling water bath for 30 minutes. Cool. Makes 7 pints.

Sliced Cucumber Pickles

10 *pounds brown sugar*
3   *pints vinegar*
50 *medium cucumber pickles, cut into 1 inch slices*
1   *dozen garlic cloves, cut in half*
1   *tablespoon whole peppercorns*
1/2 *tablespoon cloves*
1/2 *cup olive oil*

In a large saucepan dissolve the sugar in the vinegar over low heat. In a 5-gallon jar layer the sliced cucumbers, a little of the garlic, a few peppercorns, several cloves and a little of the oil until all of the ingredients are used. Pour the hot vinegar mixture over the cucumber slices in the jar. Seal the jar well and do not use for 3 or 4 weeks. Remove from the large jar, pack in hot sterilized pint jars, seal with hot lids and process in a hot water bath for 10 minutes.

Creole Sauce for Steak

3 large onions, chopped
4 cloves garlic, chopped
2 large green peppers, seeded and chopped
½ cup (1 stick) butter
8 large tomatoes, peeled, seeded and chopped
6 cups water
1 tablespoon sugar
1 teaspoon pepper
3 tablespoons Worcestershire sauce
Red pepper sauce to taste

In a heavy kettle sauté the onions, garlic and green pepper in the butter. Add the remaining ingredients and simmer for 2½ hours. Season with red pepper sauce. Serve with broiled steak. Makes about 1 quart.

Apple Pear Chutney

1 lemon, chopped
6 very crisp apples, peeled and chopped
2½ cups dark brown sugar
1½ cups raisins
¾ cup crystallized ginger or 3 ounces chopped
1½ teaspoons salt
¼ teaspoon cayenne pepper
2 cups cider or white wine vinegar
1 onion, finely minced
1 green pepper, finely chopped
1 tablespoon whole cloves

In a non-aluminum kettle gently simmer all of the ingredients together until very tender, at least 1 hour. Pack in hot, sterilized jars and seal with sterilized lids. Makes 4 pints.

Sweet Tomato Chutney

6 peppers, seeded and cut into chunks
18 ripe tomatoes, peeled, seeded and quartered
2 tablespoons salt
1 tablespoon celery seed
Black pepper to taste
2 teaspoons cinnamon
½ tablespoon ground cloves
2 pounds brown sugar
1 quart vinegar
2 garlic cloves, minced
8 medium onions, cut up
¼ cup horseradish

In a large bowl or pan mix the peppers and tomatoes with the spices and let stand. In a large kettle boil the sugar and vinegar to a thick syrup. Add the garlic, onions, tomatoes and peppers and boil until thick; add horseradish and more salt if necessary. Pack into hot sterilized pint jars and seal. Makes about 20 pints.

Basic Vinaigrette Sauce

1 teaspoon Pommery or Dijon-style mustard
⅓ cup wine vinegar
½ teaspoon salt
Generous grinding of black pepper
¼–½ cup snipped fresh dill
1 clove garlic, minced
⅔ cup olive oil or ⅓ cup olive oil and ⅓ cup salad oil

In a blender quickly blend the mustard, vinegar, salt, pepper, herbs and garlic. Pour in the olive oil a little at a time until all has been added and the sauce is thick. Makes about 1 cup.

NOTES: This sauce keeps well in the refrigerator; it is an excellent accompaniment for green beans, artichokes, and other green vegetables.

Hot Pepper Jelly

- 1½ cups cider vinegar
- 2 large green peppers, seeded and chopped
- ⅓ cup finely chopped hot peppers
- 6½ cups sugar
- 1 6-ounce bottle liquid fruit pectin
  Melted paraffin

Place ½ cup vinegar into a blender, add the peppers and reduce to a fine puree. Strain the pepper mixture through a fine cheesecloth, squeezing hard. Pour the juice into a large, flat-bottomed kettle and add the remaining 1 cup vinegar and the sugar. Bring the mixture to a full rolling boil that cannot be stirred down, stirring constantly. Remove the mixture from the heat and cool for 5 minutes. Skim off the thick foam that rises to the top. Add the liquid pectin and stir well. Pour into hot sterilized glasses. Cover the jelly with melted paraffin ⅛ inch thick. Makes seven 8-ounce glasses.

NOTES: This jelly can also be sealed in hot sterilized jars with lids. Always wear rubber gloves when handling hot peppers.

Hot Pepper Sauce

- 4 dozen small very hot peppers
- 1 clove garlic, minced
- 1 teaspoon honey
- ½ cup cider vinegar

Wash the peppers and remove the stem ends. In a medium saucepan simmer the peppers and the garlic in water to cover until very tender. Puree the mixture in a food processor and then strain out the seeds. Add the honey and vinegar to the puree and stir until well blended. Pack in bottles to store. Makes 1½ cups.

Spicy Pecans

- 1 egg white, room temperature
- 2 tablespoons water
- 1½ cups pecan halves
- ⅔ cup sugar
- 2 teaspoons cinnamon
  Pinch cayenne pepper
- ½ teaspoon ground ginger
- ¼ cup cornstarch

Preheat oven to 250° F.

In a medium bowl beat the egg white with the water; add the pecans and stir until well moistened. In another bowl combine the sugar, cinnamon, ginger, cayenne and cornstarch; sift into a shallow pan. Toss the pecans in the sugar mixture until well coated. Spread the coated pecans on a cookie sheet and bake for 1½ hours, stirring often. Makes ¾ pound.

Corn Bread Stuffing with Pecans

5	cups crumbled corn bread
6	cups breadcrumbs
2	tablespoons salt
1/2	teaspoon pepper
1/2	teaspoon powdered sage
1	small yellow onion, chopped
1 1/2	cups broken pecans
1/2	cup (1 stick) butter, melted
1/4	cup milk

Preheat oven to 325° F.

In a mixing bowl lightly toss together all of the ingredients except the melted butter and milk. Sprinkle the butter and milk over the dry ingredients, tossing lightly until combined (the dressing should be barely moist). Place the dressing in an ovenproof casserole and bake for about 40 minutes. Serve with Baked Duck.

NOTE: This excellent dressing can be used to stuff ducks or other poultry. Stuff the body and neck cavities with the dressing and roast the ducks, uncovered, for 20 to 35 minutes per pound in a 325° F. oven, basting frequently with small amounts of white wine. This mixture will stuff 2 ducks.

Corn Bread Stuffing for Duck or Other Fowl

5	cups crumbled corn bread (made without sugar)
6	cups soft breadcrumbs
2	teaspoons salt
1/2	teaspoon pepper
1	teaspoon sage, crumbled
1/2	cup chopped celery
1	large onion, chopped
3/4	cup (1 1/2 sticks) butter, melted
3/4	cup chicken broth

In a mixing bowl lightly toss together all the ingredients except the melted butter and broth. Add the butter and broth, tossing lightly until combined (add a few more tablespoons of broth if you prefer a moist dressing). Stuff the mixture lightly into the body and neck cavities of 1 or 2 ducks or a small turkey. Place leftover dressing, if any, in a buttered 1-quart casserole and bake in a 325° F. oven for about 40 minutes. This amount will stuff 2 ducks.

Meat Stuffing for Turkey

1	pound beef, ground
1	pound ham, ground
1	pound veal, ground
2	onions, chopped
1/2	green pepper, chopped
1/2	pound fresh mushrooms, sliced
1/2	cup raisins
1/2	cup almonds
1	8-ounce can tomato sauce
1	egg
1/4	cup breadcrumbs
1/2	teaspoon garlic salt

In a large mixing bowl combine the meats. In a large skillet sauté the onions, green pepper and mushrooms in a little butter until the onions are transparent. Add the meat mixture and brown; remove from the heat. Add the remaining ingredients, combine well and stuff the turkey. This amount will stuff a 20-pound bird.

Oyster Dressing for Fowl

2 cups diced white onions
3 cups diced celery
1/2 cup salad oil
8 slices stale white bread, torn into small pieces
3 cups buttermilk cornbread
3 cups chicken broth
1/2 cup oyster liquor
1 teaspoon sage (optional)
1/2 teaspoon black pepper
1/2 cup chopped fresh parsley
2 pints oysters, drained and chopped
3 eggs, well beaten

In a skillet sauté the onions and celery in the oil over low heat until transparent. Place the stale bread is a slow oven and toast until golden. In a mixing bowl combine the crumbled cornbread with the chicken broth and oyster liquor; mix well. Add the sautéed onion, celery and the oil from the skillet, the sage, pepper and parsley; stir to combine. Grind the toasted white bread chunks in a blender and stir them into the cornbread mixture. Add the chopped oysters and the beaten eggs and mix well. The mixture can be used to stuff a turkey, or baked in a large greased baking dish at 375° F. for about 1 hour or until browned. Serve with giblet gravy.

Pecan-Rice Stuffing for Poultry

1 tablespoon butter
1/2 cup chopped celery
1/4 cup chopped onion
1 1/2 cups cooked white rice
1/3 cup chopped pecans
3 tablespoons chopped fresh parsley
1/4 teaspoon salt
Pepper to taste

In a heavy skillet melt the butter; sauté the celery and onion until transparent. Stir in the rice, pecans, parsley, salt and pepper. This mixture may be used to stuff pheasants, quail, partridge or chicken. This amount will stuff 2 pheasants or a 5-pound chicken.

Pickled Beets

6 large beets, washed, simmered until tender and cooled in the cooking liquid
1 cup beet liquid
1/2 cup vinegar
1/2 cup sugar
Salt to taste
1/4 teaspoon whole black peppercorns

Peel the cooled beets and slice them into a saucepan. Pour 1 cup of the cooking liquid over the beets. Add the vinegar, sugar and salt and simmer until very hot. Remove from the heat and pack into hot, sterilized jars. Add a few peppercorns to each jar and seal at once with hot, sterilized lids. Let stand for at least 2 weeks to fully develop the flavor.

Salsa Forte

2   tomatoes, chopped
2   tablespoons olive oil
1   fresh jalapeño pepper, seeded and
        chopped
3   tablespoons fresh lemon juice
1   clove garlic, minced
3   scallions, sliced
1   tablespoon chopped fresh cilantro

In a blender or food processor puree the
tomatoes, olive oil, pepper, lemon juice and
garlic until smooth. Garnish with sliced
scallions and cilantro. Makes 1½ cups.

NOTE: Be sure to wear rubber gloves to
handle the pepper.

Salsa Verde

8–10   large green chilies, peeled, seeded,
            deveined and finely minced
2   large ripe tomatoes, peeled, seeded and
        very finely diced
1   clove garlic, minced
1   yellow onion, finely chopped
        Salt to taste

In glass bowl combine all ingredients. Let
stand an hour or more before serving or
storing.

NOTE: Always use rubber gloves when
handling hot chili peppers.

Sauce Verte

1   cup homemade mayonnaise
½   cup sour cream
1   teaspoon dry mustard
1   cucumber, peeled, seeded and finely
        chopped
¼   cup finely chopped parsley
        Salt to taste
        Pepper to taste

In a small bowl combine all of the ingredients
and mix well. Chill for at least 2 hours. Serve
with cold poached fish or shellfish. Makes
about 2 cups.

Pesto Sauce

¼   cup (½ stick) butter, softened
¼   cup grated Parmesan cheese
½   cup chopped parsley
1   clove garlic, minced
1   cup fresh basil leaves, packed tightly
¼   cup olive oil
¼   cup chopped pine nuts

In a food processor process the butter, cheese,
parsley and garlic for 10 seconds. Add the
basil and process until smooth. Add the olive
oil in a thin stream until all is incorporated.
Add the pine nuts and process for 10 seconds.
Serve with Minestrone Soup.

NOTE: It is very important to use *fresh* basil in
this recipe.

Watermelon Rind Pickle

7   pounds watermelon rind (1 large
    watermelon)
1   small bottle Lilley lime
½   tablespoon salt
6   pounds sugar
1   tablespoon whole allspice
1   tablespoon whole cloves
4   sticks cinnamon
2   quarts vinegar (approximately)

Cut the green skin and red meat from watermelon. Discard the skin and reserve the meat for another use. Cut the pale green rind into small pieces or strips. Soak the rind in the lime overnight, then wash 3 times in clear water.

In a large pot cover the rind with water, add the salt and boil for 25 minutes. Wash 3 times again; drain.

Cook the sugar and spices in the vinegar until clear. Leave overnight; then boil for 10 minutes. Pack the pickles in hot, sterilized jars and pour the syrup over them; seal with hot sterilized lids. Makes 10 pints.

NOTE: Lilley lime is available in most drug stores.

Lemon Garlic Salad Dressing

½   cup fresh lemon juice
1¼ cups salad oil
1   teaspoon salt
1   clove garlic, minced

Blend all the ingredients together in a blender, or shake them together in a covered jar. Chill. Makes ¾ cup.

Green Tomato Relish

½   head cabbage, chopped
3   large onions, chopped
12 pounds green tomatoes, thinly sliced
5   red and green bell peppers, seeded and
    sliced
    Salt
1   bunch celery, chopped
3   cups red cider vinegar
1½ pounds sugar
½   cup all-purpose flour
1   tablespoon mustard seeds
½   tablespoon celery seed
½   teaspoon ground turmeric
¼   teaspoon alum

In a large enamel or stainless steel kettle place the cabbage, onions, tomatoes, and peppers; sprinkle them with a good-sized handful of salt and let stand overnight. The next morning, drain off the liquid and heat the vegetables in the kettle. Add the chopped celery and enough fresh water to cover. Bring to a boil over medium high heat; drain. Add the vinegar, sugar, flour, mustard and celery seeds and turmeric. Cook for 15 minutes or until tender; taste for seasonings and adjust if necessary. Add alum to the mixture and heat thoroughly. Pour into hot sterilized jars and seal immediately. Makes 20 pints.

Texas Barbecue Sauce

1/4	cup Worcestershire sauce
1/2	cup chopped onions
1	cup butter, melted
1/4	cup brown sugar
1	cup catsup
1	teaspoon dry mustard
2	teaspoons red pepper
1	tablespoon freshly ground black pepper
3	cloves garlic, finely chopped
2	teaspoons chili powder
1	cup salad oil
	Juice of 3 lemons
	Red pepper sauce to taste
2	teaspoons salt

In a saucepan combine all of the ingredients. Bring to a boil, reduce the heat and simmer for 15 minutes.

NOTE: This sauce will keep for several weeks in the refrigerator.

Creole Tartar Sauce

3	tablespoons tomato paste
2	tablespoons Dijon-style mustard
2	tablespoons olive oil
1	tablespoon white wine vinegar
1/2	teaspoon paprika
3/4	teaspoon red pepper sauce
1/4	cup finely chopped scallions
1/4	cup finely chopped celery
1/4	cup finely chopped parsley

In a small bowl stir together the tomato paste, mustard, oil, vinegar, paprika and red pepper sauce until combined. Stir in the scallions, celery and parsley. Makes about 3/4 cup.

Blender Hollandaise Sauce

3	egg yolks
1–2	tablespoons lemon juice
1/4	teaspoon salt
	Dash cayenne pepper or red pepper sauce
1/2	cup (1 stick) butter, melted

Blend the first 4 ingredients in a blender on high speed, then slowly add the melted butter. The sauce will keep at room temperature for 1 hour before serving. Makes 1 cup.

NOTE: This sauce was created by the late James Beard, one of the foremost contemporary American cooks.

Tomato Relish

15	large ripe tomatoes, coarsely ground
4	large green peppers, coarsely ground
3	large onions, coarsely ground
2	cups sugar
1 1/3	cups vinegar
3	jalapeño peppers
	Salt to taste
	Pepper to taste
3	tablespoons mixed pickling spices, tied in cheesecloth

In a large saucepan combine all the ingredients and simmer over low heat for 2 hours until the vegetables are tender. Pour the relish into hot sterilized pint jars; seal with warm, sterilized lids and process in a hot water bath for 10 minutes. Makes 6 pints.

Bearnaise Sauce

2   tablespoons tarragon vinegar
1   teaspoon chopped fresh parsley
3   shallots, finely chopped
½   teaspoon finely chopped fresh
    tarragon
½   teaspoon chervil
    salt to taste
    Pepper to taste
¾   cup hollandaise sauce

In a saucepan bring to a boil all of the
ingredients except the hollandaise sauce;
simmer until all the liquid is evaporated. Beat
in the hollandaise sauce and keep warm over
hot water until ready to serve.

Cucumber Dressing
(Vinaigrette)

1   cup peeled, seeded and minced
    cucumber
½   teaspoon salt
2   tablespoons rice vinegar
1   tablespoon chopped fresh chives
1   tablespoon snipped fresh dill
1   cup crème fraiche
    Red pepper or red pepper sauce to taste

In a medium bowl sprinkle the minced
cucumber with the salt. Soak for 30 minutes
and drain well; squeeze dry. Stir in the
vinegar, chives, dill and crème fraiche. Season
with pepper or red pepper sauce. Makes about
1½ cups.

Marinade for Venison
or Beef

1   cup beef stock
1   cup red wine
⅓   cup soy sauce
1½   teaspoons salt
¼   cup chopped onion
2   tablespoons lime juice
2   tablespoons honey or
     brown sugar

In a shallow pan combine all of the
ingredients. Marinate the meat overnight in
this mixture. Drain, pat dry and cook as
desired. Enough marinade for 4 pounds of
meat.

Chili Sauce

12   over-ripe tomatoes, peeled
     and chopped
6   small onions, chopped
6   large green peppers, seeded
     and chopped
1   cup white wine vinegar
¾   cup sugar
1   tablespoon salt
2   teaspoons cinnamon
2   teaspoons ground cloves
2   teaspoons ground allspice
1   teaspoon red pepper
2   teaspoons black pepper

In a kettle bring all of the ingredients to a
boil. Simmer for 1 hour or until thick, stirring
often. Makes about 2 pints.

BREADS

Corn Bread Muffins

1	cup cornmeal
1	cup bread flour
1¼	cups milk
2	tablespoons melted butter
2	eggs, well beaten
1	teaspoon salt
1	teaspoon baking powder

Preheat oven to 450° F.

In a large bowl stir together the dry ingredients. In a separate bowl beat together the milk, butter and eggs; add the mixture to the dry ingredients. Beat the mixture lightly until thoroughly combined. Heat small muffin tins for 5 minutes in the oven. Fill the muffin tins ⅔ full and bake the muffins for 15 to 20 minutes. Serve hot. Makes about 2½ dozen small muffins.

Corn Bread Sticks

2	cups buttermilk
½	teaspoon baking soda
1½	cups cornmeal
¾	cup flour
1	teaspoon salt
2	teaspoons baking powder
2	eggs, beaten
8	tablespoons salad oil

In a mixing bowl combine the buttermilk and soda and let stand for 30 minutes. Combine the remaining dry ingredients, make a well in the center and add the eggs and the buttermilk mixture, blending well. Let stand 30 minutes.

Preheat oven to 450° F.

Grease iron breadstick pans with some of the oil and heat them in the oven until the oil sizzles. In a small saucepan heat the remaining oil, pour it into batter and stir well. Fill the pans ½ full with batter. Bake for 17 minutes in the top third of the oven. Makes 22 corn sticks.

Skillet Corn Bread

1½	cups yellow cornmeal
1	teaspoon salt
½	teaspoon baking soda
1	egg, beaten
1½	cups buttermilk
1	tablespoon butter

Preheat oven to 400° F.

In a large bowl combine the dry ingredients; add the egg and buttermilk, mixing well.

Grease a 9-inch cast-iron skillet with butter and heat it in the oven for 3 minutes or until very hot.

Pour the batter into the hot skillet and bake for 20 to 25 minutes or until golden brown. Eight to ten servings.

Assorted Corn Breads

Sally Lunn Bread

1   *package active dry yeast*
1/4   *cup lukewarm water*
1   *teaspoon sugar*
6   *tablespoons butter, melted*
6   *tablespoons lard or shortening,*
      melted
1   *cup milk*
4   *cups flour*
1/3   *cup sugar*
2   *teaspoons salt*
4   *eggs*
      Melted butter

In a small bowl dissolve the yeast in the warm water; add the teaspoon of sugar and set aside. Let the melted butter and lard cool in the milk until lukewarm. In a mixing bowl stir together the flour, sugar and salt. In a separate bowl beat the eggs thoroughly; add the milk mixture and the yeast mixture to the beaten eggs and beat well to combine. Add the flour mixture and beat well. Cover the batter with a clean towel and let rise for at least 2 hours, beating it down every 20 minutes, covering it again and letting it rise again in between (this procedure produces the light texture of the bread). After the last beating place the dough in a well-greased bundt or other tube pan, cover with a towel and let rise again (about 1½ hours). Preheat oven to 325° F.

Bake the bread for 45 to 60 minutes, basting with the melted butter during the last 10 minutes of baking time. Fifteen servings.

Texas-Style Grits Bread

4   *cups water*
1/2   *teaspoon salt*
1   *cup grits*
1/2   *cup salad oil*
3–4   *canned jalapeño peppers*
1½   *cups grated Longhorn cheese*
2   *eggs, beaten*

Preheat oven to 350° F.

In a large saucepan bring the water to a boil and add the salt. Stir in the grits and boil until thick. Remove from the heat and add the oil, peppers, cheese and eggs. Pour into a greased 2-quart baking dish and bake for 1 hour. Six servings.

NOTES: If you prefer very hot bread, add more peppers. You can vary the taste by using 1 4-ounce can chopped green chilies instead of the jalapeños.

The Stockpot's Apricot-Banana Bread

1/4   *cup chopped dried apricots*
1/4   *cup good sherry or brandy*
1   *cup unbleached flour*
3/4   *cup whole wheat flour*
2   *teaspoons baking powder*
1/2   *teaspoon salt*
3   *tablespoons walnut or peanut oil*
1/3   *cup sugar*
1   *egg, beaten*
1   *cup mashed banana*
1/2   *cup chopped walnuts*

The night before making the bread, soak the chopped dried apricots in the sherry or brandy (do not, under any circumstances, use cooking sherry).

Preheat the oven to 350° F.

Sift together the flour, baking powder and salt; set aside. In a large bowl blend the oil and sugar. Beat into the mixture the egg and mashed banana. Add the sifted ingredients to the mixture a little at a time, beating it until smooth. Fold in the walnuts and apricots. Pour the batter into a greased loaf pan and bake for about 1 hour. Makes 1 loaf.

Onion-Zucchini Bread

3 cups unbleached white flour
1 medium onion, chopped
1/2 cup grated Parmesan cheese
5 teaspoons baking powder
1/2 teaspoon baking soda
3 tablespoons butter, melted
1 cup buttermilk, heated to lukewarm
2 eggs, well-beaten
3/4 cup grated zucchini

Preheat oven to 350° F.

In a medium bowl stir together the flour, onion, 2/3 of the Parmesan cheese, the baking powder and baking soda. In a small bowl mix together the butter, buttermilk, eggs and zucchini. Stir the liquid ingredients into the dry ingredients. Spoon the batter into a well-greased 9- or 10-inch round cake pan. Sprinkle with the remaining Parmesan cheese. Bake for 45 to 50 minutes or until a knife inserted in the center comes out clean. Cool for 10 minutes before removing the bread from the pan. Twelve servings.

Banana Bread

2 1/4 cups sugar
3/4 cup (1 1/2 sticks) butter
3 eggs
1 1/2 teaspoons vanilla
4 very ripe bananas, mashed
3 cups flour
1 teaspoon baking soda
1 teaspoon baking powder
3/4 teaspoon salt
1/3 cup sour cream
1 cup chopped pecans (optional)

Preheat oven to 350° F. Butter and sugar two 9- x 5- x 3-inch pans.

In a large bowl cream together the sugar and butter until light and fluffy. Add the eggs, one at a time, beating well after each addition. Add the vanilla and stir to combine. Add the mashed bananas and mix well.

In another bowl stir together the flour, baking soda, baking powder and salt. Add the dry ingredients to the banana mixture, alternating with the sour cream and mixing well after each addition. Stir in the chopped nuts, if desired. Divide the batter between the 2 prepared pans and bake for 30 to 40 minutes or until a tester inserted in the center comes out clean. Cool the bread slightly in the pans; turn out onto wire racks to cool completely. Makes 2 medium loaves.

Cajun Rolls

1	cup milk
1/3	cup butter
1/2	cup sugar (reserve 1 teaspoon for yeast)
1/2	teaspoon salt
1	package active dry yeast
2	tablespoons warm water
4 1/2–5	cups all-purpose flour
3	large eggs
1	tablespoon melted butter

ICING

2	cups confectioner's sugar
5	tablespoons milk
1	teaspoon vanilla

In a saucepan cook the milk, butter, sugar and salt over medium heat until the butter is melted. Remove from the heat and cool to lukewarm. Dissolve the yeast in the warm water to which the reserved sugar has been added. In a large bowl add the dissolved yeast to the milk mixture; add 1 cup of the flour and beat well. Cover the bowl with waxed paper and a clean towel and place in a cold oven beside a large bowl of very hot water. Let the dough rise for 1 hour. Add the beaten eggs and mix well. Add enough flour to make a firm dough (about 4 cups), beating well with a spoon.

On a floured board knead the dough until it is smooth and elastic, about 10 to 15 minutes. Roll out the dough into a 1/4-inch-thick rectangle, spread lightly with melted butter, cover, and move to a warm place; let rise for 3 hours.

Cut the dough into pieces 4 inches long and 1/2 inch wide; twist the ends in opposite directions, bring the ends together and press in the center with your thumb. Place the rolls on a greased cookie sheet and let rise, uncovered, for another 3 hours. Preheat oven to 400° F.

Bake the rolls for 15 to 20 minutes or until golden brown.

Meanwhile, to make the icing, in a medium bowl combine the confectioner's sugar, milk and vanilla; blend well. Spread the icing on the rolls while they are hot. Makes 2 dozen.

Potato Rolls

1	package active dry yeast
1/2	cup lukewarm water
1	cup milk, scalded
2/3	cup shortening
1/2	cup sugar
1	teaspoon salt
1	cup mashed potatoes
	Flour
2	eggs, beaten

In a small bowl dissolve the yeast in the warm water; set aside. In a mixing bowl add the milk to the shortening, sugar, salt and mashed potatoes; cool to lukewarm and add the yeast. Mix thoroughly and add just enough flour to make a thin batter, like pancake batter. Cover the bowl and set it in a warm place until the mixture has doubled in bulk. Add the eggs and stir in eough flour to make a stiff dough (the dough will leave the sides of the bowl when stirred). Turn the dough out onto a lightly floured board and knead thoroughly until smooth and elastic, at least 10 minutes. Place in a greased bowl and turn to coat all sides. Cover with a clean cloth and place in the refrigerator. When ready to make the rolls, pinch off the dough, shape it into rounds and place the rolls on a greased baking sheet. Let rise until doubled in bulk (1½ to 2 hours). Preheat oven to 400° F.

Bake the rolls for 15 to 20 minutes. Serve hot. Makes about 5 dozen rolls.

Parker House Rolls

½   cup shortening or lard
½   cup boiling water
½   cup sugar
¾   teaspoon salt
1   egg, beaten
1   package active dry yeast
½   cup lukewarm water
3   cups or more all-purpose flour

In a large bowl pour the boiling water over the shortening; add the sugar and salt and beat until the mixture is smooth. Let cool. Beat in the eggs. Dissolve the yeast in the lukewarm water and add to the egg mixture. Add the flour, blending well. Place the dough in a greased bowl and turn to coat it; cover and let rise in a warm place until doubled in bulk. Knead the dough on a floured board several times and roll it out to a thickness of about ⅜ inch. Cut small circles of dough, crease each circle slightly off center and fold

to form rolls. Arrange the rolls in a greased jelly roll pan, cover and let rise again until doubled in bulk. Preheat oven to 375° F.

Bake the rolls until nicely browned, about 10 minutes. Makes 2½ dozen.

French Breakfast Puffs

⅓   cup butter or lard
½   cup sugar
1   egg
1½   cups sifted flour
1½   teaspoons baking powder
½   teaspoon salt
¼   teaspoon nutmeg
½   cup milk
½   cup sugar
1   teaspoon cinnamon
⅓   cup butter, melted

Preheat oven to 350° F. Grease a muffin tin or tins.

In a large bowl blend together thoroughly the butter and sugar. Add the egg, mixing well to combine. In another bowl stir together the flour, baking powder, salt and nutmeg; add the dry ingredients to the butter mixture alternately with the milk.

Fill the muffin cups ⅔ full and bake for 20 to 25 minutes until the muffins are golden brown. While the muffins are baking combine the sugar and cinnamon in a small bowl. Remove the muffins from the tins immediately, roll them in the melted butter and then in the cinnamon-sugar. Serve hot. Makes 12 to 16 muffins.

Pecan Muffins

1	cup sugar
2	cups all-purpose flour
1/4	teaspoon salt
2	teaspoons baking powder
4	teaspoons cinnamon
1	cup chopped pecans
1	cup milk
1/2	cup shortening (butter and lard mixed), melted
2	eggs, beaten

Preheat oven to 425° F.

In a large bowl stir together the dry ingredients; add the nuts. In a separate bowl mix together the milk, melted shortening and beaten eggs. Combine dry and liquid ingredients quickly with little stirring (mixture should be barely moist). Fill greased muffin tins ⅔ full and bake for about 15 minutes. Makes 1 dozen muffins.

Jalapeño Corn Bread Muffins

1	cup yellow cornmeal
1	cup all-purpose flour
4	teaspoons baking powder
	Salt to taste
1	cup milk
1	egg
1/4	cup shortening or bacon drippings
1	cup corn cut from the cob
1	jalapeño pepper, peeled, seeded and chopped
1/4	cup diced red pepper

Preheat oven to 350° F. Grease a medium-sized muffin pan.

In a large bowl stir together the cornmeal, flour, baking powder and salt. Add the milk, egg, melted shortening and corn; mix just until moistened (the batter will be lumpy). Stir in the peppers. Pour the batter into the muffin pan, filling the cups ⅔ full. Bake for 20 to 30 minutes. Makes about 1 dozen medium-sized muffins.

NOTE: Always wear rubber gloves when handling fresh hot chili peppers.

Bran Muffins

2	cups bran
2	cups buttermilk
2	cups whole wheat flour
1	tablespoon baking soda
1	teaspoon baking powder
1	teaspoon salt
1/2	cup sugar
2	eggs, lightly beaten
2/3	cup salad oil
1/2	cup water

Preheat oven to 400° F. Grease large muffin tins.

In a large bowl soak the bran in the buttermilk. In another large bowl combine the remaining ingredients. Add the bran mixture. Fill muffin cups ⅔ full and bake for 12 minutes. Serve warm with butter. Makes about 2½ dozen muffins.

Oatmeal Muffins

1 *cup quick-cooking rolled oats, uncooked*
1 *cup buttermilk*
1 *egg, beaten*
½ *cup firmly packed brown sugar*
½ *cup salad oil*
1 *cup all-purpose flour*
1 *teaspoon baking powder*
½ *teaspoon baking soda*
½ *teaspoon salt*
½ *cup raisins, plumped in warm water and drained*

Preheat oven to 400° F.

In a large bowl combine the oats and the buttermilk; let stand for 1 hour. Add the beaten egg, sugar and oil, stirring well to combine.

In a medium bowl combine all of the remaining ingredients except the raisins. Add this mixture to the oats mixture, stirring just until moistened (the batter should be lumpy, not smooth). Stir in the raisins.

Spoon the batter into greased muffin pans, filling them ⅔ full. Bake for about 18 minutes. Makes 1½ dozen.

Buttermilk Corn Sticks

½ *cup sifted all-purpose flour*
1 *cup cornmeal*
½ *teaspoon baking soda*
1 *teaspoon salt*
1 *egg, beaten*
1 *cup buttermilk*
2 *tablespoons melted shortening (bacon fat is best)*

Preheat oven to 425° F.

Sift the flour once, measure it, add the cornmeal, baking soda and salt and sift together. In a small bowl combine the egg and buttermilk; add to the flour mixture, stirring only enough to blend. Add the melted shortening.

Grease iron corn stick pans with melted shortening and heat them in the oven until the oil sizzles.

Spoon the batter into the corn stick pans, filling them ½ full, and bake for 20 to 25 minutes. Makes 12 corn sticks.

NOTE: This recipe also makes delicious corn bread. Add crumbled bacon to the batter to make it even better.

Corn Fritters

2 *cups corn cut from the cob*
½ *small onion, minced*
  Pepper to taste
3 *eggs, beaten*
1 *tablespoon or more butter*

In a medium bowl combine the corn, onion, pepper and beaten eggs.

Melt the butter in a 10-inch skillet. For each fritter drop 2 tablespoons of the corn mixture into the hot skillet. Flatten the batter into a thin cake and brown quickly on 1 side; turn and brown on the other side. Makes 8 fritters.

NOTE: These are good plain or with cane syrup or honey.

Pecan Waffles

1   cup sifted cake flour
1   cup unbleached flour
2   teaspoons baking powder
½   teaspoon baking soda
    Salt to taste
2   tablespoons brown sugar
3   eggs separated, yolks beaten, whites
        beaten until stiff peaks form
1½ cups buttermilk
¼   cup (½ stick) butter, melted
¾   cup chopped pecans

In a large bowl mix together all of the dry ingredients. Add the egg yolks, buttermilk and melted butter; stir in the pecans. Fold in the beaten egg whites. Pour the batter into a hot waffle iron and bake until golden. Six servings.

Corn Cakes

1   cup white cornmeal
1   cup boiling water
2   teaspoons shortening
¼   teaspoon salt
1   egg
1   cup milk

In a mixing bowl scald the cornmeal with the boiling water, stirring well. Add the shortening and salt. In another bowl beat the egg with the milk; add to the cornmeal mixture, stirring to combine. Drop the batter by tablespoonfuls onto a greased, slow griddle, making the cakes about 3 inches in diameter. The batter will be thin; the cakes should bake with a crisp, lacy edge. Makes about 2½ dozen.

Alabama Spoonbread

2   cups milk
½   cup white cornmeal
½   teaspoon baking powder
1   teaspoon salt
3   eggs, separated, yolks well beaten, whites
        beaten until very stiff peaks form
3   tablespoons butter, melted

Preheat oven to 275° F.

In a saucepan scald the milk; slowly stir in the cornmeal. Cook over low heat until the mixture is the consistency of soft grits. Add the baking powder, salt, and egg yolks. Beat in the melted butter. Fold in the egg whites. Bake in a well-greased casserole for 30 minutes. Serve immediately. Eight servings.

Hoe Cake

1   cup white cornmeal
½   teaspoon salt
1   teaspoon sugar
    Milk or boiling water
    Butter

In a mixing bowl stir together the cornmeal, salt and sugar. Stir in enough milk or boiling water to make a very stiff batter.

Grease and preheat a griddle. Drop the batter by tablespoonfuls on the hot griddle and cook slowly until well browned on the bottom. Dot the uncooked surfaces with butter and then turn the cakes. Continue cooking until the cakes are browned on both sides (the cakes will be thick). Serve with butter and jelly rather than syrup. Six to eight servings.

Spoonbread

2   cups milk
½   cup white cornmeal
½   teaspoon baking powder
1   teaspoon salt
3   eggs, separated, yolks well beaten, whites
        beaten until stiff peaks form
3   tablespoons butter, melted

Preheat oven to 275° F.

In a saucepan scald the milk and slowly stir in the cornmeal. Cook over low heat until the mixture is the consistency of soft grits. Add the baking powder, salt and well-beaten egg yolks and stir to combine. Stir in the melted butter, then fold in the stiffly beaten egg whites. Bake in a well-greased casserole for 30 minutes. Serve immediately. Eight servings.

Bacon Spoonbread

¾   cup cornmeal
1½   cups cold water
8   ounces Cheddar cheese, coarsely grated
2   cloves garlic, crushed
¼   cup (½ stick) butter
½   teaspoon salt
1   tablespoon chopped parsley
1   cup milk
4   eggs, separated, yolks beaten, whites
        beaten until stiff peaks form
½   pound bacon, fried crisp and crumbled

Preheat oven to 325° F.

In a saucepan combine the cornmeal and water. Cook over low heat until the mixture is the consistency of mush. Add the cheese, garlic, butter, salt and parsley; stir until the cheese is melted. Add the milk and the beaten egg yolks; add the crumbled bacon. Fold in the egg whites. Pour the batter into a greased 2-quart soufflé dish and bake for about 60 minutes. Six servings.

Batter Bread

¼   cup sugar
1½   cups warm water
1   package dry yeast
3   eggs, beaten
3½   cups all-purpose flour
1   cup rolled wheat or oats
1½   teaspoons salt
½   cup dry milk powder
½   cup melted butter
     Additional butter, softened
     Additional oats

In a large bowl dissolve the sugar in the water; add the yeast and stir to dissolve completely.

Combine the beaten eggs with the yeast mixture. In a separate bowl stir together the dry ingredients. Slowly stir the combined dry ingredients into the egg mixture; add the melted butter.

Spread the batter into a lightly greased 9- x 13-inch pan. Brush the top with soft butter and sprinkle with more oats. Let rise for 1 hour or until doubled in bulk.

Preheat oven to 375° F.

Bake the bread for 30 minutes or until done. Cut into squares and serve hot with butter. Twelve servings.

Irish Scones

2 cups flour
1 teaspoon baking soda
1 tablespoon sugar
¾ teaspoon salt
¼ cup (½ stick) butter
¾ cup buttermilk

In a large bowl stir together the flour, baking soda, sugar and salt. Cut in the butter and then blend in the buttermilk. Turn the dough out onto a lightly floured board and knead gently several times. Roll out the dough to a thickness of ¼ inch; cut the dough into rectangles, then into triangles. Cook the scones on an oiled griddle over very low heat for about 4 minutes on each side until golden and still moist. Serve with butter and jam. Makes about 4 dozen.

Sweet Potato Biscuits

2 cups sifted all-purpose flour
4 teaspoons baking powder
1 teaspoon salt
⅔ cup shortening or butter
1 cup mashed cooked sweet
    potatoes
3 tablespoons or more milk

Preheat oven to 400° F.

Into a large bowl sift together the dry ingredients. Cut in the shortening or butter and blend in the mashed sweet potatoes. Add enough milk to make a soft dough. Knead the dough lightly for about 1 minute. Roll the dough on a lightly floured board to a thickness of about ¾ inch; cut into squares or rounds with a biscuit cutter. Bake on an ungreased baking sheet for 15 to 20 minutes. Serve warm. Six servings.

Angel Biscuits

2 cups buttermilk
1 cup vegetable shortening or lard
1 package active dry yeast
¼ cup warm water
4 tablespoons sugar
5 cups all-purpose flour
1 teaspoon salt
1 tablespoon baking powder
    Melted butter

In a heavy saucepan heat the buttermilk and the shortening or lard, stirring to melt. Cool. Soften the yeast in the warm water and add the mixture to the saucepan. Beat in the sugar.

Sift together the flour, salt and baking powder; add the dry ingredients to the buttermilk mixture and stir to combine. Cover with a damp cloth and an inverted plate; chill overnight.

Roll out the dough to a ¼-inch thickness, cut into 1½-inch rounds and brush each round with melted butter. Stack the rounds by twos and place them in a greased pan, almost touching. Let rise for 1 hour in a warm place. Preheat oven to 400° F.

Bake the biscuits for 10 minutes or until done. Makes 5 dozen.

French Bread

½ cup milk, scalded
1 cup boiling water
1½ packages active dry yeast
¼ cup lukewarm water
1½ tablespoons salad oil
1 tablespoon sugar
4 cups sifted unbleached flour
2 teaspoons salt
2 teaspoons sugar
   Cornmeal
1 egg white, beaten
1 tablespoon cold water

Add the boiling water to the scalded milk and let the mixture cool to lukewarm. In a small bowl dissolve the yeast in the warm water; let rest for 10 minutes. Add the yeast mixture to the milk; add the oil and 1 tablespoon sugar. In a large bowl stir together the flour, salt and 2 teaspoons sugar. Make a well in the center of the dry ingredients and pour in the milk and yeast mixture. Stir thoroughly but do not knead; the dough will be soft. Cover the bowl with a damp clean towel and transfer it to a warm place to rise. Let stand for about 2 hours for the first rising.

Punch down the dough and place it on a lightly floured board. Roll the dough out into rectangles. Roll each rectangle into a French loaf by rolling jelly-roll fashion. Continue rolling, pressing outward with the hands, until you have fashioned a long thin loaf. Grease a baking sheet and sprinkle it lightly with cornmeal. Place the loaves on the prepared baking sheet and cut diagonal slits across the top of each loaf. Set the loaves in a warm place and let rise for about 45 minutes. Preheat oven to 400° F.

Place a small pan of hot water in the bottom of the oven. Bake the loaves for 15 minutes, reduce the heat to 350° F. and bake for 30 minutes more, spraying the oven from time to time with water during the last 30 minutes. Cool the bread on a wire rack. Makes 2 loaves.

Pappas' Restaurant's Garlic Greek Bread

½ pound (2 sticks) butter
6 cloves garlic, finely minced
2 long loaves of Greek or French bread

Preheat broiler.

In a saucepan melt the butter and add the garlic; heat through. Slice the bread 1½ inches thick and toast under the broiler on both sides until golden brown. Generously brush both sides of the hot bread with the garlic butter, place on a cookie sheet and return to the broiler to brown. Do not burn. Ten servings.

Pain Perdu

1 egg, beaten
1 teaspoon vanilla
2 tablespoons sugar
1 cup milk
¼ teaspoon salt
½ teaspoon cinnamon
4 tablespoons butter
6 slices day-old bread, halved

In a large bowl beat together the first 6 ingredients. In a skillet melt the butter over low heat. Dip the bread slices into the egg mixture, increase the heat to medium-high and fry the bread slices in the butter until golden brown and crusty on both sides. Serve with confectioner's sugar, sorghum molasses, cane syrup or any other appropriate accompaniment. Three to four servings.

Orange Crumb French Toast

2   eggs
1/4   teaspoon salt
2/3   cup orange juice
1 1/2   cups fine dry breadcrumbs
1   teaspoon grated orange
      peel
8   slices white bread
1   tablespoon lard
2   tablespoons butter
      Sorghum molasses or
         cane syrup

In a medium bowl beat together thoroughly the eggs, salt and orange juice. In a plate or shallow bowl combine the breadcrumbs with the orange peel. Dip the bread slices in the orange-egg mixture and then in the breadcrumb mixture, turning the slices to coat them evenly.

On a heavy griddle melt the lard and butter; brown the bread on both sides. Serve immediately, accompanied by the molasses or syrup. Four servings.

Pumpkin Bread

3 1/2   cups all-purpose flour
3   cups sugar
1 1/2   teaspoons salt
2   teaspoons baking soda
1   teaspoon ground cinnamon
1   teaspoon ground nutmeg
1   cup salad oil or melted
      butter
4   large eggs, room
         temperature
2/3   cup water
2   cups pumpkin puree
1   cup chopped pecans or
         walnuts
      Additional flour

Preheat oven to 350° F. Grease and flour 2 standard loaf pans.

In a large bowl stir together the dry ingredients until well mixed. Combine the oil, eggs, water and pumpkin puree and beat until well blended. Add the dry ingredients slowly and beat well. Dust the nuts with the flour and stir them into the batter.

Pour the batter into the greased loaf pans. Bake for 1 hour and 15 minutes. Cool the bread for 10 minutes before removing from the pans; continue cooling on wire racks. Makes 2 loaves.

NOTE: To store, wrap the bread in foil and keep it in the refrigerator, or freeze it.

Beignets

½ **cup (1 stick) butter**
1 **cup water**
2 **teaspoons sugar**
1 **cup cake flour**
2 **eggs and 1 egg yolk**
  Oil for deep frying
  Confectioner's sugar

In a heavy-bottomed pot bring to a boil the butter, water and sugar. Add the flour all at once and stir vigorously over medium heat until the mixture leaves the sides of the pot. Place the mixture in a bowl and cool it slightly, beating all the time. Add the eggs and egg yolk one at a time, beating thoroughly after each addition.

In a heavy skillet heat the oil to 350° F. Drop the batter by tablespoonsfuls into the hot oil and fry until brown. Drain, sprinkle with the confectioner's sugar and serve immediately. Makes about 1 dozen.

Hush Puppies

1½ **cups white cornmeal**
½ **cup sifted all-purpose flour**
2½ **teaspoons baking powder**
1 **teaspoon salt**
¼ **teaspoon pepper**
⅓ **cup finely chopped onion**
½ **cup milk**
1 **egg, beaten**
3 **tablespoons salad oil or melted shortening**
  Oil for deep frying

Into a large bowl sift together the dry ingredients. Add the remaining ingredients and stir only until blended. In a large, deep skillet heat the oil to 350° F. Drop the batter by tablespoonfuls into the deep fat and fry for 2 to 3 minutes or until golden brown. Drain on paper towels; serve hot. Makes 18 hush puppies.

Buttermilk Hush Puppies

½ **teaspoon salt**
½ **teaspoon baking powder**
1 **cup white cornmeal**
¼ **teaspoon baking soda**
½ **cup buttermilk**
1 **egg, well beaten**
½ **large onion, finely minced**
  Fat or oil for deep frying

In a mixing bowl stir together the salt, baking powder and cornmeal. In a small bowl mix together the baking soda and buttermilk. Combine the buttermilk mixture with the dry ingredients; add the beaten egg and mix well. Add the minced onion and stir to combine.

In a large skillet or deep fryer heat the fat to 400° F. Shape the batter into small balls or drop the batter off a teaspoon into the hot fat; fry until golden brown. Serve very hot. Makes about 2 dozen.

Honey Whole Wheat Bread

  1   *package active dry yeast*
 ¼   *cup lukewarm water*
1¼   *cups hot water*
 ¼   *cup honey*
  2   *tablespoons butter*
1½   *teaspoons salt*
2½   *cups whole wheat flour*
  2   *cups sifted all-purpose flour*

In a small bowl sprinkle the yeast into the lukewarm water to soften. In a large bowl combine the hot water with the honey, shortening and salt. Stir the mixture until the honey and shortening are melted. Cool the mixture to lukewarm and stir in the yeast. Gradually stir in 1½ cups whole wheat flour and 1 cup sifted all-purpose flour; beat until well combined. Add 1 cup each of all-purpose flour and whole wheat flour or enough to make a moderately stiff dough. Turn the dough out onto a well-floured board and knead until it is very smooth and elastic, at least 10 minutes. Transfer the dough to a well-greased bowl and turn once to coat the dough; let stand, covered, in a warm place away from drafts for about 1½ hours, or until doubled in bulk. Punch down the dough, turn it out onto a floured board and form it into a ball. Let the dough stand, covered, for 10 minutes. Shape the dough into a loaf and place in a well-greased loaf pan. Let rise, covered, until doubled in bulk, about 45 minutes. Preheat oven to 375° F.

Bake for 40 to 45 minutes, or until the loaf is golden brown on the top and sounds hollow when tapped. Turn the loaf out onto a wire rack and let it cool.

West Texas Corn Bread

     Melted butter or bacon fat
  2   *eggs*
 ½   *cup vegetable oil*
  1   *cup sour cream*
  1   *cup yellow cornmeal*
  1   *cup cream-style corn*
  3   *teaspoons baking powder*
  1   *cup shredded Cheddar cheese*
  1   *4-ounce can chopped green chilies or chopped hot jalapeño peppers.*

Preheat oven to 400° F. Grease an iron skillet with melted butter or bacon fat.

In a large bowl beat together all the ingredients. Pour the batter into the skillet and bake for 30 to 40 minutes. Twelve servings.

DESERTS

Strawberry Shortcake

SHORTCAKE

2½   cups all-purpose flour
     Pinch salt
3   teaspoons baking powder
3   tablespoons sugar
⅓   cup butter
1   egg
¾   cup milk
2   tablespoons butter, softened

1   quart strawberries
¾   cup sugar
1   cup heavy cream, whipped

Preheat oven to 375° F.

In a bowl mix together the flour, salt, baking powder and sugar. Cut in the ⅓ cup butter until the mixture resembles coarse meal. In a separate bowl beat the egg with the milk. Stir into the flour mixture to form a stiff dough. Turn the dough onto a floured board and knead for 1 minute. Separate the dough into 2 parts. Roll out ½ the dough to fit an 8-inch cake pan. Generously flour the top of the layer. Roll out the second ½ of the dough and pat it on top of the first layer. Bake for 25 minutes. Separate the layers and spread the bottom layer with the softened butter.

Stem and cut up ½ of the strawberries and mix them with the sugar. Spread a little whipped cream on the bottom layer of the shortcake. Top with the sweetened berries and cover with the second layer of the cake. Spread the second layer generously with the remaining whipped cream and arrange the reserved whole berries on top. Serve in wedges. Six servings.

Deep Dish Peach Apricot Bake

3   large peaches, peeled, pitted and
     sliced
6   apricots, peeled, pitted and sliced
⅓   cup honey
6   tablespoons (¾ stick) butter
     Nutmeg to taste
½   cup flour
½   cup sugar
½   cup milk
1   teaspoon baking powder

Preheat oven to 350° F.

In a deep casserole combine the peaches, apricots, honey, butter and nutmeg. In a medium bowl combine the flour, sugar, milk and baking powder; mix well. Pour the flour mixture over the fruit in the casserole and bake for 1 hour. Serve with vanilla ice cream. Six servings.

Yellow Cake

11   egg yolks, at room temperature
2   cups sifted sugar
1   cup milk, scalded
2   teaspoons baking powder
1/4   teaspoon salt
2 1/4   cups all-purpose flour
1/2   cup butter, melted
2   teaspoons vanilla

Preheat oven to 325° F. Grease and flour a 10-inch tube pan and line it with waxed paper.

In a large bowl beat the egg yolks until light and fluffy. Add the sugar gradually, beating until light. Add the hot milk slowly and continue beating. In a separate bowl stir together the baking powder, salt and flour. Beat the flour mixture into the milk mixture until smooth. Stir in the butter and vanilla. Pour the batter into the prepared pan. Bake for 1 hour and 15 minutes or until the cake tests done. Cool and remove from the pan. Frost with Caramel Icing. Twenty to twenty-two servings.

Caramel Icing

4   cups sugar
    Salt to taste
1   cup milk
1   egg
1   tablespoon butter
    Vanilla to taste

In a saucepan combine 3 1/2 cups sugar, salt, milk and egg; stir and bring to a boil. At the same time brown 1/2 cup sugar in a small skillet; when dark brown and melted pour it into the boiling mixture, stirring constantly to keep it from boiling over. When the mixture forms a soft ball in cold water, remove from the heat. Add the butter and vanilla and beat until creamy. Makes enough for a 2-layer cake.

Chocolate Cake

4   1-ounce squares unsweetened
      chocolate
1/2   cup (1 stick) butter
2   tablespoons very strong coffee
2   cups buttermilk
2   teaspoons vanilla
2 1/2   cups all-purpose flour
1/2   teaspoon salt
2   cups sugar
2   teaspoons baking soda

Preheat oven to 350° F. Grease and flour two 8-inch cake pans.

In a double boiler melt the chocolate and butter together with the coffee over hot water. Cool.

In a large bowl beat the eggs with the buttermilk; add the vanilla and stir to combine. In another bowl stir together the flour, salt, sugar and baking soda; add the dry ingredients to the egg mixture. Add the chocolate mixture and beat in thoroughly.

Pour the batter into the pans and bake for about 30 minutes or until a cake tester inserted in the center comes out clean. Cool the cake in the pans for ten minutes, turn the layers out onto wire racks and cool completely. Fill and frost with Chocolate Fudge Frosting.

Chocolate Fudge Frosting

4	ounces unsweetened chocolate
1/2	cup (1 stick) butter
1	pound confectioner's sugar
1/2	cup milk
2	teaspoons vanilla

In a double boiler melt the chocolate and butter over hot water. In a medium bowl combine the sugar, milk and vanilla and beat until smooth; add the chocolate mixture. Set the bowl in a pan of ice and water and beat the frosting with a wooden spoon until it is thick enough to spread. Sufficient to fill and frost a 2-layer cake.

Old Fashioned Spice Cake

1	tablespoon butter, softened
1	cup dark brown sugar
1	egg yolk
1 1/2	cups all-purpose flour
1	teaspoon baking soda
2	teaspoons cinnamon
1/4	teaspoon ground cloves
1/2	teaspoon ground nutmeg
2/3	cup buttermilk
1	cup raisins, boiled, well drained and tossed in flour
1	cup black walnuts, chopped

Preheat oven to 350° F. Grease and flour two 9-inch cake pans and line them with waxed paper.

In a mixing bowl cream together the butter and sugar until light. Beat in the egg yolk. In another bowl stir together the flour, soda and spices. Add the buttermilk and the flour mixture alternately to the butter mixture, stirring well after each addition. Stir in the raisins and walnuts.

Divide the batter evenly between the 2 prepared cake pans. Bake for about 25 minutes or until the cake pulls away from the sides of the pan. Cool for 10 minutes, turn out onto wire racks and cool completely. Fill and frost with Caramel Frosting.

Caramel Frosting

1	cup granulated sugar
1	cup dark brown sugar, packed
1/2	cup milk
3	tablespoons butter

In a saucepan combine all the ingredients and bring the mixture to a boil. Remove from the heat, place the pan in a large bowl of ice cubes and beat the frosting until it is thick and spreadable. Enough to fill and frost a 2-layer cake.

Mary Snyder's Key Lime Pie

CRUST

2	*cups flour*
1/2	*teaspoon salt*
1/3	*cup lard*
1/3	*cup ice water*

FILLING

4	*tablespoons cornstarch*
4	*tablespoons flour*
1/4	*teaspoon salt*
1 1/4	*cups sugar*
1 1/2	*cups water*
4	*egg yolks, beaten*
4	*teaspoons grated lime peel*
1/4	*cup fresh key lime juice*
2	*tablespoons butter*

MERINGUE TOPPING

4	*egg whites*
6	*tablespoons sugar*
1/2	*teaspoon vanilla*

Preheat oven to 425° F.

To make the crust, in a mixing bowl stir together the flour and salt; cut in the lard with a pastry cutter until the mixture resembles coarse cornmeal. Add the ice water all at once and mix until the dough holds together in the bowl. Roll the pastry out on a lightly floured board, handling as little as possible. Line 10-inch pie plate with the crust and crimp the edges with your thumb. Prick the surface of the crust with a fork and bake for 16 to 18 minutes until just lightly browned.

To make the filling, in a saucepan combine the cornstarch, flour, salt, sugar and water. Cook until the mixture is clear and thick, about 2 minutes. Remove from the heat and whip about 1 cup of this mixture into the beaten egg yolks. Stir the egg yolk mixture back into the cornstarch mixture and cook for 3 minutes more. Add the grated lime peel, key lime juice and butter; stir to combine and let cool to room temperature. Pour the mixture into the cooled baked crust.

To make the meringue topping, in a mixing bowl combine the egg whites with the sugar, stirring all the while. Set the bowl in a pan of hot water and stir the mixture until the egg whites feel warm. Add the salt and vanilla and beat the mixture until it is stiff and shiny. Pour the meringue over the cooled lime pie, making sure the meringue touches the crust all the way around with no gaps or air holes. Place the pie under the broiler until the top browns in peaks; watch carefully—it will brown very quickly. Cool the pie to room temperature before serving. Eight servings.

Black Bottom Pie

20	*gingersnaps, crumbled*
5	*tablespoons melted butter*

FILLING

1	*tablespoon unflavored gelatin*
4	*tablespoons warm water*
1/2	*cup sugar*
4	*eggs, separated*
2	*cups milk, scalded*

1   tablespoon cornstarch
1½ squares (1½ ounces) unsweetened
      chocolate, melted
1   teaspoon vanilla
4   tablespoons bourbon or rum
¼   teaspoon cream of tartar
    Dash vanilla
1   cup heavy cream, whipped with 3
      tablespoons confectioner's sugar
½   square (½ ounce) bittersweet chocolate,
      grated

Preheat oven to 250° F.

Roll the crumbled gingersnaps, add the butter and mix well. Pat the mixture evenly into a deep pie pan and bake for 10 minutes.

To make the filling, soften the gelatin in the warm water; set aside. In the top of a double boiler beat together the sugar and the egg yolks. Stir in the milk and cornstarch. Cook the mixture over hot water until the custard coats a spoon, about 20 minutes. Remove from the heat and measure 1 cup of custard. In a small bowl add the melted chocolate to the measured custard and beat well; cool and add the vanilla. Pour the mixture into the baked crust.

While the remaining custard is still hot, blend in the gelatin; cool, but do not allow to stiffen. Add the whiskey. In a separate bowl make a stiff meringue by beating the egg whites until frothy, adding the cream of tartar and beating until stiff. Fold the meringue into the custard and add a dash of vanilla while the custard is still soft. As soon as the chocolate custard in the crust has begun to set, cover with the fluffy custard and chill until firm.

When ready to serve, spread with the sweetened whipped cream and sprinkle with the grated chocolate.

Chocolate Pie

3   egg yolks
1   can sweetened condensed milk
3   ounces (3 squares) unsweetened
      chocolate
    Pinch salt
1   teaspoon vanilla extract
¼   cup (½ stick) butter
1   cup whole milk
1   baked 9-inch pie shell

MERINGUE

2   tablespoons sugar
3   egg whites
    Dash vanilla

In a mixing bowl beat together the egg yolks and condensed milk. Place the chocolate in the top of a double boiler; add the egg yolk mixture and the whole milk and cook until thickened. Remove from the heat and beat in the salt and butter. Strain the mixture and pour it into the baked pie shell. Preheat oven to 400° F.

To make the meringue, in a mixing bowl beat the ingredients together until stiff peaks form and the mixture is glossy. Top the chocolate mixture in the pie shell with the meringue and bake for 10 minutes or until the meringue is golden brown.

Ann Cashion's Mississippi Mud Cake

½ pound semisweet chocolate
½ pound butter
5 eggs, separated
1⅓ cups sugar
¼ cup bourbon
1½ cups sifted cake flour
1 cup chopped pecans
3 cups miniature marshmallows

ICING

½ pound semisweet chocolate
3 tablespoons butter
⅓ cup heavy cream

Preheat oven to 350° F.

In a double boiler or over very low heat melt the chocolate with the butter. Beat the egg whites with half of the sugar until they form peaks but are not yet stiff. Set aside. Beat the egg yolks with the remaining sugar until the mixture is pale yellow. Add the chocolate mixture and the bourbon to the egg yolk mixture, then add the flour and the nuts. Carefully fold in the egg whites. Turn the batter into an 8- x 11-inch buttered and floured pan and bake for 25 minutes. Remove the cake from the oven, distribute the marshmallows over the surface, return the cake to the oven and bake until the marshmallows have melted and browned. Cool the cake in the pan.

To prepare the icing, in a double boiler or over very low heat melt the chocolate and butter with the cream. Pour the mixture

through a sieve onto the surface of the cooled cake. Spread the frosting evenly over the cake and let it set.

Sunshine Cake

7 eggs, separated
1 teaspoon cream of tartar
1½ cups sugar
3 tablespoons cold water
1 teaspoon vanilla
1 teaspoon lemon extract
1¼ cups cake flour, well stirred
½ teaspoon baking powder
Salt to taste
Confectioner's sugar

Preheat oven to 350° F.

In a mixing bowl beat the egg whites with the cream of tartar until stiff peaks form. Beat in ½ cup sugar, 1 tablespoon at a time, until the mixture is smooth and glossy.

In a large bowl beat together the remaining sugar, the egg yolks, water, vanilla and lemon extract. In a separate bowl stir together the cake flour, baking powder and salt. Beat the flour mixture into the egg yolks until very light.

Gently fold the egg whites into the batter. Blend well, but do not break down the whites. Pour the batter into an ungreased tube pan and bake for 45 minutes. Remove the cake from the oven, cool, and invert the pan to transfer the cake to a wire rack. Cool completely before serving. Dust with confectioner's sugar. Twelve servings.

Lady Baltimore Cake

1   cup butter
3   cups sugar
4   eggs
1   cup milk
3½ cups cake flour
4   teaspoons baking powder
2   teaspoons vanilla
2   teaspoons almond extract
½   cup water

FROSTING

3   cups sugar
1   cup water
1   tablespoon corn syrup
3   egg whites, beaten until stiff peaks form
2   cups seeded raisins, plumped in hot
      water, drained, dried and finely
      chopped
2   cups toasted pecans or walnuts, finely
      chopped
12 dried figs, finely chopped
      Almond extract to taste
      Vanilla extract to taste

Preheat oven to 350° F. Grease and flour two 11-inch cake pans.

In an electric mixer cream the butter and add 2 cups of sugar gradually; beat until the mixture is the consistency of whipped cream. Add the eggs, one at a time, and beat thoroughly. In a mixing bowl stir together the flour and baking powder; add to the butter mixture alternately with the milk, using a wooden spoon and beating well after each addition. Pour the batter into the prepared

pans and bake for 30 minutes. In a small saucepan simmer the remaining 1 cup sugar with ½ cup water until thick. Cool the syrup and add the almond and vanilla. Spread the syrup over the cake layers as soon as you remove them from the pans.

To make the frosting, in a saucepan combine the sugar, water and corn syrup. Cook until it forms a hard ball in cold water (250° F.). Pour the syrup gradually into the egg whites, beating constantly until the mixture is cool, about 10 minutes. Add the raisins, pecans and figs. Add the almond and vanilla and stir to combine. Spread the frosting between the layers and on the top and sides of the cake.

Maple Bourbon Cake

½   cup (1 stick) butter, softened
½   cup sugar
2   eggs
2½ teaspoons baking powder
2   cups flour
½   teaspoon salt
      Freshly grated nutmeg
½   cup maple syrup
½   cup bourbon whiskey
1½ cups coarsely chopped pecans
      Confectioner's sugar

Preheat oven to 350° F.

In a mixing bowl cream together the butter and sugar until light. Add the eggs, one at a time, beating after each addition. In another bowl stir together the baking powder, flour, salt and a generous grating of nutmeg. Add the maple syrup and bourbon to the dry ingredients alternately with the butter mixture; stir in the pecans. Pour the batter into a greased standard loaf pan and bake for 45 to 50 minutes. Sprinkle with confectioner's sugar. Six to eight servings.

Ginger Pudding

½   cup (1 stick) butter
½   cup white sugar
½   cup brown sugar
1   egg, well beaten
1¾ cups flour
1   cup unsweetened applesauce
1   teaspoon baking soda
2   tablespoons unsulphured molasses
1   teaspoon cinnamon
¼   teaspoon ground cloves
2   teaspoons ground ginger
⅓   cup crystallized ginger, chopped
    Whipped cream

SAUCE

1   cup sugar
½   cup (1 stick) butter
4   tablespoons heavy cream
1   teaspoon vanilla

Preheat oven to 375° F.

In a mixing bowl cream together the butter and both sugars until light and fluffy. Add the egg and beat well. Add the flour and applesauce alternately, mixing well after each addition. In a small bowl dissolve the soda in the molasses; add to the applesauce mixture and combine well. Add the spices and the crystallized ginger and stir to combine. Pour the mixture into a greased loaf pan and bake for 1 hour.

To make the sauce, in the top of a double boiler combine the sugar, butter and cream and cook until clear and thick. Add the vanilla and stir to combine.

Turn out the baked pudding and serve hot or warm with the sauce and whipped cream. Eight servings.

Old Time Rice Pudding

3   cups milk
½   cup uncooked rice
    Salt to taste
1   cinnamon stick
1   cup sugar
½   cup raisins, plumped in boiling water
      and drained
3   eggs, beaten
1   teaspoon vanilla

In a large saucepan combine 1 cup of the milk with the rice, salt and cinnamon stick and bring to a boil. Reduce the heat and simmer until all the milk is absorbed; discard the cinnamon stick. Add the sugar and the remaining 2 cups of milk to the saucepan and simmer until the rice is very tender. Stir in the raisins, eggs and vanilla, and bring just to a boil. Reduce the heat and simmer for 3 minutes; do not boil hard. May be served warm or chilled. Six servings.

Bananas Foster

4   tablespoons butter
½   cup brown sugar
1   teaspoon cinnamon
1   teaspoon nutmeg
6   bananas, ripe but not soft, peeled
¼   cup rum

In a heavy skillet melt the butter; add the sugar, cinnamon and nutmeg. When the sugar has dissolved arrange the bananas in the syrup and simmer, spooning the syrup over the bananas, until the bananas are browned and tender. Pour the rum over the bananas, heat and ignite. Serve the bananas very hot with the syrup spooned over them. Six servings.

NOTE: Some devotees like vanilla ice cream with this dish.

Buttermilk Ice Cream

⅔   cup sugar
     Pinch salt
1   8¼-ounce can crushed pinapple with juice
2   cups buttermilk
1   teaspoon vanilla

In a saucepan combine the sugar, salt and pineapple. Cook over medium heat just until the sugar and salt dissolve; remove from the heat. Add the buttermilk and vanilla and mix well. Freeze in an electric ice cream freezer according to the manufacturer's directions. Let

stand in the freezer of your refrigerator for 2 hours before serving to develop the flavor. Four to six servings.

Banana Pudding

½   cup all-purpose flour
1   cup sugar
2   tablespoons cornstarch
2   cups milk
3   eggs, separated
1   teaspoon vanilla
2   tablespoons butter, softened
1   box vanilla wafer cookies
3   ripe bananas, sliced
3   tablespoons sugar

In a medium saucepan stir together the flour, sugar and cornstarch with enough milk to make a smooth paste. Beat in the eggs yolks, then add the remaining milk and stir well to combine. Simmer over medium heat until thick, stirring constantly. Let cool for 5 minutes. Stir in the vanilla and butter. Cool the mixture to lukewarm.

In a soufflé dish make a layer of vanilla wafer cookies. Add a layer of bananas and spoon half of the pudding mixture over them. Repeat the layers, ending with the remaining pudding mixture. Preheat oven to 350° F.

In a mixing bowl beat the egg whites with the 3 tablespoons sugar until stiff and glossy; spread over the top of the pudding. Bake for 10 to 12 minutes or until the meringue is golden. Cool to lukewarm before serving. Eight servings.

Pear and Quince Tart

4   cups ripe quinces, peeled, cored and
      chopped
2   tablespoons water
1   cup plus 2 tablespoons sugar
3   cups Bartlett pears, peeled, cored and
      finely chopped
1   tablespoon lemon juice
1/2 teaspoon cinnamon
2   tablespoons brandy
1   pie shell, baked blind for 10 minutes

TOPPING

1/4 teaspoon cinnamon
1   tablespoon sugar
1/2 cup chopped walnuts

Preheat oven to 375° F.

In a large, heavy saucepan combine the quinces, water and 1 cup sugar. Cook over low heat, stirring frequently, until the quinces give up their moisture. Simmer for 20 to 30 minutes until the fruit is soft and transparent but not falling apart (the time will depend on the ripeness of the fruit); stir often to prevent sticking. When the quinces are cooked, most of the moisture will have evaporated. Turn the mixture into a mixing bowl and set aside.

In a saucepan combine the pears, lemon juice and remaining sugar; slowly bring the mixture to a simmer. Cook, stirring often, for 15 to 25 minutes, or until the pears are soft and falling apart and most of the juice has evaporated (mixture should have a consistency similar to applesauce). Combine the pear mixture with the quince mixture, adding the cinnamon and the brandy. Fill the cooled pie shell with the mixture.

To make the topping, combine the ingredients in a small bowl. Sprinkle the topping mixture evenly over the top of the tart. Bake for 20 minutes or until the crust is lightly browned. Cool on a wire rack before serving. Six to eight servings.

Refreshed Fruit

3/4 cup sugar
1 1/2 cups water
      Juice of 1 lemon
1/2 cup dry white wine
1   ripe cantaloupe, cut into balls or
       wedges
3   navel oranges, peeled and sectioned
2   green apples, unpeeled, cored and
       diced
2   red apples, unpeeled, cored and diced
3   bananas, sliced
1   cup seedless green grapes
1   cup purple or red grapes, halved and
       seeded

In a 1-quart saucepan dissolve the sugar in the water. Bring to a boil and reduce the heat; simmer, uncovered, for about 10 minutes and remove from the heat. Stir in the lemon juice, cover and refrigerate until cold. Add the wine. In a large bowl combine all the fruits. Pour the lemon syrup over them and toss gently until the fruit is evenly coated. Cover and refrigerate. Twelve servings.

Baked Pears

12   large cooking pears
2   cups sugar or 1 cup sugar and 1 cup
     maple syrup
2   cinnamon sticks, broken
1/4 teaspoon vanilla
1/2 (1 stick) butter

Preheat oven to 350° F.

Wash and peel the pears, cut them in half lengthwise and remove the cores. Place the pears in a 4-inch-deep baking dish that has a top. Sprinkle the sugar, cinnamon and vanilla over the pears; slice the butter and dot it over the pears. Cover and bake for 1 hour. Twelve servings.

Baked Apples

6   large MacIntosh apples, cored and
     peeled halfway down
1/4 cup melted butter
1/2 cup sugar
1/4 cup raisins, plumped in 1/4 cup rum
1/4 cup sugar
1   teaspoon lemon juice
1/2 cup chopped pecans
2   tablespoons butter
1/3 cup hot water
     Heavy cream

Preheat oven to 300° F.

Roll the apples in the melted butter and then in the 1/2 cup sugar. Arrange the apples in a shallow baking dish. Drain the raisins. In a small bowl mix together the raisins, 1/4 cup sugar, lemon juice and pecans. Fill the cored apples with the raisin mixture and dot with the butter.

Pour the hot water into the bottom of the baking dish around the apples. Bake for 1 hour; do not baste. Serve hot, warm or cold with heavy cream. Six servings.

Blackberry Jam Cake

1   cup butter
1 1/2 cups sugar
3   eggs
1   cup seedless blackberry or raspberry jam
      or preserves
3   cups all-purpose flour
2   teaspoons nutmeg
2   teaspoons ground cloves
2   teaspoons cinnamon
1   teaspoon baking soda
1   cup buttermilk
2   teaspoons bourbon whiskey or vanilla
      extract

Preheat oven to 350° F. Grease well a 9-inch angel food or bundt cake pan.

In a large bowl cream together the butter and sugar until light and fluffy; beat in the eggs one at a time. Fold in jam or

In a separate bowl stir together the dry ingredients; add to the egg mixture alternately with the buttermilk, folding in lightly. Fold in the bourbon or vanilla. Spoon the batter into the greased pan and bake for 35 to 45 minutes. Cool the cake for 10 minutes before turning it out of the mold.

Flan

¾ cup sugar
2½ cups milk
2 cups cream of coconut
6 eggs
5 egg yolks
2 teaspoons vanilla, Mexican
    if available
1 cup sliced almonds

Preheat oven to 325° F.

Caramelize the sugar by melting in a skillet over medium heat, watching constantly so that it does not burn. As the sugar bubbles, lift the pan off the heat, tilting to move the caramel around the surface of the pan. When the sugar is caramelized, quickly pour the caramel syrup into a 10-inch round cake pan or 8 individual flan molds, tilting to coat evenly. (If the caramel hardens, return the pan to the heat to liquefy, then continue to coat the pan or molds.) Place the pan or molds in a larger pan filled with hot water.

In a mixing bowl beat the eggs and egg yolks lightly with a whisk. Add the remaining ingredients except the almonds, whisking together to make a custard.

Pour the custard into the caramelized pan or molds and sprinkle the almonds evenly over the top. Cover all the pans with aluminum foil and bake for 1 hour or until a knife inserted in the custard comes out clean. Remove the flan from the water bath and refrigerate. When ready to serve, invert the pan or molds onto a serving platter.

Crème Caramel

½ cup sugar
¼ cup water
⅓ cup sugar
2 cups milk, scalded
2 eggs
2 egg yolks
1½ teaspoons vanilla

Preheat oven to 350° F.

In a saucepan dissolve the ½ cup sugar in the water and cook over low heat until the mixture turns a golden brown color; *do not burn*. Pour the hot caramel mixture into a mold and turn the mold to coat the bottom and the sides with the caramel.

In another saucepan dissolve the ⅓ cup sugar in the scalded milk. In a mixing bowl beat the eggs and the egg yolks until light. Beat a little of the hot milk into the eggs and pour the eggs into the rest of the milk. Simmer for 1 minute, cool slightly and then beat in the vanilla.

Strain the mixture into the prepared mold. Set the mold in a pan of hot water and bake until set, about 45 to 50 minutes; remove from the oven and cool. Refrigerate until ready to serve.

Unmold the crème caramel onto a serving plate and spoon any remaining caramel sauce over the top. Eight to ten servings.

Bread Pudding with Bourbon Sauce

6 *slices white bread, toasted and lightly buttered*
1 *cup hot water*
½ *cup seedless raisins, plumped in bourbon whiskey*
2 *eggs, beaten*
⅓ *cup sugar*
   Salt to taste
1 *cup light cream*
1 *teaspoon vanilla*
¼ *cup sugar mixed with ½ teaspoon cinnamon*

BOURBON SAUCE

½ *cup butter*
1 *cup dark brown sugar*
¼ *cup water*
1 *teaspoon cornstarch*
⅓ *cup bourbon*

Preheat oven to 350° F. Lightly butter a 1-quart baking dish.

Break up the toast and pile it into the bottom of the baking dish. Pour the hot water over the toast. In a mixing bowl beat together the eggs, sugar, salt, cream and vanilla. Pour the mixture over the toast and let stand for 10 minutes. Sprinkle with the cinnamon-sugar. Bake for 30 minutes.

Meanwhile, to make the bourbon sauce, in a heavy saucepan melt the butter and sugar. In a small bowl stir the cornstarch into the water until the mixture is smooth. Add the cornstarch mixture to the sugar mixture. Stir in the bourbon and heat until thick.

Serve the bread pudding hot with the bourbon sauce over the top. Six servings.

Rice Custard with Lemon Sauce

2 *cups milk*
1 *cup cooked rice*
1 *tablespoon butter*
⅓ *cup sugar*
½ *teaspoon cinnamon*
¼ *teaspoon salt*
⅓ *cup raisins*
2 *eggs, beaten*

SAUCE

½ *cup sugar*
1 *tablespoon cornstarch*
   Salt to taste
   Pinch nutmeg
1 *cup boiling water*
2 *tablespoons butter*
1½ *tablespoons lemon juice*

Preheat oven to 350° F.

In a saucepan heat the milk to scalding; add the rice and butter and stir to combine. Stir the sugar, cinnamon, salt and raisins into the beaten eggs; slowly stir the egg mixture into the hot milk mixture and simmer for 2 minutes. Pour the custard mixture into a greased baking dish, set the dish in a pan of hot water, and bake for 1 hour or until set.

To make the sauce, in a saucepan combine the sugar, cornstarch, salt and nutmeg; gradually stir in the boiling water. Cook, stirring, until the sauce is thick and clear. Beat in the butter and lemon juice. Serve the sauce over the custard. Four servings.

Lemon/Orange Trifle Dessert

6   eggs, yolks beaten, whites beaten until stiff peaks form
1½ cups sugar
¼   cup lemon juice
½   cup orange juice
3   teaspoons grated lemon peel
¼   teaspoon vanilla
1   tablespoon unflavored gelatin
¼   cup warm water
1   cup heavy cream, whipped
3   dozen lady fingers, torn into pieces
⅓   cup red port or sherry

In the top of a double boiler combine the egg yolks, ¾ cup of the sugar, the lemon and orange juices and grated lemon peel. Cook over low heat until the mixture is the consistency of custard and coats a spoon; remove from the heat. Soften the gelatin in the warm water, add it to the egg yolk mixture, return to the heat and stir briefly until the gelatin dissolves completely. Beat in the vanilla, then fold in the egg whites. Fold in the whipped cream.

In a glass serving bowl build the dessert in layers. Start with the lady fingers and sprinkle them with the port or sherry. Spoon on some custard, add another layer of lady fingers, and continue layering until the custard and lady fingers have been used, ending with the lady fingers. Serve from the dish. Eight servings.

Louisiana Yam Custard With Pecan Topping

2   pounds fresh sweet potatoes, peeled and boiled until tender
1½ cups half and half cream
1   tablespoon melted butter
2   eggs, slightly beaten
¾   cup sugar
1½ teaspoons pumpkin pie spice
1   tablespoon dark rum

TOPPING

1½ tablespoons butter, softened
⅓   cup brown sugar
⅓   cup chopped pecans

    Heavy cream

Preheat oven to 400° F.

In a large bowl mash the potatoes; measure 2 cups. In a food processor puree all the ingredients except those for the topping. Pour the mixture into a greased 9- x 9-inch pan and place in a pan of hot water. Bake for 50 minutes. Cool.

Meanwhile, to make the topping combine the butter, sugar and pecans. When the custard has cooled, reheat the oven to broiling temperature. Crumble the topping mixture over the baked custard and broil until the topping bubbles. Serve warm from the oven with heavy cream. Eight servings.

Sweet Potato Pie with Candied Ginger Topping

4   tablespoons (½ stick) butter
2   cups mashed cooked sweet potatoes
½   cup white sugar
¼   cup brown sugar
½   teaspoon cinnamon
½   teaspoon nutmeg
¾   cup heavy cream
3   eggs, well beaten
1   9-inch unbaked pastry shell
1   cup heavy cream, whipped (optional)

TOPPING

4   tablespoons (½ stick) butter
⅓   cup brown sugar, packed
¾   cup crystallized ginger
    Fresh lemon juice

Preheat oven to 350°. F.

In a large bowl mash the butter with the potatoes and add the sugar, cinnamon, nutmeg, cream and eggs, beating well. Pour the mixture into the pastry shell and bake for 25 minutes.

To make the topping, cream together the butter and brown sugar. Gently rinse any excess sugar from the ginger and pat dry with paper towels; chop the ginger coarsely. Add the chopped ginger and the lemon juice to the butter-sugar mixture and stir to combine.

After the initial 25 minutes of baking time, remove the pie from the oven and gently spread the topping mixture over the pie. Return the pie to the oven for an additional 25 minutes or so, checking at intervals for browning. Serve with whipped cream, if desired.

Sopaipilla Dulce (Mexican Fried Cookie)

4   cups flour
1   teaspoon salt
2   teaspoons baking powder
4   tablespoons lard
1   cup sugar
4   eggs, beaten
2   cups milk (approximately)
    Oil for deep frying
2   teaspoons cinnamon

Sift together the flour, salt and baking powder into a mixing bowl; cut in the lard until the mixture resembles coarse meal. Stir in ½ cup sugar, then stir in the beaten eggs. Add enough milk to make a medium dough. Let the dough stand for 30 minutes.

Roll out the dough to a thickness of ¼ inch; cut into 1½-inch squares. In a large skillet heat the oil to 350° F.; fry the cookies until they are brown. Drain.

To make a topping, combine the cinnamon with the remaining ½ cup sugar and mix well. While the cookies are still hot, roll them in the cinnamon-sugar or shake them with it in a brown paper bag until coated. Serve the cookies warm with strong coffee. Makes 2 dozen.

Spanish Almond Cookies

1	cup (2 sticks) butter, softened
1½	cups sugar
2	eggs
1	rounded teaspoon ground cloves
1	rounded teaspoon ground cinnamon
3	cups flour
½	pound blanched almonds

In a mixing bowl cream together the butter and sugar. Add the eggs, one at a time, blending well after each addition. Stir the spices into the flour, sift together and add to the creamed mixture. Add the almonds, mixing by hand if necessary. Shape the dough into rolls and store in the refrigerator until very firm. Preheat oven to 375° F.

Slice the dough into thin slices with a sharp knife and bake on an ungreased cookie sheet for 5 to 10 minutes. Store the dough in the freezer between batches to keep its shape. Makes about 5 dozen.

Praline Cookies

½	cup butter
½	cup sugar
1	cup tightly packed brown sugar
1	egg, beaten
	Pinch salt
1	cup all-purpose flour
1	cup pecans, coarsely chopped
1	teaspoon vanilla

Preheat oven to 375° F.

In a large bowl cream together the butter and sugar until light; add the egg, then the salt, flour, nuts and vanilla. Mix well. Shape the dough into balls the size of walnuts on a greased cookie sheet. Flatten out the cookies by dipping fingers in cold water and pressing to ⅛ inch or thinner. Bake for 10 to 12 minutes or until brown. Makes 3 dozen.

Natillas

4	cups milk
4	eggs, separated, whites beaten until very stiff peaks form
1	cup sugar
	Salt to taste
	Cinnamon

In a large saucepan scald the milk. Drop the beaten egg whites into the hot milk by spoonfuls; do not allow the milk to boil. Cook the egg whites in the milk for 5 to 6 minutes. Remove the egg whites from the hot milk with a slotted spoon and arrange them in a glass serving bowl; reserve the hot milk in the saucepan.

In a medium bowl beat the egg yolks with the sugar and salt. Beat the egg yolk mixture into the hot milk. Simmer until smooth and thickened, stirring constantly.

Strain the custard over the egg whites in the serving bowl and dust with cinnamon. Serve hot or at room temperature. Four to six servings.

Mint Sherbet

2 cups fresh mint leaves
   Juice of 4 lemons
1 cup boiling water
2 scant cups sugar
2 cups water
   Juice of one large orange
2 egg whites, beaten until
      stiff peaks form

Place the mint leaves in a mixing bowl, add
the lemon juice and pour the boiling water
over all; let stand for 15 to 20 minutes. In a
saucepan bring the sugar and the 2 cups water
to a boil and simmer for 5 minutes; cool.
Strain the liquid from the mint leaves and add
to the cooled sugar syrup. Chill the mixture
and add the orange juice. Freeze in an electric
ice cream freezer according to the
manufacturer's instructions. When the mixture
is half frozen fold in the beaten egg whites;
freeze completely. Eight servings.

Lemon Ice Cream

2 cups heavy cream
1 tablespoon grated fresh lemon peel
1 cup sugar
⅓ cup fresh lemon juice
   Fresh mint leaves for garnish (optional)
   Whole fresh strawberries for garnish
      (optional)

In a large bowl combine the cream and sugar;
stir until the sugar is dissolved. Blend in the

lemon peel and lemon juice. Pour the mixture
into a shallow pan and freeze until firm (about
4 hours) or freeze in an electric ice cream
freezer according to the manufacturer's
instructions. To serve, garnish with fresh mint
leaves and strawberries if desired. Makes 3
cups.

Caramel Ice Cream

1½ cups heavy cream
1½ cups half and half cream
⅛ teaspoon salt
6 egg yolks
1½ cups sugar
1 teaspoon vanilla
½ cup plus 1 tablespoon water

In a saucepan scald together the heavy cream
and half and half cream. Add the salt and
bring just to a boil; cover and let stand for at
least 15 minutes.

In a mixing bowl beat the egg yolks and ½
cup of the sugar until thick and lemon
colored. Stir part of the hot cream into the
eggs, then slowly add the remaining egg
mixture to the rest of the hot cream. Cook
over medium heat, stirring until the mixture
thickens slightly. Do not boil. Cool slightly and
add the vanilla. Cool completely and
refrigerate for at least 4 hours or up to 3 days.

In a small saucepan combine the remaining
1 cup sugar with ½ cup water and bring to a
boil. Cook, stirring constantly, until the
mixture caramelizes and turns dark brown.
Remove from the heat and slowly add the

remaining tablespoon of water. Stir the syrup into the cream mixture; chill. Transfer the mixture to an electric ice cream freezer and freeze according to the manufacturer's directions. Makes 1 quart.

Peppermint Stick Ice Cream

3   cups half and half cream
1   cup sugar
1   teaspoon vanilla
½   pound peppermint stick candy, crushed

In the top of a double boiler heat the cream; add the sugar and beat until it is dissolved. Cool. Stir in the vanilla, then stir in the crushed peppermint candy. Freeze in an electric ice cream freezer according to the manufacturer's directions. Six to eight servings.

Lemon Sherbet

2   cups sugar
2   cups water
1   lemon, very thinly sliced
    Juice of 6 lemons combined with 1 cup
        water
4   egg whites, beaten until stiff peaks form

In a saucepan boil the sugar, water and lemon slices for 5 minutes. Strain, cool and add the lemon juice and water. Freeze in an electric ice cream freezer according to the manufacturer's instructions. When the mixture is half frozen, fold in the beaten egg whites; freeze completely. Eight to ten servings.

Apricot Ice Cream

2   cups sugar
1   tablespoon unflavored gelatin
4   tablespoons warm water
4   cups apricots, peeled
½   cup water
    Juice of 1 lemon
2   cups heavy cream, whipped stiff

In a saucepan boil the sugar in 1 quart of water for 5 minutes. In a mixing bowl dissolve the gelatin in the warm water; add the sugar syrup, stir to combine and let cool. In a saucepan simmer the apricots in the ½ cup water until tender. Remove the pits, mash the apricots and let cool. Add the apricots and the lemon juice to the gelatin mixture; pour into trays and freeze until partially set. Pour the mixture into a large bowl, stir in the whipped cream, return to the trays and freeze completely. Twelve servings.

Sherried Pecan Balls

1½   cups sugar
½   cup sweet sherry
1   teaspoon cinnamon
3   cups pecan halves

In a saucepan cook the sugar and sherry together to a soft boil stage or 225° F. on a candy thermometer. Add the cinnamon and the pecans and stir until the mixture becomes cloudy. Drop by teaspoonfuls onto waxed paper; let cool. Peel the pecan balls off the waxed paper and serve or store. Makes about 3 dozen balls.

Rhubarb Ring with Strawberries

1	*tablespoon salad oil*
2	*pounds fresh rhubarb, trimmed, washed and cut into ½-inch pieces (about 4 cups)*
1	*cup plus 1 tablespoon sugar*
1½	*cups water*
1	*tablespoon finely sliced fresh ginger*
2	*envelopes unflavored gelatin*
2	*cups fresh ripe strawberries, hulled Confectioner's sugar*
1	*cup chilled heavy cream whipped with 1 tablespoon rum*

Lightly brush the oil evenly over the inside surfaces of a 1-quart ring mold.

In a large enameled or stainless-steel saucepan combine the rhubarb, 1 cup of the sugar and 1 cup of the water and bring to a boil over high heat, stirring until the sugar dissolves. Add the ginger, reduce the heat to low and simmer, partially covered, for about 10 minutes or until the rhubarb is tender but still intact.

Meanwhile, sprinkle the 2 envelopes of gelatin into the remaining ½ cup of water and let it soften for 4 to 5 minutes. Add the gelatin to the rhubarb mixture and stir until it dissolves completely. Pour the mixture into the oiled ring mold, spreading it and smoothing the top. Cool to room temperature, cover and refrigerate for at least 3 hours.

To unmold and serve the rhubarb ring, run a thin knife around the sides of the mold and dip the bottom briefly into hot water. Place an inverted serving plate on top of the mold and invert. Rap the plate on a table and the rhubarb ring should slide out easily. Sprinkle the strawberries with the confectioner's sugar, garnish the mold with the strawberries and the flavored whipped cream and serve. Six servings.

Christmas Shortbreads

1	*cup (2 sticks) butter, softened*
¾	*cup confectioner's sugar*
1	*teaspoon vanilla extract*
1¾	*cups all-purpose flour*
6	*1-ounce squares semisweet chocolate*
1	*teaspoon vegetable shortening*
1½	*cups chopped pecans*

In a large mixing bowl, cream together the butter, sugar and vanilla. Add the flour and mix well.

Form the dough into a long roll, about 18 inches; wrap in waxed paper and chill for several hours or overnight.

Preheat oven to 300° F.

Cut the roll of dough into ¼-inch slices, then cut the rounds in half, forming half circles. Bake on ungreased cookie sheets for 16 to 20 minutes (cookies should be dry but not browned). Cool.

Melt the chocolate and shortening over hot, not boiling, water. Dip the tip of each cookie into the chocolate, then into the pecans. Cool on cookie sheets in the refrigerator until the chocolate is set. Store in the refrigerator. Makes 4 to 5 dozen cookies.

Brandied Rice Ring with Custard Cream

¼   cup candied fruit (or
       diced dates and
       figs)
¼   cup seedless raisins
¼   cup brandy
1½ cups sugar
½   cup water
5½ cups milk
1   cup raw rice
2   tablespoons butter
1   vanilla bean
⅛   teaspoon salt
4   eggs, separated
½   teaspoon vanilla extract
1   teaspoon brandy

Preheat oven to 375° F.

Plump the fruit and raisins in the ¼ cup brandy and set aside. In a shallow skillet melt 1 cup sugar in the water, heating until the syrup is golden brown. Quickly pour the syrup down the sides and bottom of a 6-cup ring mold, tilting to coat evenly.

In a large saucepan combine 4 cups of the milk, the rice, butter, vanilla bean and salt; bring to a boil. Reduce the heat and cook, stirring frequently, for 35 minutes or until the rice is tender and the liquid is absorbed. Remove the vanilla bean, stir in the fruit and brandy and cool. In a bowl beat the egg whites until frothy. Add ¼ cup sugar and beat until stiff but not dry. Fold the egg whites into the fruit mixture and pour the mixture into the caramel-lined ring mold. Bake for 35 minutes or until set. While still hot, carefully invert onto a serving dish.

To make the custard cream sauce, beat the egg yolks and the remaining ¼ cup sugar in a small saucepan. Scald the remaining 1½ cups milk, then slowly pour it into the sugar mixture. Cook over low heat, stirring constantly, until smooth and thickened. Remove from the heat, beat in the vanilla extract and the brandy. Spoon the warm sauce over warm or cold slices of the rice ring. Twelve servings.

Frozen Charlotte Russe

1   tablespoon unflavored gelatin
2   cups milk
6   egg yolks
⅔   cup sugar
1   teaspoon vanilla
1   dozen lady fingers
1   pint heavy cream, whipped

In a saucepan combine the gelatin with the milk and simmer, stirring, until the gelatin is dissolved. In a mixing bowl beat the egg yolks with the sugar; add the egg yolk mixture to the simmering milk mixture, stirring constantly over low heat until the mixture is thick. Strain the mixture, stir in the vanilla and cool until it begins to set.

Line a lightly buttered mold with the lady fingers. Gradually fold the whipped cream into the custard until thoroughly blended. Pour the mixture into the lined mold and freeze. Ten servings.

Hilltop Herb Farm's Rose Geranium Pound Cake

Rose geranium leaves sufficient to cover the bottom of a 9- or 10-inch pan
- 3 *cups sugar*
- 1½ *cups (3 sticks) butter, room temperature*
- 5 *eggs*
- 3 *cups flour*
- ½ *teaspoon ground mace*
- 6 *ounces club soda*
- 1 *tablespoon lemon juice*
- 1 *tablespoon lime juice*

Generously grease and flour a 9- or 10-inch tube pan. Line the bottom of the pan with overlapping rows of rose geranium leaves (the leaves will shrink during the cooking process, so use plenty). Preheat oven to 375° F.

In a mixing bowl cream together the sugar and butter until light and pale yellow. Add the eggs one at a time, beating with an electric mixer at high speed for 1 minute after each addition. Add the flour and mace alternately with the club soda and fruit juices; beat for 1 minute more. Pour the batter into the prepared pan, taking care not to disturb the leaves. Bake for 1 hour or until a toothpick inserted in the center comes out clean. Cool the cake in the pan for 20 minutes, turn the cake out onto a wire rack and cool completely.

NOTE: Fresh basil leaves can be substituted for the rose geranium leaves (the flavor, of course, will not be the same).

Glazed Orange Slices in Ginger Sauce

- 6 *navel or Temple oranges*
- 1 *cup dry white wine*
- 2 *tablespoons red wine vinegar*
- ¾ *cup sugar*
- 1 *½-inch cinnamon stick and 10 whole cloves, wrapped together in cheesecloth*
- 2 *tablespoons Grand Marnier or other orange liqueur (optional)*

With a small sharp knife remove the peel from two of the oranges without cutting into the bitter white pith beneath. Cut the peel into strips about ⅛ inch wide and drop the peel into boiling water to cover; boil for about 2 minutes. With a slotted spoon transfer the strips to paper towels to drain.

Cut the white outer pith and membrane from the 2 skinned oranges. Cut away and discard the peel, pith and all the white outside membrane from the remaining 4 oranges. Cut the oranges into thick slices.

In a large enameled or stainless-steel saucepan combine the wine, vinegar, sugar, cheesecloth-wrapped cinnamon and cloves and the ginger and bring to a boil over medium heat, stirring until the sugar dissolves. Add the orange slices and the strips of orange peel, and turn them with a spoon to coat them evenly with the syrup. Reduce the heat to low and simmer, uncovered, for 15 minutes, turning the orange slices over frequently but gently.

With a slotted spoon transfer the orange slices and peel to a deep bowl. Pick out and discard the cheesecloth bag of spices and taste the syrup for sweetness. If using the liqueur, add it to the syrup and stir to combine. Pour the syrup over the orange slices and cool to room temperature. Cover the bowl tightly and refrigerate for at least 2 hours. Six servings.

Cassis Mousse

8	egg yolks
1½	teaspoons unflavored gelatin, softened in ½ cup warm water
½	cup currant jam or more to taste
¼	cup water
¾	cup heavy cream, whipped
7	egg whites, whipped until stiff peaks form
12	lady fingers
½	cup heavy cream, whipped, flavored with 2 tablespoons Cassis

In a medium bowl beat the egg yolks thoroughly; add the gelatin and stir to combine. In a heavy saucepan bring the currant jam to a boil with the water; remove from the heat and cool for a few minutes. Beat the egg yolk mixture into the jam. Return the saucepan to the heat and bring the mixture to a boil. Remove from the heat and cool thoroughly. Gently fold in the whipped cream and the beaten egg whites.

Line the bottom and sides of a chilled 10-inch ring mold with a layer of lady fingers and pour in the mousse. Top with the flavored whipped cream and refrigerate. Six to eight servings.

Pecan Pie

1	unbaked 9-inch pie shell
2	cups pecan halves
3	eggs
⅛	teaspoon salt
¾	cup sugar
1	cup dark corn syrup
½	cup (1 stick) butter
½	teaspoon vanilla

Preheat oven to 350° F.

Chop about ¼ cup pecans and set aside. In a medium bowl beat the eggs and the salt with a wooden spoon until the mixture thickens. Gradually beat in the sugar. Add the corn syrup, melted butter and vanilla; stir well to combine. Stir in the chopped pecans. Pour the mixture into the pie shell, spread the remaining pecans over the top and bake for 1 hour.

Lemon Chess Pie

¼	cup (½ stick) butter
1½	cups sugar
4	eggs
	Juice of 2–3 lemons
1	scant tablespoon cornmeal
1	unbaked pastry shell

Preheat oven to 350° F.

In a mixing bowl cream together the butter and sugar until light. Add the eggs and stir until blended. Add the lemon juice and cornmeal. Pour the mixture into the pie shell and bake for about 25 minutes. Serve warm or cold.

Chocolate Almond Soufflé

Butter
Confectioner's Sugar
3   *egg yolks*
½   *cup sugar*
2   *teaspoons almond extract*
4   *ounces (4 squares) unsweetened*
      chocolate, melted over hot water
⅛   *teaspoon cream of tartar*

Preheat oven to 400° F. Butter a 1-quart soufflé dish and dust it with confectioner's sugar.

In a mixing bowl beat the egg yolks; add the sugar and continue to beat until the mixture is light in color. Stir in the almond extract. Fold in the melted chocolate and cool slightly.

In a separate bowl beat the egg whites with the cream of tartar until stiff peaks form. Fold the beaten egg whites into the chocolate mixture and pour into the prepared soufflé dish. Place in the oven and immediately reduce the temperature to 375° F. Bake for 20 to 30 minutes until the mixture has at least doubled in bulk and the top is lightly browned. Serve immediately. Four to six servings.

Fig Soufflé

3   *eggs, separated*
3   *tablespoons sugar*
2   *tablespoons butter*
2   *tablespoons flour*
¾   *cup milk*
2   *tablespoons butter, softened*
12 *large fresh figs, stemmed and diced*

Preheat oven to 350° F. Beat egg whites with sugar until stiff peaks form.

In a heavy saucepan melt the butter; stir in the flour and cook over low heat for 2 minutes. Stir in the milk all at once and beat until smooth. Cook for about 3 minutes, or until the mixture begins to thicken.

Remove the mixture from the heat and beat in the egg yolks, one at a time. Stir in the softened butter, then stir in the chopped figs. Gently fold in the beaten egg whites.

Generously butter and sugar a 1-quart soufflé dish. Spoon the soufflé mixture into the prepared dish. Bake for 40 minutes and serve at once. Four to six servings.

Coconut Ice Cream

6   *cups freshly grated coconut*
4   *cups hot milk*
1   *cup sugar*
1   *teaspoon vanilla*
¼   *cup dark rum*
     Grated coconut for garnish

Pour the grated coconut into a large bowl and pour the hot milk over it; let stand for 30 to 40 minutes. Strain the milk into a large bowl through cheesecloth, squeezing to extract all the liquid. Discard the pulp.

Beat the sugar, vanilla and rum into the milk. Freeze in an electric ice cream maker according to the manufacturer's directions.

Freeze the ice cream in freezer of refrigerator for an additional 2 hours to develop the flavor. Serve garnished with grated coconut. Eight servings.

Pumpkin Pecan Soufflé

1½ *cups sugar pumpkin puree*
2   *teaspoons cinnamon*
½   *cup sugar*
4   *eggs, separated*
4   *additional egg whites*
¼   *cup dark rum or ¼ cup hazelnut liqueur*
¾   *cup chopped pecans*
1   *tablespoon softened butter*
    Heavy cream, whipped (optional)

Preheat oven to 350° F.

Place the pumpkin, cinnamon and sugar in a saucepan and add ½ cup water. Simmer until the pumpkin is very tender. Add the 4 egg yolks one at a time, beating after each addition. Beat in the rum or liqueur, pecans and butter.

Beat the 8 egg whites until stiff peaks form; fold into the pumpkin mixture. Pour the mixture into a buttered 1½-quart casserole and bake for 35 to 40 minutes or until golden brown. Serve at once, topped with whipped cream if desired. Four to six servings.

Ice Box Cake

1   *pound butter*
1   *pound sugar*
1   *dozen eggs, separated, whites beaten until stiff peaks form*
4   *1-ounce squares unsweetened chocolate, melted over hot water*
1   *pound pecans, chopped*
2   *dozen macaroons*
½   *cup whiskey*
1½ *dozen lady fingers*

In a large bowl cream the butter and sugar together for 20 minutes. Beat the egg yolks for 6 minutes and add them to the sugar mixture. Pour in the melted chocolate and stir to combine. Fold in the stiffly beaten egg whites. Add the nuts.

Soak the macaroons in the whiskey. Place the lady fingers around the inside of a springform pan. Place a layer of macaroons on the bottom of the pan.

Add the cake mixture and the macaroons to the lined pan in alternate layers until the pan is full. Refrigerate.

NOTE: If you wish, additional macaroons can be substituted for the lady fingers when lining the pan.

Margarita Sorbet

1   *cup sugar*
2   *cups water*
1   *cup freshly squeezed lime juice*
3   *tablespoons grated lime peel*
4   *tablespoons tequila*
    Additional tequila
    Fresh lime slices for garnish

In a medium saucepan boil the sugar and water for 5 minutes. Cool. Stir in the lime juice, lime peel and tequila. Freeze in an electric ice cream freezer according to the manufacturer's directions.

Serve with additional tequila poured over each serving. Garnish with a slice of fresh lime. Six servings.

Almond Macaroons

1 cup (½ pound) almond paste
1 cup confectioner's sugar
3 large egg whites, room temperature
   Dash salt
½ teaspoon vanilla extract
   Granulated sugar

Preheat oven to 300° F.

On a cutting board chop the almond paste; add the confectioner's sugar and work the paste with the fingers until the sugar is blended.

Add the egg whites, one at a time, blending well after each addition. Use only enough egg white to make a soft dough that will hold its shape when dropped from a spoon. Add the salt and vanilla.

Drop spoonfuls of dough to the size of a quarter onto greased and floured cookie sheets. Sprinkle each cookie with granulated sugar and bake for 20 minutes. Makes 40 cookies.

NOTE: Almond paste is available in most supermarkets in 8-ounce cans or 6-ounce rolls.

Pralines

2 cups white sugar
1 cup brown sugar
¾ cup water
1 tablespoon white corn syrup
1 scant teaspoon salt
1 teaspoon vanilla
1 cup chopped pecans

In a saucepan combine the sugar, water, corn syrup and salt. Cook until a soft ball forms when dropped in water or a candy thermometer shows 236° F. Add the vanilla and remove from the heat; cool for 5 minutes. Add the pecans and beat until the liquid clouds. Drop from a tablespoon onto waxed paper and let stand until firm. If the mixture hardens in the pot, place the pot in hot water to soften the contents. Makes 18 pralines.

NOTE: If you use the praline mixture for praline ice cream, do not beat after adding the pecans.

Guava Turnovers

1½ cups flour
½   cup butter
¼   cup boiling water
½   teaspoon salt
    Guava paste

Preheat oven to 325° F.

Sift the flour and blend together with the butter, boiling water and salt. On a floured board roll out the pastry thin and cut into circles 4 inches in diameter. Slice the guava paste ¼ inch thick and place 1 slice on half of each circle of pastry. Fold the pastry over the guava paste, moisten the edges with water and crimp the edges with a fork to seal the turnovers. Place the turnovers on an ungreased cookie sheet and bake for 15 to 20 minutes. Makes about 2 dozen.

NOTE: Guava paste is available in many supermarkets and in Spanish grocery stores.

Brandy Snaps

3/4   cup (1 1/2 sticks) butter
1/2   cup sugar
1/4   cup dark brown sugar
1/2   cup dark molasses
3/8   teaspoon ground ginger
3/4   teaspoon grated orange peel
3/4   teaspoon ground cinnamon
1/8   teaspoon salt
1 1/2 cups all-purpose flour
1   tablespoon brandy

Preheat oven to 300° F.

In a saucepan melt the butter; add the sugars, molasses, ginger, orange peel, cinnamon and salt. When the sugars have melted, stir the mixture well to blend the ingredients. Remove from the heat; add the flour, stirring until smooth. Add the brandy and stir to combine.

Drop the batter by scant teaspoonfuls several inches apart onto an ungreased cookie sheet. Bake 10 to 12 minutes or until golden brown. Remove from the oven and wait 2 minutes before carefully removing the cookies with a spatula and placing them on a flat surface to cool. Makes 6 dozen 2-inch cookies.

Bourbon Balls

2 1/2 cups crushed vanilla wafers
1   cup pecans
2   tablespoons cocoa
1   cup confectioner's sugar
3   tablespoons white Karo syrup
1/4   cup bourbon
      Confectioner's sugar

In a food processor or blender grind the vanilla wafers and pecans. In a mixing bowl combine the cocoa and sugar; add the ground wafer mixture. In a small bowl stir the Karo into the bourbon; pour the mixture over the dry ingredients. Mix the batter until it is moist and then shape it into small balls. Roll the balls in the confectioner's sugar. Makes 3 dozen.

The Stockpot's Persimmon Mousse

1   tablespoon freshly grated
        orange peel
1/4   teaspoon powdered ginger
1/4   cup Grand Marnier
6-8   persimmons, peeled and seeded
2   cups whipping cream
1/4   cup powdered sugar

In a small bowl add the orange peel and ginger to the Grand Marnier and set aside. Puree the persimmons and measure 2 cups puree; set aside. In a chilled bowl with chilled beaters, whip the cream with the powdered sugar until stiff. Pour the seasoned Grand Marnier into the persimmon puree and mix well. Fold the puree mixture into the whipped cream and blend well; spoon into glasses or individual bowls and chill for 1 hour. Six servings.

NOTE: Persimmons vary in size and type as well as sweetness. This will affect the number of persimmons and amount of sugar needed.

Buttermilk Pie

Pastry for 1-crust pie, baked 15 minutes
or until golden
4 *tablespoons flour*
4 *tablespoons water*
1 *cup buttermilk*
¾ *cup dark brown sugar*
2 *eggs, separated*
2 *tablespoons butter, softened*
2 *tablespoons sugar*

Preheat oven to 350° F.

In a small bowl beat the flour and water together until smooth. Pour into the top of a double boiler, add the buttermilk and cook over boiling water until thick, stirring frequently. Beat in the sugar, egg yolks and butter and continue to cook until the mixture is thick and clear. Remove from the heat.

Pour the mixture into the cooled pie shell.

In a large bowl beat the egg whites with 2 tablespoons sugar until stiff peaks form. Pour the meringue over the custard in the pie shell and bake for 8 to 10 minutes or until the meringue is golden. Chill before serving.

Orange Cookies

½ *cup (1 stick) butter*
1 *cup sugar*
Peel of 2 oranges, grated
1 *egg, lightly beaten*
½ *cup fresh orange juice*
3 *cups all-purpose flour*
½ *teaspoon cinnamon*
4 *teaspoons baking powder*

Preheat oven to 325° F.

In a mixing bowl cream together the butter, sugar and orange peel. Gradually add the egg, orange juice, flour, cinnamon and baking powder, mixing well to combine. Drop the batter by teaspoonfuls onto an ungreased cookie sheet and bake for 10 to 12 minutes or until the cookies are lightly browned. Makes 6 dozen.

Chocolate Ice Box Pie

2 *cups crushed vanilla wafers*
⅓ *cup soft butter*
1 *12-ounce package semisweet chocolate*
morsels
1 *whole egg*
2 *eggs, separated, whites beaten until stiff*
peaks form
1 *teaspoon rum*
2 *cups heavy cream, whipped stiff*

In a large bowl combine the wafer crumbs and butter; press the mixture into a springform pan or deep pie pan.

In a double boiler melt the chocolate over simmering water. In a separate bowl beat 1 whole egg and 2 egg yolks until light; add to the melted chocolate. Add the rum. Fold the beaten egg whites and half the whipped cream into the chocolate mixture. Pour the mixture into the crust and freeze for several hours. Top with the remaining whipped cream before serving. Six to eight servings.

Syllabub

½   cup brandy
½   cup dry sherry
¼   cup fresh lemon juice
3   tablespoons superfine sugar
2   cups heavy cream
½   cup sugar
2   egg whites, beaten until soft
      peaks form

In a mixing bowl beat together the brandy, sherry, lemon juice and superfine sugar. In a separate bowl beat the cream with ½ cup sugar until soft peaks form. Fold the egg whites into the whipped cream. Blend ¼ cup of the wine mixture carefully into the cream mixture. Spoon the remaining wine mixture into the bottoms of 8 large glasses. Top with the cream mixture and serve at once. Eight servings.

Strawberry Pie

1   quart fresh strawberries, washed and
      hulled
¾   cup sugar
2   tablespoons cornstarch
1   baked pastry shell
½   pint heavy cream

In a saucepan mash 1 pint of the strawberries; cook over medium heat and add the sugar and cornstarch. Simmer the mixture for 10 minutes. Stir in 1 pint of whole strawberries and pour the mixture into the baked pastry shell. Whip the cream just until stiff and spoon over the top of the pie.

Calas

½   cup raw rice
3   cups boiling water
½   package yeast
½   cup lukewarm water
2   eggs, beaten
½   cup sugar
6   tablespoons all-purpose
      flour
1   teaspoon vanilla
1   teaspoon cinnamon
      Salad oil or vegetable oil
       for deep frying
      Confectioner's sugar

In a saucepan add the rice to the boiling water, cover, reduce the heat and cook for about 25 minutes or until the rice is very soft. Drain and cool. In a small bowl stir the yeast into the lukewarm water until it dissolves. Mash the rice and mix it well with the yeast. Set the mixture in a warm place to rise overnight or for about 12 hours.

Add the beaten eggs to the rice mixture, then stir in the sugar, flour and flavorings. Let rise for 15 minutes. Shape the mixture into balls or cakes.

In a heavy skillet bring the oil to 370° F. Fry the cakes until golden brown, drain, sprinkle with confectioner's sugar and serve hot. Makes about 2 dozen.

Peach and Pecan Ice Cream

2   eggs, well beaten
3   cups light cream
1   can sweetened condensed milk
1½   cups thoroughly mashed fresh
        peaches
½   cup coarsely chopped pecans,
        toasted
1   teaspoon vanilla extract
½   teaspoon almond extract

In a large bowl stir together all of the ingredients; pour into an ice cream freezer container and freeze according to the manufacturer's instructions. Let stand for at least 2 hours in the freezer of your refrigerator to develop the flavor. Makes 1½ quarts.

Cassava Pudding

2   cups peeled, grated cassava, soaked in
        water and drained
1½   cups milk
1¾   cups sugar
1   teaspoon vanilla
6   tablespoons butter, softened
3   eggs
1½   teaspoons salt
3   cups light cream
1   cup grated coconut

Preheat oven to 350° F.
   In a large bowl mix together all of the ingredients. Pour the mixture into a 13- x 9-inch pan and bake for 30 to 40 minutes or until set. Serve warm. Ten servings.

Pecan Crispies

½   cup shortening
½   cup butter
2½   cups dark brown sugar
2   eggs, well beaten
2½   cups all-purpose flour
½   teaspoon salt
½   teaspoon baking soda
1   cup chopped pecans

Preheat oven to 350° F.
   In a large bowl cream together the shortening, butter and sugar until light and fluffy. Add the eggs and beat well. Sift together the dry ingredients and add them to the batter, stirring well to combine. Add the nuts and stir. Drop the batter by teaspoonfuls onto a greased cookie sheet about 2 inches apart. Bake for 10 to 12 minutes or until crisp. Makes 3 dozen.

Chess Pie

1½   cups sugar
½   cup water
1½   tablespoons cornmeal
1½   tablespoons flour
½   cup melted butter
6   egg yolks
1   teaspoon vanilla
1   unbaked 9-inch pie shell

Preheat oven to 250° F.
   In a mixing bowl combine all of the ingredients; beat well and pour the mixture into the pie shell. Bake for about 1 hour or until firm. Six to eight servings.

Coconut Pecan Cake

1 *cup butter or margarine, room temperature*
2 *cups sifted sugar*
6 *large eggs, room temperature, separated*
3½ *cups all-purpose flour*
3 *teaspoons baking powder*
Salt
½ *cup bourbon*
½ *cup milk*
1 *7-ounce package extra moist, sweetened, thin coconut flakes*
1 *cup chopped pecans*
3 *tablespoons flour*

Preheat oven to 300° F. Grease a 9-inch tube pan or two 5-inch tube pans and line them with waxed paper.

In a very large mixing bowl cream together the butter and sugar using medium speed on an electric mixer. Beat the egg yolks until thick and add them to the butter mixture. Stir together the flour, baking powder and salt; add to the egg mixture alternately with the bourbon and the milk. Stir in the coconut. Toss the pecans in the flour; stir them into the batter.

Beat the egg whites on high speed until stiff but not dry; fold into the batter. Spoon the batter into the pan or pans. Bake a large tube pan for 1 hour and 10 minutes, small tube pans for 1 hour or until a toothpick inserted in the center comes out clean. Cool on a wire rack for 15 minutes before removing from pan. Twenty-two to twenty-four servings.

Pecan Bars

½ *cup (1 stick) butter*
¼ *cup confectioner's sugar*
1 *cup cake flour (reserve 2 tablespoons for the second layer batter)*
1½ *cups brown sugar*
½ *teaspoon baking powder*
2 *eggs, lightly beaten*
1 *cup pecans, broken*

Preheat oven to 375° F.

In a mixing bowl combine the butter, confectioner's sugar and cake flour (less 2 tablespoons); blend thoroughly. Spread the mixture in a 9- x 12-inch baking pan. Combine the brown sugar, reserved cake flour, and baking powder; add the mixture to the beaten eggs and mix until smooth. Add the nuts. Spread the mixture on top of the first layer in the pan. Bake for 30 to 40 minutes. Cool slightly, cut into squares and let cool completely. Makes about 15 large squares.

RESOURCE GUIDE

This Resource Guide is meant to assist you in obtaining ingredients for the recipes in this book if you have difficulty finding them locally. We suggest you write to (or call) the companies listed below to obtain further information.

ANDOUILLE
TASSO

Oak Grove Smokehouse Inc.
17618 Old Jefferson Highway
Prairieville, Louisiana 70769
(504) 673-6857

CHILIES

Mexican Chile Supply
304 East Belknap Street
Fort Worth, Texas 76102
(817) 332-3871

CRAB AND SHRIMP BOIL

Central Grocery Company
923 Decatur Street
New Orleans, Louisiana 70116

CRAYFISH

Battistella Seafood
910 Touro Street
New Orleans, Louisiana 70116
(504) 949-2724

CREOLE CONDIMENTS

Creole Delicacies
533 Ann Street
New Orleans, Louisiana 70116

CREOLE SPICES
FILÉ POWDER
GUMBO MIXES

Gazin's
2910 Toulouse Street
P.O. Box 19221
New Orleans, Louisiana 70179
(504) 482-0302

FRESH HERBS

Hilltop Herb Farm
P.O. Box 1734
Cleveland, Texas 77327
(713) 592-5859

**FRESH SEAFOOD
TURTLE MEAT**

Smith Knaupp Company
450 W. McNab Road
Fort Lauderdale, Florida 33309

GOURMET RICES

Konriko Company Store
301 Ann Street
P.O. Box 296
New Iberia, Louisiana 70560
(800) 55l-3245

MESQUITE

Forrest-Shelton Chipping Co.
P.O. Box 196
Sanford, Texas 79078
(800) 432-6280

PECANS

H.M. Thames Pecan Company
The Nuthouse
P.O. Box 2206
Mobile, Alabama 36652
(800) 633-1306

QUAIL

Quail Roost Quail Farms
8942 S.W. 129 Terrace
Miami, Florida 33176
(800) 323-5028

Many state and local organizations and fine purveyors have issued attractive and interesting regional cookbooks. The following are among the many excellent ones available.

America's Country Inn Cookbook, available by mail from The R. T. French Company, Consumer Services Kitchens, 1 Mustard Street, Rochester, New York 14692.

Authentic Cajun Cooking, available by mail at a cost of $1.75 from McIlhenny Company, Avery Island, Louisiana 70513.

Bayou Cuisine, available by mail at a cost of $9.95 plus $2.00 for postage and handling from St. Stephens Episcopal Church, Box 1005, Indianola, Mississippi 38751.

The Best Little Cookbook in Texas, available by mail at a cost of $10.95 plus $1.50 for postage and handling (Texas residents please add $.55 per copy for local sales tax) from The Junior League of Abilene, Inc., 774 Butternut, Abilene, Texas 79602.

Delectable Dishes from Termite Hall, available by mail at a cost of $9.80 postage-inclusive from The Madaloni Press, 355 Saint Michael Street, Mobile, Alabama 36602.

From the Land of Tabasco Sauce, available by mail from McIlhenny Company, Avery Island, Louisiana 70513.

The Gasparilla Cookbook, available by mail at a cost of $10.50 plus $1.25 for postage and handling (Florida residents please add $.42 per copy for local sales tax) from The Junior League of Tampa, P.O. Box 10223, Tampa, Florida 33679.

Guten Appetit!, available by mail at a cost of $11.43 plus $1.25 for postage and handling (Texas residens please add $.57 per copy for local sales tax) from The Sophienburg Memorial Association, Inc., New Braunfels, Texas 78130.

The Secrets of Creole Cooking, available by mail from B. F. Trappey's Sons, Inc., P. O. Drawer 400, New Iberia, Louisiana 70560.

Southern Sideboards, available by mail at a cost of $11.95 plus $1.55 for postage and handling (Mississippi residents please add $.60 per copy for local sales tax) from The Junior League of Jackson, Mississippi, P. O. Box 4553, Jackson, Mississippi 39216.

INDEX

➤

(page numbers in italics indicate illustrations)

ACKNOWLEDGMENTS

The following have granted permission to reprint photographs in this volume:

Antiques Magazine/Helga Photography, frontispiece; Annunciation Greek Orthodox Church, page 10; Florida Department of Natural Resources, Bureau of Marketing and Extension Services, pages 17, 91; McIlhenny Company, Makers of Tabasco® brand products, pages 25, 37, 83; Catfish Farmers of America, pages 31, 111; the R. T. French Company, page 45; Maryland Office of Seafood Marketing, page 53; Glade Bilby II, page 69; Courtesy B. F. Trappey and Sons/Greg Greer, page 125; Ellen Foscue Johnson, page 181.

The following have granted permission to reproduce their recipes in this volume:

Rice Council of America, Antoine's Crab Meat Étouffée, Antoine's Creole Gumbo, Broussard's Quail in Red Wine with Dirty Rice, Broussard's Brandied Rice Ring with Custard Cream, Broussard's Crawfish Cardinale with Rice Pilaf, Green Rice; reprinted with the permission of the McIlhenny Company, taken from their recipe booklet, "Authentic Cajun Cooking" by Chef Paul Prudhomme, Paul Prudhomme's Redfish Courtbouillon, Paul Prudhomme's Chicken and Andouille Smoked Sausage Gumbo, Paul Prudhomme's Seven-Steak, Tasso and Okra Gumbo; McIlhenny Company, Makers of Tabasco® brand products, Texas Chili, Hot Cabbage Slaw, Fried Marinated Perch, Creole Tartar Sauce, Spicy Pecan Ham Mold; The Stockpot of Longview, Texas, Seafood Diablo, Spicy Stockpot Ribs, Persimmon Mousse, Apricot-Banana Bread; Hilltop Herb Farm, Rose Geranium Pound Cake; Bayley's Restaurant, Mobile, Alabama, West Indies Salad; Highlands Bar and Grill, Birmingham, Alabama, Mini Crab Cakes, Lamb with Cognac and Mint; Mr. Eugene Walter, Mme. Huger's Oyster Omelette, Pickled Red Snapper, Veal Kidneys Flambes à la Eugene; Mrs. Sydney Adair Smith, Escalloped Chicken, Baked Duck, Corn Bread Stuffing with Pecans; Mary Snyder, Cold Avocado Soup, Hearts of Palm Salad, Seafood Kebabs (Jewels from the Sea), Key Lime Pie; Florida Department of Natural Resources, Gulf South Atlantic Fisheries Development Foundation, Inc., Smoked Fish Salad, Broiled Swordfish with Sauce Dijon; Catfish Farmers of America, Catfish with Artichoke Sauce, Baked Catfish, Baked Catfish Continental, Catfish Baked in Foil, Crisp Fried Catfish, Hush Puppies.

We wish to thank the following individuals for their help and cooperation:

Richard and Frances Stitt of the Highlands Bar and Grill, Birmingham, Alabama; Mrs. Sydney Adair Smith; Mrs. Mary Snyder; Mr. Eugene Walter of The Madaloni Press; Mr. Donald Davidson of the Marketing Corporation of America; Mr. Walter S. McIlhenny and Mr. Paul C.P. McIlhenny of the McIlhenny Company; Ms. Eleanor Cooper of Dudley-Anderson-Yutzy; Mr. John Frazier of Peter A. Mayer Advertising, Inc., in New Orleans; Ms. Isabel Kellogg of Manning, Selvage & Lee; Ms. Magdalene Felts of the Annunciation Greek Orthodox Church of Pensacola, Florida.

The staff of Media Projects Incorporated would like to acknowledge the help, support and cooperation of Robert Frese, Kathy Ferguson and Dominique Gioia of Taylor Publishing Company. And we would like to express our thanks to Barry Kastner and the staff of David E. Seham Associates for fine work and extraordinary service.

Have Better Homes and Gardens® magazine delivered to your door.

For information, write to:

ROBERT AUSTIN, P.O. BOX 4536, DES MOINES, IA 50336.